Transgenerational Family Therapies

THE GUILFORD FAMILY THERAPY SERIES
Alan S. Gurman, *Editor*

TRANSGENERATIONAL FAMILY THERAPIES

LAURA GIAT ROBERTO

Foreword by Alan S. Gurman

THE GUILFORD PRESS
New York   *London*

© 1992 The Guilford Press
A Division of Guilford Publications, Inc.
72 Spring Street, New York, NY 10012

Printed in the United States of America

This book is printed on acid-free paper.

Last digit is print number: 9 8 7 6 5 4 3 2 1

Library of Congress Cataloging-in-Publication Data

Roberto, Laura Giat.
    Transgenerational family therapies / Laura Giat Roberto.
        p.   cm. — (The Guilford family therapy series)
    Includes bibliographical references and index.
    ISBN 0-89862-107-0
    1. Family psychotherapy.   2. Intergenerational relations.
I. Title.   II. Series.
    [DNLM: 1. Family Therapy—methods.   WM 430.5.F2 R642t]
RC488.5.R63   1992
616.89'156—dc20
DNLM/DLC
for Library of Congress   92-1530
                                                                    CIP

To my children,
AARON JESSE
my cedar of Lebanon,
and
JORDANA NAOMI
my rose,
in the garden of our family

Foreword

To many problem-centered, solution-focused, present-oriented family therapists, transgenerational therapy approaches often seem to have some of the properties of gases: They appear to have neither a definite shape nor volume. Like gases, transgenerational models also seem, to their critics, to expand to fill any space available. To carry this unfortunate metaphor just a bit further, we can say that Laura Giat Roberto's *Transgenerational Family Therapies* is certainly the strongest demonstration to date of the essential solidity of these approaches. When examined more closely than current trends in the various mental health fields at times would allow, they are shown to contain clear conceptions of personality development in both its healthy and unhealthy forms, and of individual and systemic change. Moreover, while the concepts of transgenerational family therapies seem to critics to lead too often to rather vaporous descriptions of actual therapeutic technique, this state is shown to inhere not in the doing, but in the telling. As Roberto makes undeniable, these time-sensitive methods of therapy include therapist interventions that are far more describable, repeatable, and teachable than many family therapists are aware. I dare say that even a good number of transgenerational therapists themselves will be pleasantly surprised to read Roberto's book and discover this side of the transgenerational approaches.

As if these contributions were not enough, Roberto provides another service of conceptual and clinical significance that perhaps is best appreciated in historical context. The major transgenerational models of family therapy, while influential over more than three decades, have, curiously, begotten only relatively small coteries of adherents in the second and third generations of the field. As a result, the followers of Whitaker, Bowen, Boszormenyi-Nagy, etc., have had rather little sustained interaction. This, in turn, had led to a substantial lack of awareness of the commonalities among these methods. The isolation from the rest of the field of family therapists loyal to object relations theory has driven still deeper wedges of understanding between psychodynamic and systemic types. Roberto's penetrating analysis of the convergences among these approaches offers both an illumination of what has preceded in this segment of the field, and the basis for advancement into a more coherent meta-perspective for transgenerational therapists. This advancement is Roberto's own uniquely integrative vantage point on how to connect therapeutically the past and the present. Nowhere, for example, is there a more clearly described model for family assessment through a transgener-ational lens than in this book. And common clinical strategies, such as the use of cotherapy, take on new salience when considered and refined in Roberto's model.

Altogether, this book is two most valuable books in one: a systematic and thorough description, analysis, and critique of the major extant models of transgenerational family therapy, on the one hand, and, on the other, a powerful and innovative clinical framework for the practice of transgenerational therapy.

ALAN S. GURMAN
Professor of Psychiatry
University of Wisconsin Medical School

Preface

In October 1990, as this book was being completed, the family therapy community mourned the death of Murray Bowen, M.D. It is with deep sadness, as well as joy in having known him, that this text is offered with its review of his work and that of others. There is no easy way to describe the excitement, the hope, and the confidence that he and his colleagues generated through their ground-breaking exploration of how family values, mandates, myths, dreams, and legends make their way through generations of living to find expression in the present—often, literally, worlds away from the taproots of family history.

Although I was never trained by Murray Bowen, my apprenticeship with his colleague Carl Whitaker gave me the privilege of understanding the perspective gained at a time when biological psychiatry formed the substrate of the mental health field. As a clinical psychologist, I was trained to believe that physiological as well as emotional dysfunction is always interactive with the environment; transgenerational family theory presented to me an interactive "biology of the family." Now, in 1992, as biological psychiatry and its financial backing in Washington once again gain precedence in the social sciences, it seems more imperative than ever that we extend our knowledge of the deep resources and emotional stressors that are represented in extended family networks. I believe that it is to these deep resources that we will always turn as social scientists, whether we define the objects of our intervention as disease, socially induced madness, relational conflict, or existential "problems in living," as Harry Stack Sullivan called them.

LAURA GIAT ROBERTO

Contents

Transgenerational Family Therapies

Introduction

This book emerged from a decade of family therapy teaching and supervision. During that decade, from 1980 to 1992, the field of family therapy lost its innocence (witness the great debates of objectivism and constructivism in systemic theory); launched from its home in the psychiatric community, it sought to leave adolescent rebellion behind with the medical model of dysfunction and to enter adulthood. In that decade, journal editors, clinicians, and theorists re-examined the question "Why do research?" Scientists chided practitioners for lack of outcome studies to validate the efficacy of certain marital and family therapy techniques, and well-validated instruments such as the Family Adaptability and Cohesion Evaluation Scales (FACES-III; Olson, Portner, & Lavee, 1985) and the Structural Analysis of Social Behavior (SASB; Benjamin, 1974) saw greatly increased use in family interaction research. The American Family Therapy Association held its first symposium dedicated especially to the interface between family practice and family research, focused on questions of divorce, gender, and biological influences, in November 1990.

Feminist scholars turned courageously toward the theories of their own mentors and colleagues, and developed a critique of such therapeutic concepts as "neutrality" so cogent that it has impelled third- and fourth-generation therapists to begin reformulating the techniques they were taught within a gender-sensitive context (Walters, Carter, Papp, & Silverstein, 1988; Goodrich, Rampage, Ellman, & Halstead, 1989). The American Family Therapy Association began in June 1990 to hold annual men's and women's institutes, to investigate the personal and professional concerns of leaders in the field regarding male and female gender roles in our own organizations.

The American Family Therapy Association also appointed task forces to establish liaisons with social policy-making bodies in our government, as advocates for social and political reforms for American families. Family therapists from Iron Curtain countries increasingly joined our

1

American organizations, and American therapists were in turn enjoined to join the International Association for Marriage and Family Therapy. Finally, the Communist bloc dissolved in 1992. Considerable controversy arose in national organizations concerning the proper position of members on social and political problems: proactive, analytical, or neutral? In the "young adulthood" of our field, we have begun the work of contextualizing our theories to fit the contextual nature of our practice settings, our communities, and our national identities. Lyman Wynne, Susan McDaniel, and Timothy Weber edited a book on systemic consultation, which looked specifically at the impact of unique practice settings on the way that family therapy is conducted (Wynne, McDaniel, & Weber, 1986).

Yet, despite this shift toward greater complexity and contextualization of our family systems theories, we still have difficulty incorporating the elements of history and time. To some extent, this surely reflects our American preoccupation with newness and change—"better living through chemistry," as Dow Chemicals' motto used to state. To another extent, it reflects the buried trauma of post-World War II Europe, familial memories of death and genocide, and the toils of immigration and resettlement. There are no bombed-out churches to reconstruct in America, reminders of past political regimes and lessons of history. There was no Berlin Wall for the populace to tear down. There are, to be sure, the battlefields of our own Civil War, with their mounds of earth from old bunkers hidden in the forest glades. But the reminders of this war are earth and a few old cannons; the wooden buildings used for housing are long gone. In America especially, we forget that we are part of the flow of history, on both a national level and a familial level.

Our theoretical blindness to time and history, when it is carried into our family systems theories, produces an ahistorical therapy that ignores a crucial level of context. Gregory Bateson (1972) reminded American philosophers and social scientists in the 1970s that environmental context is the "difference that makes a difference" in the process of social change. But social contexts have a dimension of time, and are longitudinal and chronological. For example, the cybernetic concept of "double description," or description of an interactional event from two viewpoints, often involves relational differences that are *generational*—differences between parent and child, grandparent and parent. An ahistorical, cross-sectional "structural" or systemic description of family interaction does not allow for the recognition of generation (though it does recognize the entity of decision-making "hierarchies"). In a society in which extended families are separated by the mobilization of working adults and their offspring, can an ahistorical therapy address the unspoken concern that these families have for the parents and grandparents left far away? How can such a therapy strengthen extended family bonds over distance and time in order to compensate for their stress and isolation? In what terms can an ahistorical therapy discuss the covert, sometimes conflictual, feelings of obligation and attachment that a successful son or daughter has for the elders who provided the family home, educated him/her, or granted him/her financial and emotional security?

Finally, when family realities are examined within the context of all members, the larger community, and the surrounding culture, we cannot leave out the element of the passage of time and the contribution of historical change to the values, beliefs, and mores of families and their members. In the 1990s, it is a common problem for grown sons and daughters to struggle with parents and grandparents over such issues as religious intermarriage; ethnic and racial intermarriage; career changes, which leave the old family business or profession behind; residential transience, which leaves the hometown behind; differences in sexual and reproductive decisions, such as abortion and artificial insemination; and differences in child-rearing practices. As James Framo has pointed out, each adult son or daughter must reconcile the opposing forces of adaptation to current social and cultural mores, and the traditions and values that have shaped his/her family in the past. Only the transgenerational models of family therapy speak directly to this dilemma.

Our tendency toward ahistorical thought and analysis has obscured not only our ability to evaluate the role of *generation,* but also our ability to evaluate the role of phenomena such as *power* in influencing the course of human relationships. On this problem, Luepnitz (1988) criticizes the cybernetic model and its later constructivist modification as explicated by Bateson, Varela, Maturana, and others. She points out that

> . . . in fact, family therapy has not produced nearly as many books and tapes on family violence as it has on anorexia nervosa, although many more deaths are caused by the former than the latter. Instead of throwing away the small map of cybernetics, family therapy has redefined [its] territory in terms that its map can locate. (p. 73)

A model of family relationships that concentrates on ahistorical, interactional analysis is certainly simpler; it meets the scientific requirement called "Occam's Razor," which states that the less complex, more "elegant" solution is likely to have greater generalizability (one type of validity). However, in adopting and teaching primarily structural, interactional, problem-focused, and solution-based theories to frame relational problems, we cut out analysis of certain long-term, slow-changing familial processes that also come to fruition in the appearance of emotional symptoms and distress.

For example, a purely interactional therapy model has little to offer the parents who, having adopted a child who later becomes dysfunctional, feel that their child has "bad genes" and lose their hope for the future of the family. Neither can a problem-focused or solution-based approach easily aid a couple in which the husband or the wife is unwilling to conceive a child while the other spouse pines for one. Some family problems have roots in extended family issues that have developed over periods of at least 30 or 40 years, and that "feed forward" into the present life of the couple or family to restrict adaptation now. As the Old Testament so profoundly stated, "The fathers [or mothers?] have eaten bitter fruit, and the children's teeth are set on edge" (Ezekiel 18:2).

This book was written over the passage of time in the process of consulting with families who struggle to form and maintain a sense of identity and group values in a world that is changing increasingly rapidly. Attempting to master conflict and internal dissension over their individual and collective life cycles, and to preserve intimacy, families in the 1990s face dwindling community and state resources, impoverished schools, decreased aid to poor women and their children, the demise of government-funded aid programs and job training, and the empowerment of multinational corporate structures that have no local or regional loyalties. They also struggle against high divorce rates, a soaring cost of living that takes two parents out of the home, and the severe health risks that threaten their smaller broods of children in the form of designer drugs and lethal venereally transmitted disease. They establish homes in a world that is currently marked by the increasing use of terrorism and mercenary wars for profit, and by the proliferation of lethal weapons available through catalogues to children who are bright enough to falsify their ages on an order form. In the context of these social changes, we can see why the field of family therapy must itself become more *time-sensitive*—sensitive to slowly forming political climates; problems of social violence and "downward drift" over three to four generations of the underprivileged; the universal and ancient roots of gender and racial inequity; and the growing environmental protection crisis.

The models of therapy reviewed in this book are those that attempt to preserve the context of time in the analysis and treatment of relational problems. They are reviewed with an aim toward synthesizing central concepts for use in theory and practice, by those who wish their therapy to be more time-sensitive. Because transgenerational theories and their clinical models of treatment were developed in different areas of the country with different populations, the reader will find that I first review, in Part I, the contributions of four separate, equally powerful schools: the natural systems, symbolic-experiential, contextual, and object relations models. Each model created a somewhat different vocabulary of meanings for the slow-changing family processes it sought to describe. Chapters 5 and 6 provide a synthesis of the central terms and concepts that provide the practitioner with a conceptual "bridge," drawing together one coherent model of transgenerational theory.

Part II of this book discusses the rich compendium of techniques that have been developed by the transgenerational models, including genogram construction and three-generational assessment methods; creating a framework for therapy; and working with extended family networks in consultation or ongoing family therapy. The innovations of Donald Williamson and James Framo are presented, as well as "purist" techniques. Finally, Part III contains recommendations for the training therapy of the family therapy trainee who wishes a personal experience that will prepare him/her for transgenerational work.

·I·

TRANSGENERATIONAL FAMILY THEORIES

·1·

Murray Bowen:
Natural Systems Model

History of the Model

Murray Bowen's model, which he termed "natural systems theory," was developed in the course of family research on dyadic interaction between mothers and their schizophrenic offspring. While working on inpatient units at the National Institutes of Health between 1954 and 1959 in Bethesda, Maryland, Bowen attempted to formulate principles that would describe and predict dysfunctional patterns of behavior between a parent and a psychotic child (Bowen, 1972/1988). In this way, he sought to establish and test a rigorous theory of transgenerational processes in the development and maintenance of schizophrenia. He was particularly interested at the outset in the way in which overly connected, or "enmeshed," families' interactions contributed to poor self-awareness and ego boundaries in schizophrenic offspring.

Bowen further used as a criterion of validity that if these transgenerational patterns were indeed present in symptoms and treatment of acute schizophrenia, then addressing the patterns must lead to therapeutic change in family therapy sessions (Bowen, 1972/1988). Early research observations were restricted to the mother–child dyad, and only later were expanded to include observation of the roles of the father in dysfunctional interactions (Bowen, 1972/1988).

One early assumption made in natural systems theory was that triangular processes were *causal* in symptom formation. "The first research hypothesis . . . *knew* the origin and development of schizophrenia as a product of the two-person mother–patient relationship" (Bowen, 1972/1988, p. 470). After a time, the model was also generalized to less impaired families, so-called "normal" families, and intrastaff relationships in the workplace.

A "nodal point" in Bowen's career, as he described it, was his presentation of a paper based on work with his own family of origin and focused on the principle of "differentiation," which he had defined in his research on psychosis. The presentation, at a national conference in 1967, described how he had for the previous 12 years made "trial-and-error" efforts to change emotional "triangles" between himself and his parents, based on his research observations (Bowen, 1972/1988). Bowen concluded that the triadic emotional tension, or triangle, between oneself and one's own parents is the most important relationship over the life span, leading to interactional patterns that remain relatively fixed in *all* relationships.

After the 1967 conference, Bowen began to focus his model of therapy on the establishment of "person-to-person" relationships within families of origin. He began to experiment with helping clients to see their family members as people rather than symbolic images from the past; to observe their own behavior in key emotional triangles; and to de-triangle themselves.

As Bowen developed and refined his theoretical concepts, his shifts in teaching methods were carried home by trainees to their own families of origin in a manner that appeared spontaneous (i.e., not strategically planned). Later, assignments and reports back to the family therapy seminar became a standard teaching modality for therapists in training (Bowen, 1974/1988).

By 1968, Bowen noticed that the trainees (psychiatry residents) who engaged in this family-of-origin work performed more effectively in therapy with clinical families. They also seemed as effective in problem solving with their spouses and children as residents who were in weekly therapy for their own marriages or families, if not more so. Gradually, by 1971 he concluded that individuals focused on making change with their families of origin (especially parents) were effectively raising their functional levels of differentiation and defusing intense emotional triangles, thereby increasing their ability to function in marriages, child rearing, and professional psychotherapy.

Key Concepts

In natural systems theory, six interrelated concepts make up the structures and processes to be observed in families. They are defined and described below. Their relationship to healthy function and dysfunction in marriages and families is examined later in the chapter.

Triangles

"Triangles," as noted above, are considered the basic building blocks of any emotional (relational) system (Bowen, 1966/1988; Piercy, Sprenkle,

& Associates, 1986). In a relational system of three persons, during conflict-free periods two members are allied with the third present as an "outsider." Anxiety in the dyad involves the vulnerable third party, who may appear highly attractive, and the inclusion of the third party reduces anxiety in the original dyad.

Triangles extend and interlock in larger groups as tension increases. According to Bowen, "one of the basic concepts considers 'the triangle' (three-person system) the 'molecule' of any emotional system, whether it exists in the family or in a larger social system" (1972/1988, p. 469). Triangles comprise the smallest stable relational systems. Emotional forces inside a triangle constantly shift in a series of chain reactions. Within a family or group, some triangles are more significant than others. They form when a dyad becomes stressed, because dyads are considered inherently unstable (Bowen, 1972/1988).

Alliances within triangles constantly shift. During periods of calm, one ally is favored; under stress, the third member is approached; as the third member becomes stressed, he/she may further approach one or the other members of the original dyad. If a third member becomes unavailable, another member is found. In this fashion, old triangles expand and interlock with new members who likewise become stressed (Bowen, 1972/1988). Here are some examples:

mother–child dyad; father peripheral in calm periods.
wife–husband dyad; mother-in-law peripheral in calm periods.
mother–child dyad; sibling peripheral in calm periods.

A variety of "secondary triangles" can form when two or more individuals ally as one corner of a triangle temporarily, on perhaps one issue only. For example, a mother and an aunt may ally in a mother–child dyad with the father peripheral, creating a secondary triangle of mother–child–aunt.

The related concept of "detriangling" means "reading" or observing the emotional triangling process among family members, usually by observing their and one's own affect, and controlling one's own participation *while not losing emotional contact* (i.e., becoming "cut off") (Piercy et al., 1986).

Differentiation of Self

"Differentiation of self" is perhaps the most central concept in the natural systems model, apart from that of triangles. Bowen described differentiation of self as a continuum that ranges all the way from "undifferentiation," or ego fusion, to a hypothetical complete differentiation of self from others, which is never really achievable. Differentiation can be thought of as emotional maturity, but it has little to do directly with emotional health, pathology, or symptoms (Bowen, 1966/1988, 1972/1988). On a continuum of low differentation (0) to high differentiation (100), individuals lower on the scale are more vulnerable to stress, and recover slowly or not at all from stress-related symptoms. The greater the undifferentiation, the greater the tendency to fuse with (react emotionally to) others. Undifferentiation, or fusion, always occurs in an interpersonal (not intrapsychic) context. It normally reaches its greatest intensity in marriage, because of the extensive interdependency between spouses.

Low differentiation is characterized by emotionality, dependency, lack of capacity for autonomy, rigidity, externalization, and psychosomatic or psychotic-level symptoms under stress. There is less ability to reason out solutions; the person's primary needs are for security and love; and there is avoidance of conflict. Events that are disruptive tend to cause anxiety and clinical symptoms (Bowen, 1972/1988). The lower the level of differentiation, the more intense the emotionality in a triangle.

High differentiation is characterized by goal direction, clear values and beliefs, flexibility, security, autonomy, conflict tolerance, and neurotic-level symptoms under stress. The person has an increasingly well-defined "basic self" and less "pseudoself" (see below); less fusion in close relationships; less energy invested in maintaining a sense of self with others; and more energy and satisfaction in goal-directed activities (Bowen, 1972/1988). The person also shows less reactivity to either praise or criticism, is more realistic in self-evaluation, and can lose himself/herself in intimacy when he/she wishes to without anxiety.

On the conceptual continuum of differentation, persons in the midrange (50–75) have definite beliefs and values on important life issues, but still tend to be overfocused on the opinions of others. They may make some decisions based on emotional reactivity, having to do with concern that they will receive disapproval from significant others. In the nuclear family, there are three major mechanisms for controlling the subjective discomfort (intensity) of fusion: (1) chronic marital conflict; (2) dysfunction in one spouse, usually the one who "gives in" and becomes dependent; and (3) transmission of marital tensions to one or more children. In most families, a combination of these three processes is found at work (Bowen, 1966/1988, 1972/1988).

Closely related to the concept of differentiation is that of "basic self." Basic self is a quality demonstrated in "I" positions, defining individual beliefs, needs, wishes, and limits. Basic self can undergo change, but only from within the individual, and must be based on new knowledge and experience. Basic self is not influenced by interpersonal patterns of behavior, in that it is not changed by coercion, pressure, approval, or power (Bowen, 1972/1988). "Pseudoself" is a more fluid shifting of self, made up of beliefs and values acquired *within a relational system*. These beliefs are learned in order to gain rewards from a relationship. They are negotiable and are usually influenced by positions taken by others. Pseudoself is the part of self that fuses in intense emotional interactions.

Family Projection Process

"Family projection process" is the means by which parents transmit problems to their children (Bowen, 1966/1988). A family with maximal projection shows a parental marriage that is apparently calm and asymp-tomatic, and demonstrates almost complete preoccupation with the wel-fare of the most involved child. The manner in which one or several children become most involved in this emotionally laden process has to do with familial selection over time. Variables that influence selection of one child for parental projections include the lifestyle of the parents and each child; traumatic events related to or coinciding with the pregnancy and birth of a particular child; the temperament of a particular child; or special relational patterns that develop over time with a particular child (Bowen, 1972/1988).

This concept is built upon the psychoanalytic definition of projec-tion as the splitting off of emotions, beliefs, and other attributes within a parent so that they are out of awareness. Projection involves perceiving these split-off attributes in the child instead, and usually creates a a a strong emotional reaction in the parent. Bowen believed that children who receive many parental projections as a familial process become drawn into an intensely emotional relationship with one or both parents, which then interferes with satisfactory individuation.

Multigenerational Transmission Process

The "multigenerational transmission process" is the means by which specific degrees of differentiation are transmitted over generations. Trans-mission of differentiation, as that of symptoms, takes place through a multigenerational interlocking of emotional fields between parents and children. It occurs via overfocusing on one or two children, which delays their maturation. These children go on to marry individuals who are at about their own level of basic differentiation, and can provide the same excessive focusing on their own children. In contrast, children who are uninvolved in this parental overfocusing can develop a higher level of basic differentiation than that of their parents.

The process of multigenerational transmission moves within families to lower and lower levels of differentiation in each generation. A vulnerable child with low differentiation marries at his/her level and produces a child at a lower level, and so forth. According to this theory, severe emotional or behavioral symptoms such as process schizophrenia occur along with progressively lower levels of self over the course of generations (Bowen, 1972/1988).

Chronic low differentiation can be manifested in marital conflict, dysfunction in one spouse, or dysfunction in one or more offspring. Some or all of these symptoms are found in families with a severe multigenerational transmission process. Again, elaboration of any or all of these problems occurs because generations of the most undifferentiated offspring marry partners at similar levels of differentiation (Piercy et al., 1986).

Nuclear Emotional Family System

Originally called the "family ego mass" (Bowen, 1966/1988), the central grouping defined as a family in the natural systems model is that of the nuclear family. Members of the nuclear family system are father, mother, current children, and progeny born later in time. The nuclear family is considered a developmental entity that evolves from a committed adult dyad, followed by shifts in the marital pair and in both families of origin, the birth of children, and the resulting emotional triangles. The early term "undifferentiated ego mass" was an attempt to describe a fused, or enmeshed, nuclear family (Bowen, 1972/1988).

Along with the concept of the nuclear emotional family system, Bowen distinguished the "emotional field" (Bowen, 1966/1988). A "field" is the relational dynamic being monitored by an observer at the moment, and may be taking place within a nuclear family grouping or an extended family grouping. The term "extended family" (Bowen, 1966/1988) was coined by Bowen to mean an entire network of living relatives, especially grandparents, parents, and children (three generations, the grouping most commonly used by all transgenerational models).

Sibling Position

"Sibling position," the sixth central concept in the natural systems model, is controversial and not as widely utilized as the other five key concepts. Bowen borrowed the term "sibling position profile" from Walter Toman (1961). Its original meaning was that in a marriage, the ordinal position of each spouse in his/her original sibling group (oldest, middle, youngest) influences the way in which the spouses will handle conflicts and adapt to life cycle tasks. Bowen (1972/1988) believed that there are "typical" behavioral and attitudinal profiles for each ordinal position. However, he also hypothesized that in a familial projection process, the selected child always becomes infantilized, regardless of ordinal position.

Theory of Healthy Functioning

General Considerations

According to Bowen (1972/1988), the degree of disturbance in a family essentially stems from the degree of emotional fusion in the parental pair. In turn, fusion reflects low differentiation of self in each spouse, a holdover from life experience in their own families of origin. The ways in which spouses handle their degree of marital fusion determines the areas in which the "undifferentation" will be absorbed, and those in which symptoms will appear during periods of stress.

Healthy or Well-Functioning Marriage

In a functional marriage, the spousal pair (or its emotional aspect, its "ego mass"; Bowen, 1966/1988) changes in its dynamics over time as shifts in the extended families and in the environment produce "reality stresses of life" (Bowen, 1966/1988, p. 171). In other words, all marriages pass through transitional stressors inherent in the family life cycle (Carter & McGoldrick, 1980). As a result, shifts take place within the couple's familiar ways of interrelating. As an example, the way in which a couple negotiates intimacy and autonomy needs changes after the birth of off-spring. In the natural systems model, these shifts are seen as normal and inevitable adaptations to the creation of new triangles around the marital system (e.g., triangles involving an infant, a father-in-law, or a minor sibling). Changes in the outside environment (e.g., critical events and societal changes) also produce new triangles (Carter & McGoldrick, 1980).

Well-Functioning Family

According to Bowen, "the highest level of differentiation that is possible for a family is the highest level that any family member can attain and maintain against the emotional opposition of the family unit in which he lives" (1966/1988, p. 175). The reference to "emotional opposition" reflects his hypothesis that, to some degree, parental undifferentiation is projected onto one or more children *in all families*.

Theory of Family Dysfunction

General Considerations

A low level of basic self, or differentiation, is a primary cause of dysfunction in individuals and families (Bowen, 1972/1988). The poorly differentiated individual is highly emotionally reactive. He/she is also dependent on significant others, expecting love, approval, and security on a consistent basis. Events that disrupt or threaten equilibrium in the relationship cause anxiety. Chronic disruption can lead to dysfunction and emergence of symptoms. These symptoms can include emotional disorders, physical illness, and interpersonal or social incapacitation (e.g., workaholism and social withdrawal).

Bowen stated that he rarely, in his clinical and professional experience, encountered individuals who could be rated over 60–75 on his 100-point scale of differentiation (Bowen, 1972/1988). This assertion has not been confirmed through controlled empirical research, yet it has not encountered significant controversy in the marital and family literature. The model posits that the lifestyle and thought patterns of individuals at one end of this scale are so different from those of individuals at the opposite end that people tend to choose spouses and close friends with approximately equal levels of differentiation (Bowen, 1972/1988). It is this selection process that is thought to bring about marriages between spouses with similar levels of basic self.

Dysfunctional Marriage

According to the natural systems model, in a symptomatic marriage one spouse shows greater passivity under stress than the other. This spouse shows greater apparent dependency, and "gives in" frequently in disagreements to the other. This spouse becomes more symptomatic than the other spouse, and often has psychosomatic stress reactions. The partner in this apparently vulnerable position is called "overadaptive" (Bowen, 1966/1988).

The overly adaptive spouse may start marriage with a functional level of differentiation equal to that of the other partner, but ends up functioning far below that original level as the partner becomes chronically "overfunctional" (Bowen, 1972/1988). This "merger" is one example of marital fusion. In effect, one spouse is giving up some functional self while the other partner gains a higher level of functional self through his/her asymptomatic status. This merger results in little overt marital conflict and permits great closeness. The dominant spouse, who gains functional self, is often unaware of the problems of the overadaptive spouse, who gives in.

I have said that within this model, marital conflict is seen as the second of three ways in which low differentiation can be manifested. Conflict occurs when neither spouse will adapt to the other in the fusion, or when the one who formerly overadapted refuses to continue (Bowen, 1972/1988). In general, marital dysfunction that serves to absorb low differentiation is quite difficult to reverse. Symptoms in a spouse can absorb large quantities of stress resulting from poor differentiation, protecting the other partner from vulnerability over long periods of time.

The Dysfunctional Family

The third path by which poor differentiation is manifested is through an intense, long-term projection process onto one or more children, leading to major symptoms in the children. At the same time, this process utilizes so much parent–child emotional energy that the parental marriage escapes overt conflict and is even neglected.

The most frequent pattern of family projection is that of the centrally involved mother who focuses extensively on a child, since she is the caregiver, while the father (if present) may be quite peripheral. This child becomes the recipient of a major portion of familial mandates, expectations, concern, and legacies, while other children become less involved over time. McGoldrick and Gerson (1985) point out that several children who are close in age or bound by a critical life event may become recipients together. The symptomatic child is the one most emotionally attached to the parent(s), and develops with a lower level of differentiation than other siblings. In contrast, siblings growing up more separate from the familial projection process can emerge with higher basic self than the parents (Bowen, 1966/1988).

The lower the overall level of differentiation in a family, the greater the intensity of emotion centering around life cycle events (Bowen, 1966/1988). The reason for this has to do with the relatively high degree of anxiety with which its members function. Anxiety, also called "unresolved emotional attachment" in Bowenian theory (Bowen, 1974/1988), includes unresolved interpersonal conflicts between parents and their families of origin, chronic dysfunction in the grandparental marriages, and/or traumatic incidents within the life cycle of the parents. After childhood, this degree of anxiety is considered relatively fixed, except for functional (contextual) changes. However, under favorable circumstances and with good fortune, the amount of unresolved attachment or anxiety in these family members may decrease; with further traumatic events or environmental stress, it may increase (Bowen, 1974/1988).

A central concept in the natural systems theory of marital dysfunction is that of the "distancer" and the "pursuer." Distancing, whether emotional or physical, is considered one mechanism for dealing with poor differentiation. The function of distancing is to maintain a family's emotional equilibrium, in the face of the recurrent interpersonal turmoil born of high reactivity. Emotional distancers may live in close physical proximity to the family of origin, but withdraw emotionally when anxious or stressed. Spontaneous interchange stops, and they become reserved and isolated. Physical distancers are extremely sensitized to the physical presence of significant others, so they seek physical withdrawal (e.g., by running away or otherwise absenting themselves from the family).

Most individuals use a combination of mechanisms to maintain intimate equilibrium when there has been differentiation failure. For example, a family member may become silent when anxious, and may use physical departure only when under intense stress, such as during a marital fight (Bowen, 1974/1988). The technical term for severe emotional *or* physical distancing is "emotional cutoff" (Bowen, 1974/1988, p. 535).

The type of behavior used to achieve distance is not an indicator of the intensity or degree of unresolved emotional attachment; those who run away are as attached as those who stay home and distance themselves emotionally. Physical distancers may differ *experientially*, in that they often fight emotional closeness, believe that they are "independent," and idealize marriage and family until stress causes them to run away again. This dynamic is seen as underlying transient relationships and multiple marriages/divorces. In contrast, emotional distancers may stay proximally involved under stress, and are more prone to physical illness, emotional symptoms such as depression, and maladaptive social behavior (Bowen, 1974/1988).

Central characteristics of emotional cutoff include denial of the intensity of unresolved emotional attachment to parents, acting or pretending to be more independent than one actually is, and severe repeated distancing. "Adolescent turmoil" is seen as another reflection of emotional cutoff reflecting poor differentation.

Emotional pursuers are individuals who attempt to cope with relational anxiety by merging with or joining with a partner, who is seen as more independent and resourceful. Pursuers frequently seek out distancers for long-term relationships and marriage, because of this appearance of (and belief in) independence and stability on the part of the distancers. To the individual who pursues closeness when stressed, the distancer seems more self-reliant; however, as I have stated, distance and cutoff reflect severe differentiation problems.

Interventions and Technique

Theory of Change

According to the natural systems model, in psychotherapy change is initiated by disturbing the equilibrium in dysfunctional marriages and families of origin. As adult offspring clarify individual values, needs, and beliefs in psychotherapy, they become less available to participate in chronic triangles in their families. The families of origin may become highly emotionally reactive to this shift toward separation; opposition may also occur in social and work systems in which a client participates. If the client can maintain a more separate stance under this reactive pressure, then a higher level of basic differentiation can be achieved (Bowen, 1966/1988).

Triangles actually lend themselves to change under therapeutic conditions, because the emotional forces inside them are highly predictable. If one can observe and control one's own role in fixed family triangles, one can begin to move outside these triangles. When one individual can control his/her own emotional responsiveness and not take sides with either party in a triangle, *and still stay connected with both parties*, the emotional intensity in the triangle will decrease. In addition, both of the other two parties in the index triangle can also move to a higher level of basic differentiation (Bowen, 1972/1988) if a substitute third party to the triangle is not drawn in.

Goals of Change

There are two major goals in natural systems therapy of individuals, marriages, and families:

1. To help individual members to increase their basic differentiation of self.
2. To "detriangle" pre-established three-person systems *in steps*, by helping the client in therapy to remain emotionally separated while original two-party tensions are addressed and resolved (Bowen, 1966/1988).

Therapeutic Techniques

In Bowenian psychotherapy, there are three general methods of intervention from which the therapist chooses:

1. Marital psychotherapy, in which an individual differentiates a self from the spouse; therapy focuses on each spouse for short periods, with the therapist as the third point of a triangle.
2. Individual psychotherapy, in which differentiation is worked on solo with guidance from a supervisor as preparation for marital work ("family therapy with one family member").
3. A less effective option of coaching only the individual (Bowen, 1966/1988).

Optimally, the method of choice is to proceed with a husband and wife together for the entire length of treatment. Bowen found that when a symptomatic client was seen alone, there was symptom relief but no change in his/her marriage. Since marital tension is seen as partly contributing to problems, marital therapy is believed to be more effective in the long term.

In the natural systems model, couples are seen together for a substantial length of time. For example, Bowen (1966/1988) recommended that couples be seen once a week for 4 years—since "it might require this amount of time for significant differentiation of self" (p. 176)!

Early dyadic techniques stressed communication of feelings verbally, and analysis of unconscious beliefs through dreams. Later, the focus was moved to externalizing and separating fantasy, feeling, and thinking systems from one another—a far more intellectual and less affective procedure. Emotions such as anxiety and reactive experiences became virtually ignored as symptoms of poor differentiation.

Bowenian psychotherapy, however intellectual it may be, does make use of the relationship between therapist and couple or individual. The therapist defines his/her "self" to the clients, by laying out what he/she would or would not do in personal life situations. This behavior can be seen as a form of role modeling. To the extent that the therapist also deliberately constructs a therapeutic triangle, he/she is also utilizing enactment to induce isomorphic dynamics in the therapy room, in order to intervene between and separate spouses.

Techniques with one member are considered preparatory work, for the purpose of beginning change in a deadlocked marriage or family of origin that is severely conflictual or enmeshed. Essentially, the therapist is electing to utilize the most motivated member to induct change in the wider family. This approach is initiated "when the family system is so stalled that efforts to work with multiple family members increases the dysfunction, or when work with multiple members reaches a cyclical impasse" (Bowen, 1966/1988, p. 181). It can be seen that preparatory individual psychotherapy is a "seeding" technique, in which one member is coached to alter behavior in familial conflicts in order to force other members to alter their behavior as well.

·2·

Carl Whitaker:
Symbolic-Experiential Family Model

Carl Whitaker received his postdegree training in child psychiatry. Like other pioneers in transgenerational family therapy, he initially focused on individual psychotherapy with children and adolescents. His early orientation was psychoanalytic, drawing on the work of Melanie Klein, August Aichhorn, and Otto Rank. He was especially influenced by Rank's conception of the therapist as an "auxiliary" or "ally" rather than a blank-screen expert (Neill & Kniskern, 1982).

Later, from 1944 to 1946, Whitaker worked with psychotic and acutely symptomatic adults at the Oak Ridge atomic weapon facility, adapting affective and "primary-process" techniques that he had developed in the treatment of children and youths. A second period of investigation began, focused on a "here-and-now," ecologically oriented view of emotional symptoms rather than a more historical, Freudian, wish–defense theory of symptom formation.

From 1946 to 1955, at Emory University in Atlanta, Georgia, Whitaker experimented with the use of "multiple therapy" or cotherapy in treating individual schizophrenics. He and his colleagues focused their efforts on decoding the symbolic meaning of statements made by psychotics. Whitaker and his colleagues became particularly interested in the concept that psychotic symptoms were a byproduct of the schizophrenic's attempts to survive his/her distorted perceptions, and to attend to personal and familial needs. From this viewpoint, psychotic symptoms could be considered attempts to adapt, and even to find solutions to daily problems in functioning. This was a radical concept at a time when schizophrenia was already considered constitutional in nature, and when individual development was posited within a conflict model rather than a growth model of change.

Periodic case conferences held with other schizophrenia researchers led to the Sea Island Conference in 1955, one of the earliest family therapy conferences held, and to publication of his second book (Whitaker, 1958). Over the course of these conferences, the members of Whitaker's group gradually moved their level of observation to the role of the nuclear family in symptom maintenance. The Emory researchers were particularly concerned with enmeshed families in which a parent—at that time, usually the mother—tended to overmonitor or infantilize psychotic offspring. Early intervention techniques emphasized creating greater interpersonal distance and fostering individuation in family members. Contrary to common belief, these techniques were highly deliberate and planned in nature, rather than spontaneous or whimsical. While the primacy of "experiential change" (change through therapeutic experience) was asserted, technique was systemic and theory-based.

In the late 1950s and 1960s, Whitaker and his colleagues John Warkentin and Thomas Malone formalized their use of cotherapy teams in the ongoing treatment of schizophrenic families. Their purpose was to help each therapist avoid assimilation into familial enmeshment, to preserve neutrality, and to provide modeling of constructive interactional patterns (Neill & Kniskern, 1982; Roberto, Keith, & Kramer, 1987).

In 1964, Whitaker moved to the Department of Psychiatry at the University of Wisconsin School of Medicine, where he was to remain for much of the next two decades. There, he taught postgraduate family systems theory in a residency program that was one of the first to approximate the later requirements of the American Association for Marriage and Family Therapy for academic marital/family therapy training programs. He also continued to consult with hospitalized psychotics and their families, even hospitalizing entire nuclear families briefly to observe interactional patterns. In his resident teaching, Whitaker pioneered the use of videotape as a medium in supervision, the use of cotherapy as a training device, and the use of family therapy rather than individual therapy for resident trainees.

Whitaker worked at the University of Wisconsin to explicate the symbolic-experiential model of individual development within the context of the family life cycle, and of the family life cycle within the context of cultural mores and constraints. His therapeutic techniques incorporated some of the later influence of the Mental Research Institute by becoming more strategic or solution-focused, rather than psychodynamic or problem-focused. However, the method he developed has remained rooted in the primacy of affective experience in the process of change; hence the appellation "symbolic-experiential" family systems theory.

Key Concepts

Symbolic Experience

The symbolic-experiential model posits that individual awareness of values, beliefs, and needs is formed in one's family of origin through the experience of interactional patterns and emotional dynamics. Experiences are internalized, in the psychodynamic sense, through the process of identification, and form the basis for expectations in intimate relationships thereafter.

Since these experiences stem from infancy on, they occur on a preverbal, emotional basis; that is, they are symbolic experiences, which may or may not be completely explicit. The symbolic nature of interpersonal belief systems and self-awareness dictates that therapeutic change also operates on a symbolic level, through learning new options for relating vis-à-vis the therapist–client relationship.

Growth

"Growth," a central concept in symbolic-experiential theory, is the biological and psychological maturation that occurs over the life cycle. Growth is actually a "metaconstruct" describing changes that take place in individuals as they successfully complete life cycle tasks. The term "maturation" in this context refers to an internal state of self-awareness that is expressed as interpersonal competence, whether vocationally or personally. Unlike the natural systems model, which posits that individuals conserve early levels of differentiation (or maturation), this model holds that there is a biological drive in humans toward growth.

Growth includes the process of making remedial change (i.e., compensating for circumstances that have hampered self-awareness), and also more far-reaching integration of new experiences over the life cycle (Neill & Kniskern, 1982). Individual efforts at growth interact with familial mandates and needs, as well as with cultural pressures. These pressures are necessary catalysts for increased interpersonal competence, but may at times interfere with maturation (especially if chronic relational dysfunction is present). Growth, like the Bowenian concept of "differentiation" (see Chapter 1), is an ideal construct that is rarely achieved to its fullest extent.

Impasse

"Impasses" are plateaux in intimate relationships, in which change and individual growth does not occur. An impasse does not simply "freeze" a relationship permanently, but leads to deterioration so that the relationship becomes less of a resource for the participants. In this sense, impasses lead to what Boszormenyi-Nagy has called "stagnation" (see Chapter 3).

Impasses, in symbolic-experiential theory, are defined as failure to progress to a deep level of emotional interchange and/or negotiation of important needs, values, and beliefs. Impasses are always bilateral, and constitute positive feedback loops in which moves toward change trigger disengagement or reappearance of old relational patterns. Impasses may lead to triangulation of third parties into the problematic relationship, to diffuse tension.

Scapegoat

A "scapegoat" is the symptom bearer in a marriage or family. An identified symptom bearer is frequently the recipient of close monitoring by other family members, so that his/her problems in functioning become highlighted in a persistent manner. Over time, these problems become reified so that he/she becomes "the problem." Like other transgenerational family models, the symbolic-experiential model holds that conflictual family values, and overly rigid or difficult mandates from the past, tend to be passed down over generations and deposited on particular offspring by virtue of their position in the family, biological characteristics, and/or circumstances of birth.

Special offspring, because they are persistently monitored, create a channel for diverting other marital or family stresses. Because they are faced with emotional demands that are difficult to fulfill, Stierlin (1974) has termed these offspring "bound delegates"—a term closely resembling "scapegoat." The affect and concern about unaddressed transgenerational stressors also become focused on the symptom bearer; hence the term "scapegoat."

Culturally Invisible Pathology

The symbolic-experiential model does not base diagnosis solely on assessment of a marital or family symptom bearer. Perhaps uniquely, it also highlights the role of the "white knight"—the family member(s) with symptoms that are highly valued by our Western culture and hence are not treated. There are many culturally invisible pathologies present in dysfunctional families: the "Type A" personality, or workaholic; the distant/disengaged father; the successful sociopath who is "all business"; political heroes who embezzle and divert public funds. Symbolic-experiential theory defines "culturally invisible" symptom bearers to be as dysfunctional, from a relational and systemic point of view, as those whose symptoms debilitate them in terms of performance.

Countertransference

An important concept in cotherapy, "countertransference" is redefined in this model as the therapist's experience of affective engagement with a couple or family. A strong level of engagement is crucial for change to take place. Countertransference emerges in the dynamic process of joining a family, intervening in its process, and separating.

Accompanying affect includes the therapist's beliefs about and attitudes toward his/her own family of origin, and more here-and-now identification with one or more members of the treatment family (Whitaker, 1958; Whitaker, Felder, & Warkentin, 1965). The affect itself is considered nontherapeutic, but is important evidence of the degree of the therapist's engagement with a clinical family. Understanding and resolving countertransference affect take place not with the clinical family, but in cotherapy or peer consultation.

Resistance

"Resistance" is defined in the symbolic-experiential model as an ambivalence about change or as later-stage therapeutic impasse, rather than as a reaction to therapy. This ambivalence is thought to reflect differential motivation to make change among the individuals within a couple or family. However, one person expressing reluctance to make change may be speaking for a subgroup in the family. Resistance is regarded as a belief that the couple's or family's solutions for current symptoms are the best solutions. Another way of defining resistance is as an absence of anxiety about the solutions being used to deal with problems.

Theory of Healthy Functioning

General Considerations

The symbolic-experiential model distinguishes a family's structural organization from its interpersonal and affective (individual internal) process (Roberto, 1991). "Structure" refers to relational boundaries, subgroup composition, roles, allocation of responsibility and authority, and distribution of privileges and rewards. A couple's or family's current structure can be more or less functional, depending on the flexibility, consistency, and clarity of its structure. A family structure must also meet the age-appropriate needs of its members in order to be functional. For example, a family whose eldest child serves as a partner to the divorced father will be likely to develop symptoms.

"Process" refers to emotional dynamics, including the presence and degree of intimacy, bonding, and empathy with children; sexuality between the adult partners; differentiation of members from one another; degree of emotional commitment to the marriage and/or family; and ways of expressing and resolving conflict. The degree of connectedness between and among members in the face of their individual life cycle tasks also makes a couple or family more or less functional.

It is a myth that functioning marriages and families are free of difficult or even chronically recurring problems. John Weakland (personal communication, 1983) has stated, "When you have a problem, life is just the same damned thing over and over. After the problem is solved, life is just one damned thing after another." In the symbolic-experiential model, each couple or family is seen as having its own unique organization—its own "craziness"—which both aids in adaptation and blocks the path of change. Only persistent, rigidly unsolvable problems interfere with healthy functioning.

Healthy or Well-Functioning Marriage

Marriage is viewed, in symbolic-experiential theory, as an attempt to "complete" ourselves—not only in the reproductive sense, but also in order to induce further adult development (particularly the experience of intimacy). Marriage is such an intimate relationship that many social conventions need not be observed in order for the marriage to function. "It's a kind of oneness and separation which is part of the adult pattern of our structure" (Whitaker, 1982a, p. 167).

A functional marriage is continuously balanced or "mutual," and "reciprocal" in terms of the partners' emotional responsivity and their interest in each other. Although degree of interest need not be the same between partners at all times, shifts in one spouse tends to lead to a reciprocal shift in the other partner, so that level of marital emotionality remains consistent.

Healthy marriages in the West begin with an experience of falling in love as an initial stage, although the bilateral "in love" experience gradually abates, to be replaced by a period of differentiation and increased emotional separateness. There is a high degree of bonding between marital partners. The bonding is seen in affect that is not always positive, and can include concern, anxiety, anger, or other negative emotions. This affective bonding includes sexuality, procreation, irrationality and play, or a past history of these experiences (Whitaker, 1982b).

According to this model, most enduring alliances function best with clear generational boundaries. A common symbolic-experiential metaphor is that of the "generation gap," in which families are encouraged to recognize that there are differing needs and motivations in parents and children, even while they work to cooperate along generational lines. In early marriage or commitment, it is important that each partner be separate to some extent from the concerns and goals of his/her parents, and able to focus on attaching to the new mate. Furthermore, each young partner must separate from his/her own family of origin in order to be able to tolerate separation in the spouse. Otherwise, marriage is "just two scapegoats sent out by two families to reproduce each other. . . . The battle is which one it will be" (Whitaker, 1982c, p. 368).

In a well-functioning marriage, bonding and intimacy between partners are present. Intimacy need not be expressed verbally in order to exist in a marriage; physical exchanges, cooperation, and dyadic activity can all be expressions of intimacy. Sexuality is contained between the spouses, and emerges between generations or outside the marriage only as play. Neither partner feels a need to form extramarital alliances or to turn to a child for gratification.

There is some degree of gender balancing in the roles given to husband and wife. Most Western marriages currently show "alpha" bias, or oppressive stereotyping of male and female responsibilities and choices. Some marriages show "beta" bias, which is a minimization or neglect of real differences between male and female past experiences and current needs within the marriage. Rachel Hare-Mustin (1987) has written extensively about the damaging nature of "beta" bias, which is less visible to couples and to therapists in the 1990s.

Hence, in order for marriages to attain the role flexibility necessary to promote adult growth and development *for both genders,* some degree of balance must be fostered in the marital expectations of husbands toward their culturally more restricted wives. Symbolic-experiential theory has always maintained a strong focus on gender inequality as one major contributor to dysfunctional marriages. This concern stems from the concept of "culturally invisible pathology," since gender bias is a pervasive and still poorly controlled cultural problem.

Healthy or Well-Functioning Family

In terms of its structure, a well-functioning family shows permeable boundaries both internally (between members) and externally (between the family and the community). Internal boundaries define generations and subgroups, such as siblings; external boundaries define the nuclear and extended families, significant outsiders, and the social support network. Outside relationships with nonfamily members are allowed without being perceived as a threat (Whitaker & Keith, 1981).

Healthy families, according to this model, have a three- to four-generation family identity, which is transmitted to offspring. The nuclear family integrates and modifies characteristics of the maternal and paternal families of origin, in order to produce this sense of family identity. Although there are extended family commitments at certain times, permeable boundaries allow attention to be given to extended families during the necessary periods without creating anxiety in a spouse or child.

Dyadic alliances and flexible coalitions are available for solving problems. When a family member becomes symptomatic, others can ally to advise, encourage, or confront. Pairing is not permanent, and no one is excluded completely from active triangles within the family. Triangles formed around stressful problems can also change, as the problems change. Flexible coalitions also mean that the member identified as "the problem" can change. Whitaker (1985) termed this phenomenon the "rotating scapegoat." Functional families allow each member to admit to problems at times, but also competencies. Problems are not reified permanently, but can be viewed as transient complications (Whitaker & Keith, 1981).

Flexibility in the assignment of roles allows members to show individual differences, and to change individual behavior or beliefs without creating pressure. Each member has some freedom to modify his/her decisions and values on the basis of individual life experience and developing preferences, as well as of familial legacies (traditions) and mandates (directives).

Family roles are never real and fixed; they are always products of past interactions with, and the mutual perceptions of, parents, grandparents, children, and siblings. In healthy families, transgenerational mandates or directives shape individual behavior through the influence of past events, losses, and resulting belief systems (Boszormenyi-Nagy & Krasner, 1986; Roberto, 1987; Whitaker & Keith, 1981). However, these mandates are adapted by members as they advance through the life cycle.

Negotiations do not necessarily occur smoothly; they can involve conflict, confusion, and even anger. Although these shifts may produce transient disruption, they do not result in long-term despair, perceptions of failure, or family dissolution. Well-functioning families are willing to re-examine and renegotiate their expectations periodically.

Role flexibility in general must include gender role flexibility in particular. According to the symbolic-experiential model, well-functioning families have the capacity to resist the pressure of a male-dominated culture. For example, the mother may focus on her own career without objection from her husband or children. A father may provide active parenting without questioning of his adequacy as an adult male member of the family. It is not sufficient that a family recognizes that members are in conflict or anxiety about gender role stress. A functional family takes a proactive stance toward the necessity of expanding options for partners of each gender and does not minimize the importance of creating more balance.

In terms of emotional process, the symbolic-experiential model emphasizes the importance of mutual bonding and attachment in creating a sense of well-being and self-confidence in families. Bonding with children is seen in physical proximity and monitoring by adults, and does not necessarily involve expressed sentiment.

Members can be distinguished from each other through the process of differentiation and individuation. Each member can speak for himself/ herself separately. Because there is tolerance of individual differences, the children are not perceived as a homogeneous subgroup, and the parents do not always function as a unitary "executive subsystem." Autonomy is one aspect of the individuation process, and is seen in the capacity to make individual decisions, to clarify values independently, and to take action without requiring ongoing confirmation from parents or partner. Well-functioning families can encourage and plan for individuals and their growth.

Tolerance for conflict allows disagreement to become overt and explicit. Conflict is sustained long enough for resolution to become possible, through either new framing of the problem, agreement, or compromise. Resolution may not always be formalized, but evolves as differences are acknowledged. Conflict does not destroy long-term empathy between members in healthy families.

Sexuality in well-functioning families is contained within generational boundaries. Children can experiment with sexuality as peer play or flirtation, without feeling pressure to use their sexual capacities for early gratification. Parents can express sexuality playfully with each other in front of the children, in ways that are affectionate.

Loyalty and mutual commitment create an underlying foundation of relational permanence. This permanence fosters the sense of the family as a whole, or group identity, and serves as a buffer during periods of stress and disorganization. The concept of mutual commitment closely resembles Boszormenyi-Nagy's concept of "merited trust" or earned trust (see Chapter 3).

The capacity for problem solving, or generating solutions, is another aspect of healthy functioning. This reflects the fact that every family undergoes normative stress, both developmental (life cycle events) and transgenerational (longer-term events). What distinguishes the well-functioning family is that it *possesses the resources to solve its problems.*

Alternatives and solutions are drawn from past experiences; family values; family myths and stories; creative fantasy; input from family support networks; new and untried solutions; and random trial and error (Whitaker & Keith, 1981).

Playfulness and humor are strengths in a healthy family (Keith, 1987). With some degree of self-observation and individuality, family members gain the ability to mock or satirize their own and one another's behavior and expectations. Humor diffuses tensions, "metacommunicates" about one's positions without confrontation, and adds emotional intensity to problematic situations.

Finally, in well-functioning families, some degree of acculturation occurs but still allows each to maintain some of its ethnic dimensions, despite the demands of American culture. Our culture shows "beta" prejudice (i.e., neglect of legitimate differences) toward ethnicity, as it does toward gender. Many families in the United States carry transgenerational values and legacies from distant countries within the last two generations. In well-acculturated families, there is a balance between mandates absorbed from American society, and those traditions carried forward from their unique heritages.

Theory of Family Dysfunction

General Considerations

The symbolic-experiential model assumes that symptoms appear when dysfunctional structures and emotional processes persist over time severely enough to inhibit performance of life cycle tasks. Although healthy families have transient problems, in dysfunctional families these problems rigidify and create intense emotionality and behavioral disruption (Whitaker & Keith, 1981).

Families experience stressors in one or more of three different domains: environmental events (e.g., war); developmental stress over the life cycle (e.g., teenage pregnancy); and transgenerational stress (e.g., migration). Stressors within these three domains can become impasses, through a circular interchange in which situational upheavals impinge on an already vulnerable life stage or vulnerable family (Roberto et al., 1987).

Whitaker (1976b) has written that transgenerational stress can also result from the presence of destructive myths or family legacies (traditions), which bind family members to the needs and losses of previous generations. These binding legacies have been termed "delegations" by Helm Stierlin (1974). They create pressure to remain loyal to beliefs and solutions of the past, rather than to adapt familial beliefs to conditions in the present.

In dysfunctional marriages and families, partners can be viewed as re-enacting preset roles from their families of origin within the new marriage and family of procreation. These re-enactments help to maintain the transgenerational organization of each partner's family of origin. For example, a wife may remain continually aloof from her husband in order to continue to serve as her mother's confidante, while her own mother is distant from her father, who is overcommitted to his family's business.

Whitaker has also written extensively on the idea that symptoms exist within three different contexts. These three contexts are interactional sequences, which give a family member's symptoms different therapeutic meanings. They are "[being] driven crazy," "going crazy," and "acting crazy" (Whitaker, 1982d). Although the term "crazy" seems to carry a distinct negative connotation, it most probably evolved within the framework of therapy with psychotic families. An equally valid rendering might be "being made symptomatic," "getting symptomatic," and "acting symptomatic."

An individual can be "driven symptomatic" in an interpersonal context that is emotionally toxic—for example, in a family with a pervasive pattern of disqualification or minimization. Or, the individual can feel as if he/she is "getting symptomatic," meaning that he/she is in a state of confusion, anxiety, or temporary disorganization. Finally, a symptom bearer can "act symptomatic" under stress, as a way of coping with intolerable pressure. For example, a depressed son may withdraw and cry when confronted strongly by his father.

It can be seen from this extensive discussion of symptoms that the symbolic-experiential model places heavy emphasis on the role of *dysfunctional family process* in the interpretation of symptoms. In contrast to other transgenerational models, there is relatively little weighting of intrapsychic variables (such as differentiation) in understanding and treating dysfunction. The identified client is viewed as the arbiter of family tensions, selected by virtue of individual characteristics, prescribed family roles, and random elements as well (e.g., circumstances of birth).

Dysfunctional Marriage

In the symbolic-experiential model, marriages become dysfunctional in one of three areas: in the level of bonding or attachment between spouses; in the flexibility of spouses' ways of approaching each other in conflictual or emotionally volatile areas; and in the degree of complementarity of their roles or positions in the marriage.

It is common to find spouses who have accommodated to each other in their marriage, but are not deeply invested in each other on an emotional level. These affectively "dead" marriages can appear well organized on a structural level, but are considered quite dysfunctional on a process level. For example, a husband may attend to family responsibilities and make important family decisions together with his wife, but both husband and wife may fail to communicate with each other about personal needs and desires.

Flexibility in relating between partners is lacking in certain dysfunctional marriages. In these couples, dyadic expectations and ways of engaging the spouse have become rigid and irreversible, or "too stable." Such marriages show repeated cycles of interaction that may be chronically conflictual or even explosive, creating obstacles to open problem solving or negotiation. Essentially, " . . . each individual maintains the role assigned to him and *helps the partner* in *his maintaining the role they* have worked out for him, as well" (Whitaker, 1982b, p. 193; italics Whitaker's).

Finally, in overly complementary marriages, one spouse appears to overfunction while the other spouse systematically overadapts, cannot function well autonomously, and is recurrently symptomatic (see the natural systems analysis of this pattern in Chapter 1). This pattern can be viewed as a "bilateral pseudotherapeutic marriage" (Whitaker, 1982a, p. 169), which is based on respective projections of strength and weakness, with attendant desires to help or be helped.

The Dysfunctional Family

Characteristics of the dysfunctional family include both structural and process problems. Structurally, there may be problems with overly rigid or overly diffuse internal boundaries. The family may have difficulty separating the parents from the children, the grandparents from the parents, or the like. Or there may be such strict demarcations that family members feel that they cannot turn to one another for aid—for example, in a family where one or more parents are unavailable for the needs of the children.

Overly rigid external boundaries prevent family members from forming social support networks, and create isolation and secrecy during times of stress. On the other hand, overly permeable external boundaries can lead to inclusion of outsiders in important family decisions, triangulation of community helpers into ongoing family relationships, and perceptions that the family is incompetent. For example, a family may become so mired in the juvenile justice system that parents and siblings cease to address the problems of an adolescent delinquent son themselves.

When the boundaries inside and outside a family are disorganized, its subsystems cannot function properly. Spouses do not attend to the needs of their marriage; children tend to be pulled out of their sibling groups and targeted or parentified; and extended families are drawn into their tensions. In families with poorly maintained boundaries, the children are easily overburdened with the needs of their parent(s). This triangulation can contribute to the emergence of symptoms in the overburdened children, who cannot attend to important individual life tasks such as peer socialization or school.

Another outcome of disorganized internal and external boundaries is the appearance of long-term emotional coalitions. The most common form of coalition is the "pathological triad" (Haley, 1977; Hoffman, 1981), but coalitions are not always triadic. Schachter (1982) has noted that in an alternate form, two individuals in a state of emotional tension can each acquire an ally, forming a "tetrad." For example, a father may prefer his son,while the mother favors the younger daughter, and the two parents are distant from each other.

Rigidity of roles or family positions (including sex stereotyping) is another characteristic of the dysfunctional family. The pressures underlying this rigidity are "vertical"—transgenerational mandates from families of origin which bind the current generation to avoid adaptation and openness to change. In the presence of these binding mandates, the current family frequently maintains a constricted and invariant set of choices regarding how family members must act and believe.

One example of this rigidity is seen in family businesses, where sons and daughters deny themselves career choice out of loyalty to serving an existing familial business commitment. Rigidity in familial roles produces difficulties with intimacy and identification. Members come to feel that they are accepted or "belong" only in the context of doing what has been expected and valued in the past. Frequently, this perception contributes to avoidance of negotiation and attempts to make change, producing a sense of stagnation and mistrust.

Dysfunctional processes, as opposed to dysfunctional *structure,* are problems in the way in which a family deals with the relational needs of its members. In families in which members are overly interconnected or fused (permeable internal boundaries), there is difficulty with separation and change. Shifts in the needs of one individual cause other individuals to experience disruption. In these enmeshed or fused families, there is an attempt to forestall change by reliance on members' sense of obligation to the others. Members who show differences or pursue change can become scapegoats if they are symptomatic, or "white knights" if their stress is culturally acceptable (Whitaker & Keith, 1981).

Sacrifice and codependency constitute another type of dysfunctional family process. Self-denial and self-sacrifice for others are especially characteristic of psychosomatic families (Roberto, 1986, 1988; White, 1983). Codependency is seen in psychosomatic and addictive families. Self-sacrificial behavior in families may be related to emotional maltreatment and/or physical or sexual abuse in families of origin.

Failure of parental empathy is a dysfunction that involves deficits in an adult's ability to see a child's point of view or to protect his/her needs physically or emotionally. This failure also may reflect abuse, abandonment, or neglect in the parent's family of origin. The traumatic loss or absence of nurturant parenting leaves such an individual without a model for mutual consideration, concern, and trust to incorporate into future intimate relationships (Boszormenyi-Nagy & Spark, 1973).

In dysfunctional families, conflict is experienced as aversive and even dangerous. The presence of chronic unresolved tension leaves members fearful that the tension will escalate out of control unless it is carefully managed. In enmeshed or fused families, a chief concern may be that the symptomatic member will deteriorate. In distant families with many internal boundaries, there is sensitivity toward alienating one another further. Although some distressed families are explosive, there is often significant conflict avoidance both leading up to and following each explosive incident. One pattern of conflict avoidance, "premature closure," consists of repeated brief conflicts that recur but are not sustained long enough for clarification or negotiation to take place (Roberto, 1986, 1987, 1991).

Interventions and Technique

Theory of Change

The symbolic-experiential model holds that marital and family therapy does not control the type of change that occurs in family patterns. This belief stems from the position that family therapists do not define the values that a healthy family must have, or the choices that its members will make regarding beliefs, lifestyle, and behavior. Since each family has its own culture or belief system, which is rooted in many generations of experience, it is assumed that these traditions will continue to hold influence during and after psychotherapy.

Although the type or direction of change is not prescribed in symbolic-experiential therapy, this model aims at creating a maximal degree of shift from dysfunctional structures and processes to new ones. Treatment is intended to aid a couple or family to develop its own customs more freely, without remaining bound to carry values or patterns that were set in the past or that compensate for the past (Roberto, 1991). Whitaker has compared this stance toward change with the concept of coaching: "It is like teaching tennis to an advanced player" (Whitaker & Keith, 1981, p. 208).

Goals of Change

Symbolic-experiential therapy utilizes specific goals, which are staged. That is, the area in which the therapist works to create change depends on whether a couple or family is in early-stage, midcycle, or late-stage treatment. Specific goals for each stage of therapy are described later in this chapter. Two overarching goals over the course of therapy are (1) to increase a family's experiential sense of cohesiveness and mutuality, while supporting members' different needs; and (2) to make members' affective sides more available to them as a tool for investigating their own values and potentials.

The techniques utilized to promote change are planned for three different effects. The first is disorganization of rigid, repetitive cycling of interaction. The second is activation and promotion of anxiety in family members other than the symptom bearer. The third purpose is support of all new decisions that are congruent with a family's dominant values and beliefs.

The object of this form of family therapy, like that of the other transgenerational models, is not simply symptom relief, but modification of the multigenerational patterns that underlie symptoms. In dysfunctional families, these relational patterns tend to be rigid, chronic, and devoid of affect. Activation of anxiety and encouragement of affective expression help to facilitate personal disclosure, which mobilizes individuals to create change (Roberto, 1991; Whitaker & Keith, 1981). Expressed emotionality and awareness of affect produce unpredictable (as opposed to chronic) behaviors and disorganize dysfunctional cycles.

Therapeutic Techniques

GENERAL CONSIDERATIONS

Symbolic-experiential therapy relies on the creation of a "therapeutic suprasystem" (Roberto, 1991), which is comprised of the treatment family or couple, and cotherapists or therapist plus consultant. Optimally, the treatment team involves a cotherapy team of two. The therapeutic dyad possesses unique assets—chiefly modeling of emotional processes, such as dyadic intimacy, conflict resolution, autonomy, and negotiation. In addition, a cotherapy pair is preferable for construction of the binocular or systemic view so crucial to working with families.

When a cotherapist is not available, an alternate therapeutic structure in the symbolic-experiential model is use of a consultant or consultation group. The consultation team does not possess many strengths of the ongoing cotherapy "marriage," particularly as a model for clinical couples and families. However, it replicates several other functions: provision of a multiple or systemic view; support for the therapist; division of roles and attendant maneuverability; and greater problem-solving potential.

Symbolic-experiential interventions seek to heighten affect and to create a sense of drama in regard to problematic relationships. This sense of drama serves to highlight areas that require change, and to motivate family members to consider alternatives that would be more personally satisfying. Teaching stories, often offered as dreams or fantasy, provide a mix of direct "educational" input and indirect input to stimulate family reaction. These techniques are metaphorical in nature, and carry the power of metaphor in that they are difficult to reject out of hand (as direct prescriptions may be rejected).

Use of "universals," or allusions to normal developmental issues, underscores specific relational impasses and encourage discussion. For example, the therapist opens discussion of in-law tensions, which arise from the nodal event of marriage or remarriage. Other universals include ubiquitous social patterns, such as inclusion–exclusion; the organization of work; conflict and cooperation; triangles and dyads; and so on.

Humor is a central technique in symbolic-experiential therapy, and is recommended as a tension release for the highly affective nature of the work. Humor buffers challenge and confrontation, preserves a therapeutic alliance, and conveys caring and proximity.

SPECIFIC TECHNIQUES

In early-phase marital or family therapy, symbolic-experiential therapists focus on building trust and credibility within the new therapeutic suprasystem (Whitaker, 1976a). Before a family can invest enough of itself emotionally to depend on an expert for help, a basis for disclosure must be created. This tenet resembles the structural technique of "joining."

Rather than assuming a neutral stance, the symbolic-experiential therapist shows open and warm interest, with clear messages of caring for each family member (Napier, 1983; Whitaker, 1975). This warmth, while it resembles therapeutic stances in the other transgenerational models, differs by emphasizing play, humor, personal interchanges, and use of self.

Joining by use of self is a concept that is often mistaken for venting oneself. "Use of self" refers to sharing of selected experiences, teaching stories, memories, and fantasies that support client initiatives, underscore the need for change, or suggest a different solution to a problem. Unresolved personal conflicts, poorly controlled symptoms, and stresses in a therapist's own family do not enter into deliberate use of self.

The cotherapists communicate to the spouses or family members that the therapy team will set the structure for the meetings (e.g., frequency, members who are invited to attend), but that the couple or family will be "in charge" of the direction of sessions and the timing and pace of the work. These communications occur via a series of conversations termed "battle for structure" and "battle for initiative" (Whitaker & Napier, 1977). Stripped of their militaristic connotations, these two early-stage techniques clarify the respective roles of the clinical family and the cotherapy team.

The "battle for structure" establishes the cotherapists' position in the therapeutic suprasystem as consultants for change (Roberto, 1991). The family is told honestly and without pressure that in order to be helpful, sessions will need to be held at recommended intervals (often biweekly), to be of significant length (often 1½ hours), and to have specific family members in attendance. The word "battle" in the term refers to initial tensions that occur while a couple or family examines its willingness to allow the therapists to structure participation in the therapy.

"Battle for initiative" (Whitaker & Napier, 1977) refers to early-stage conversation centering around the issue of what topics and themes are to be explored in therapy. The therapists take the position that the couple or family members are to decide which problems they wish to focus on, and in what order. Since the initiative for making change is theirs, it is their province to control the direction of meetings.

When a spouse or family member is unwilling to take on this initiative, the therapists examine his/her reluctance to engage, rather than taking over the direction of sessions. For example, if a husband is unsure whether to discuss his marital dissatisfactions or to file for divorce, the therapists will insist that this decision belongs to him and his wife.

In the midcycle phase of marital or family therapy, the therapists begin to intervene specifically to create "interpersonal expansion of the symptom" (Roberto, 1991; Whitaker & Keith, 1981). They make alternate framings of problematic behaviors, in such a way as to reorganize family perceptions of the problems in a relational and transgenerational light. Therapist interventions are made in a supportive rather than a confrontational fashion, to promote cohesion in the therapeutic suprasystem. Dyadic interchanges between therapist and individual family members are stressed, in order to draw out multiple views of relational tensions.

There are four central therapist strategies that contribute to expansion of symptoms: creating alternative interactions; acting as a replacement for a participant in a key conflict; expanding the focus to include others besides the symptom bearer; and avoiding blame of caretakers (frequently the mother). These strategies help family members to increase their understanding of the systemic nature of their dysfunctional relationships. For example, watching a therapist talk with an adolescent daughter about her curfew violations (replacement) may illumine for a father his own belittling tone when correcting her.

There are seven other midphase techniques used to facilitate reorganization of interactional patterns (Whitaker & Keith, 1981; Whitaker & Napier, 1977):

1. Redefining symptoms as efforts toward growth is a reframing that links symptomatic behavior to the family's need for change, but is not necessarily a positive reframing. For example, alcohol abuse may be interpreted as an attempt to self-medicate an extremely hopeless mood.

2. Highlighting covert conflict involves "making the implicit explicit," for the purpose of heightening affect and increasing awareness of dysfunctional behavior or destructive belief systems. The therapists track indirect evidence of differences or disagreement, and emphasize its presence. Chronically distant spouses may be told that they appear to be in a "cold war."

3. Fantasy alternatives to real and current stressors are utilized to encourage problem solving and a more creative, observational stance in chronically dysfunctional families. These alternatives are offered as a model, and are not meant as prescriptions (hence the term "fantasy"). For example, a therapist might ask a depressed mother if she has considered going home to her mother.

4. The therapists act to separate interpersonal stress from internal stress. Mood changes, anxiety, and negative expectancies are questioned and acknowledged, and attached to interactional patterns surrounding them (Whitaker & Keith, 1981). Individual family members are encouraged to express their own fears and beliefs about these patterns, rather than restricting the focus to "who does what to whom." For example, a defensive husband may be encouraged to discuss at length his fears about how he would fare if his angry wife should leave him.

5. Augmenting family despair is an intervention used for symptomatic patterns that have become rigidified and impersonal, such as long-term conflict or chronic sexual dysfunction. This rigidity can be challenged by increasing family anxiety deliberately.

6. Extended family reunions are extended family sessions that include as many members as possible, and draw from three or even four generations to create a large family group (Whitaker, personal communication, 1979). They are planned as one- or two-shot consultations, may range from 1 day to 1 week in length, and are planned carefully to allow for members traveling long distances. The purpose of the reunion is

to allow observation of longer-term familial patterns that typically can only be discussed anecdotally. In addition, information can be exchanged, and perceptions (and projections) of one another can be reexamined with the aid of participants who have experienced the family over many years of development.

An exercise used to prepare for an extended family reunion involves requesting personal life histories in the form of a narrative from parents or grandparents. The narrative covers the span of time up until the birth of the identified client, effectively removing him/her from the frame of reference. Resulting information can be conveyed by letter or audiotape, and often clarifies remote events in a family of origin that underlay previous decisions and behavior. This information commonly facilitates an empathic understanding of the motives of previous generations and "humanizes" the actors, making reconciliation an option (see Boszormenyi-Nagy's concept of "rejunction" in Chapter 3).

7. Role reversal allows the therapists to take the position of individuals within the couple or family, which forces those individuals into another position for that period of time (Roberto, 1991). From the vantage point of specific positions, cotherapists can make comments and predictions, and can take action to bring about change. Then the family members being represented can agree or disagree, and thereby can create new views of their roles within the family. For example, a therapist can take on the role of an angry eldest son, pushing the parents to consider the consequences of their avoidant relationship. The son, relieved of this position, can observe his own participation in their chronically constricted marriage and can reconsider whether he wishes to remain in that position and whether it is constructive.

The midphase of therapy emphasizes confrontation and challenge, as well as support of each member's viewpoints. The presence of two cotherapists adds latitude by allowing one therapist to challenge while the other supports, or to restrain a highly reactive member while the other intervenes, or to mirror different sides of a highly sensitive disagreement.

In contrast, late-phase symbolic-experiential psychotherapy puts more focus on decision-making and change efforts within the family or couple itself. The therapists play a newly peripheral role, and make more metacomments as opposed to direct intervention and dyadic interchange. Central problems and dysfunctional patterns are often reinterpreted, since formerly nonsymptomatic members often acknowledge their own distress during this stage. The therapist–family suprasystem now interacts in a context of peer interaction, rather than one of consultant–consultee. Shifting to this late-stage context utilizes three specific interventions:

1. Use of spontaneous self-disclosure, as opposed to teaching stories or illustrations, conveys the message that family members and therapists

are equally competent. The self-disclosure is present-focused, and reinforces a peer status between family members and the therapists.

2. Requests for feedback allow therapists to survey family members for their own opinions about the course of therapy thus far, satisfaction with changes already in place, and personal wishes for further work. Actively seeking out these opinions reinforces the view that the therapists have been "hired" by the couple or family, and that couple or family values are key in evaluating the efficacy of therapeutic work.

3. Discussion of termination, and anticipatory mourning, make the members of a client family aware that their development will proceed at some point without outside intervention. Explicit discussion of the end of therapy also conveys the therapists' confidence that they will be able to solve future problems themselves, emphasizing their newly acquired competence. Hearing that the therapists will miss working with them reinforces the view that each family possesses a unique culture and "personality" that is special and valuable.

·3·

Ivan Boszormenyi-Nagy: Contextual Family Model

History of the Model

Since 1965, Ivan Boszormenyi-Nagy and his colleagues have particularly examined the idea that multigenerational obligations and pressures play a direct role in the formation of emotional symptoms (Piercy et al., 1986). This "invisible web" of familial obligations can be considered an additional dimension of family functioning—essentially, an ethical dimension. The so-called "contextual model" was originally based on observations in intensive family therapy of schizophrenics (Boszormenyi-Nagy, 1962, 1965, 1972; Boszormenyi-Nagy & Spark, 1973). In this respect, its original development came at a point in time similar to that of the natural systems and symbolic-experiential models. The contextual model was developed as both a theoretical model and a method of applied psychotherapy. "As a set of premises, it informs both personal and professional relationships. As a method, it introduces a new, *ethical dimension* of relational leverages and determinants" (Boszormenyi-Nagy & Krasner, 1986, p. ix; italics added).

Boszormenyi-Nagy was a pioneer in the family therapy movement in the United States, and in 1957 became the founding director of the Department of Family Psychiatry at Eastern Pennsylvania Psychiatric Institute (EPPI) in Philadelphia. His department was a research and clinical service unit until state funding was terminated in 1980. The department focused on intensive psychotherapy and research with hospitalized schizophrenic clients. EPPI sponsored several early family therapy conferences in 1964 and 1967, and Boszormenyi-Nagy helped to found the American Family Therapy Association in the late 1970s. Originally, he was heavily influenced by Kalman Gyarfas's views on the dynamics of schizophrenia; Gyarfas was also a mentor to Virginia Satir. Beginning in 1957, Boszormenyi-Nagy attempted to synthesize object relations theory, especially the ideas of Fairbairn, with European existentialist philosophy, particularly as represented by Martin Buber (Boszormenyi-Nagy, 1989). He shared theoretical ideas with clinicians at Chestnut Lodge Sanitorium in Maryland, where Harry Stack Sullivan, Frieda Fromm-Reichmann, Harold Searles, and Otto Will worked. At that time, his concepts focused on the role of therapist trustworthiness in therapy of psychotic clients.

In the late 1950s and 1960s, Boszormenyi-Nagy began to move from individually focused interventions, as his colleagues in the field also made this epistemological shift. His contemporaries included Murray Bowen, Lyman Wynne, Nathan Ackerman, Carl Whitaker, and Donald Jackson (all of whom worked at medical schools and medical facilities). Later, in retrospect, he felt that in early conjoint family therapy, the paradigm entering the field was that of a multilateral therapeutic contract: "An implicitly ethical contractual reorientation was getting underway, but it was obscured by a side-tracking into general systems theory which left no room for dynamic concepts such as balances of entitlement or indebtedness" (i.e., internal dynamics; Boszormenyi-Nagy & Ulrich, 1981, p. 161). In the 1960s, Boszormenyi-Nagy expanded his then-clinical model of treatment into multiple-family treatment and community consultation. Jackson and Weakland (1961) considered EPPI one of the first known family therapy training programs. The body of ideas was first summarized in the late 1960s (Boszormenyi-Nagy & Framo, 1965; Zuk & Boszormenyi-Nagy, 1967).

In terms of the societal/political context that has underlain the conceptual development of the contextual model, Boszormenyi-Nagy writes:

> Its impetus has been the societal background of ripped-off, over-burdened, abandoned nuclear families. . . . We submit that the family is trying to exist in the vacuum that was left when the connection between visible relationships and intergenerational rootedness broke down and the ethical implications of that connection were lost. (Boszormenyi-Nagy & Ulrich, 1981, p. 161)

Key Concepts

All elements of the contextual model—its theories of healthy functioning and dysfunction, the process of change, and clinical intervention—are based on the idea that there are four "relational realities," or templates, for understanding and constructing the interpersonal world and through it the self. These four dimensions of relational reality are "objectifiable facts" (Dimension I); "individual psychology" (Dimension II); "systems of transactional patterns" (Dimension III); and "ethics of due consideration" (also called "merited trust"; Dimension IV) (Boszormenyi-Nagy & Krasner, 1986, p. 44).

Dimension I: Objectifiable Facts

The first dimension of functioning includes "pre-existing factors," "unavoidable conflicts," and "consequences." Pre-existing factors include genetic or temperamental determinants; physiological characteristics; developmental history; and life cycle events such as parental divorce, heritable illness, or deaths.

Unavoidable existential conflicts are developmental differences between intimate family members that involve stress and turmoil (e.g., parental concern vs. adolescent autonomy; parental self-development vs. caretaking of children; separation/divorce vs. coparenting). Essentially, these unavoidable conflicts are really complex life cycle differences that tend to present members with mutually incompatible needs and role demands.

Consequences of relational interchanges are behavioral and emotional symptoms. The symptoms are self-perpetuating and self-evident; that is, they have a life of their own, as in the case of anorexia nervosa. However, symptoms can also be seen, in addition to "objectifiable facts," as consequences of relational conflict that might profitably be reworked (Boszormenyi-Nagy & Krasner, 1986).

Dimension II: Individual Psychology

Proponents of the contextual model believe that family theory needs to incorporate individual dynamics as one of many systemic levels of human experience (Boszormenyi-Nagy, 1989). The dimension of individual psychology includes affective experience, characteristic behavior, life goals, and individual motivations. Aspects of individual functioning are considered one of the greatest resources for relationship change, in that individuals universally possess needs and desires that can be called upon in therapy to mobilize change. In addition, however, the perceptions of individual family members are also important *data* to the extent that they can be shared and understood (Boszormenyi-Nagy & Krasner, 1986).

Individual feelings and motivations are "relational indicators"; that is, they point to an interpersonal dynamic or pattern in process. For example, the experience of anger often indicates that someone has been deprived to the profit of another. Individual affect and needs must be utilized explicitly in order to identify key relationship problems, and to resolve those interpersonal conflicts productively.

It is possible to maintain a therapeutic stance in marital and family treatment that respects individual needs and wishes without producing a pathologizing or scapegoating effect. This stance, in the contextual model, is explicitly defined and is called "multidirectional partiality" (Boszormenyi-Nagy, 1966). This partiality, which is described later, allows the observer to avoid "getting caught" between conflicting needs of different family members. However, an individually responsive stance also does not necessarily mean positively connoting exploitative or destructive behavior, which may be understandable systemically but perpetuates relational dysfunction.

Attention to individual psychology also includes identifying projections between partners, or between client and therapist. In this sense, it shares a major conceptual framework with the object relations and symbolic-experiential models. The contextual therapist, like the therapist of all other transgenerational schools, distinguishes between here-and-now interactional conflict and "displaced" conflicts between individuals based on projections from their families of origin (Boszormenyi-Nagy & Krasner, 1986).

Dimension III: Systems of Transactional Patterns

Systems of transactional patterns are useful for understanding family dynamics and for planning strategic interventions. However, it must be stated that in the contextual model, interactional patterns are utilized mainly as a source of information about implicit contractual or ethical understandings within a family (Dimension IV), not as a primary target for clinical intervention. The dimension of transactional patterns includes verbal and behavioral processes that are either simple or complex—for example, simple and double-binding communications; triangles; scapegoating; framing and reframing of problems; metaphoric language; prescriptions; restraints; positive and negative connotation; and behavioral expressions of intimacy, authority, and control.

Family therapy models that are purely systemic define transactional patterns functionally, via manifest behavior, and focus on circular (relational) events. Because of this circularity, they do not address unidirectional, forward-moving impacts across generations and life cycles. Also in contrast with purely systemic models, the contextual model retains its interest in the individual, subjective vantage points accompanying circular interactions (Boszormenyi-Nagy & Ulrich, 1981; Boszormenyi-Nagy & Krasner, 1986). Moreover, a purely transactional or systemic model of family functioning can also suffer from reductionism, especially anthropomorphism, as seen in awkward descriptions such as "the family system resisted change" and the like. Intervention strategies are often aimed at this invisible, anthropomorphic agent, which is seen as maintaining symptoms. At the same time, purely systemic models neglect the fact that the structure of a current nuclear family reflects the structures and conflicts of countless preceding generations (Boszormenyi-Nagy & Ulrich, 1981).

When these considerations are omitted, a treatment model may be based on "ephemeral changes of manifest behaviors, an orientation that overlooks the relational resources in a family that are capable of improving *the quality of its members' lives*" (Boszormenyi-Nagy & Krasner, 1986, p. 56; italics added). Or, to further place the dimension of transactional systems within the contextual model,

> It is not primarily the rigid unchangeability of . . . behavior . . . that present[s] families with their fundamental dilemma. In fact, rigid insistence on family "rules" tends to reveal itself as a defense against an underlying threat of unrelatedness. The most pervasive problem of today's family life has to do with its felt loss of resources and the imminent threats of abandonment and fragmentation. (Boszormenyi-Nagy & Krasner, 1986, p. 417)

Dimension IV: Ethics of Due Consideration

The fourth dimension supersedes other previously defined dimensions of relationship, and is termed "ethics of due consideration" or "merited trust." These terms refer to the building up of trustworthiness through justifiable acts ("justifiability" meaning consideration of the needs of other family members). Basically, Boszormenyi-Nagy and his colleagues believe that "people's capacity to remain reasonably *trustworthy* keeps relationships sustainable over time" (Boszormenyi-Nagy, 1986, p. 58; italics added). Within the dimension of ethics, there are seven unique concepts to describe relevant emotional processes.

"Legacy" refers to a transgenerational mandate linking the inherited characteristics of a current generation to its obligation to children. It is seen as a uniquely positive input in the chain of family and community survival. A family examines and modifies its legacies because of its inherent obligation to help free posterity from crippling habits, traditions, and delegations from previous generations (Boszormenyi-Nagy, 1976; Boszormenyi-Nagy & Krasner, 1986).

"Trustworthiness" is seen as a bilateral bonding process built between family members. The importance of the mutual building of trust stems from the idea that relational balance, or mutuality, is the key to intimacy from the contextual viewpoint. The perception of a partner or parent as trustworthy is an outcome of (1) being given credit for one's own contributions to the family; (2) being responded to in a responsible manner when in need; and (3) observing that the partner or parent shows concern for fair distribution of familial burdens and benefits (Boszormenyi-Nagy & Krasner, 1986). In dysfunctional families, members need help in defining how to be more fair in their mutual expectations, as a way of rebuilding individual trustworthiness. Trustworthiness can also be looked at as a kind of "relational accountability."

"Merit" " . . . is a way of earning entitlement for the self through . . . contributing to and *crediting* the other" (Boszormenyi-Nagy & Krasner, 1986, p. 59). This "due crediting" means that a family member is willing to identify the contributions of the other(s) to his/her quality of life. In other words, it is a way of acknowledging the efforts of other family members openly. Due crediting, when it is done on a mutual basis, results in a balanced and equal distribution of a family's emotional resources and pressures among all members. For example, due crediting occurs when angry parents can also acknowledge a child's contributions to the family (although not necessarily approving of all his/her behavior). The outcome of giving due credit is that one earns personal merit in the eyes of partner and family.

"Earned entitlement" refers to a stance that is the opposite of dominance or control—a stance in which a family member receives caring or giving in the context of having earned or merited trust. Earned entitlement is not an interactional process, nor is it a psychological process such as a value. Instead, it is a contextual process by which a certain amount of caring is due because that individual has earned it through trustworthy behavior. This position is, however, inherent in children's relationships with their parents, without needing to be earned.

"Autonomy" is redefined, within the contextual model, as personal growth or goal-directed behavior *when it exists side by side with trustworthiness*. The trustworthiness or accountability allows continued relating. In the contextual model, consistent and caring connectedness over the long span of time is a universal requirement for healthy functioning. Without ongoing connectedness, autonomy in this model has no meaning. Autonomy with accountability means that as individuals make decisions, there is multilateral assessment of consequences. Boszormenyi-Nagy also defines autonomy as "the capacity to earn entitlement" (merit). He compares it to Erik Erikson's concept of "generativity," the creation of actualized trust (Boszormenyi-Nagy & Krasner, 1986).

The concept of the "revolving slate" refers to a relational process, in which a person's wish for revenge against someone who hurt him/her is acted out with a substitute "victim." This new target is treated as if he/she were the original offender. The term "slate" refers to a fixed accounting between people who ordinarily should be dealt with and considered in a more open-ended fashion (Boszormenyi-Nagy & Spark, 1973; Boszormenyi-Nagy & Ulrich, 1981). For example, an angry man who was humiliated and criticized by his father may target his teenage son with criticism and humiliations.

The seventh ethical concept is that of the "ledger." This abstract idea refers to the balance between two partners' merits and debts in their relationship. The "ledger" of fairness is balanced in a relationship when there has been mutual giving and taking between them. The ideal "ledger" or balance of fairness depends on whether one is observing a symmetrical (e.g., husband–wife) or asymmetrical (e.g., parent–child) relationship. In symmetrical relationships, each partner owes the other's needs the same due consideration as his/her needs are given, in order to balance the "ledger" of fairness.

In asymmetrical relationships, the child is unable to give back consideration to the same extent that he/she needs it. A fair balance or "ledger" requires "equitable but not equal reciprocity" (Boszormenyi-Nagy & Krasner, 1986, p. 417). Some of the debts and entitlements in a relationship are "vertical"—that is, they are responses to legacies passed on by a previous generation. Others are "horizontal," created by the earning of merit when family members support and care for each other over time. It must be noted that family legacies do offer examples, options, and choices to offspring, but can also bind or impose debts on them in various ways as well.

In summary, Dimension IV, or merited (earned) trust, is the heart of the contextual family systems model. It focuses on specific relational processes that Boszormenyi-Nagy and his colleagues have termed "ethical." These so-called ethical processes include the following:

1. Consequences of past decisions and actions for current relationships.
2. Impact of these consequences on all members of a family.
3. Development of relational resources with emphasis on the most vulnerable members (young children).
4. Prevention of further injury or damage in the present and future generations (Boszormenyi-Nagy & Krasner, 1986).

The dimension of ethics moves beyond the level of symptoms and their maintenance, and beyond circularity of behaviors. It moves into the context of relational and social justice, and of trustworthiness as it operates in intimate relationships. A purely considerate and trustworthy relationship is, however, an idealized goal that can be worked toward but never achieved completely. "Our multilateral concern is not . . . limited to intergenerational connections. . . . The goal of contextual therapy is to achieve a responsible orientation to intermember issues of fairness and trust on the part of both participant and therapist" (Boszormenyi-Nagy & Ulrich, 1981, p. 161).

Theory of Healthy Functioning

General Considerations

In the contextual model, healthy functioning is rarely defined interactionally, but instead ethically (between individuals), societally (within social systems), and contextually (within larger systems). Therefore, the characteristics of well-functioning marriages and families do not specify desirable behaviors between family members. Rather, the aspects listed define what might be called a constructive or healthy relational *context* within a marriage or family.

Healthy or Well-Functioning Marriage

A well-functioning marriage contains an early romantic period of intense infatuation. Both spouses possess a past ability to earn merit in friendships and other relationships in which they have been able to show trustworthiness. Each shows constructive (but not excessive) family-of-origin loyalties and family legacies. In other words, each partner has been able to separate amicably and effectively from his/her family of origin; each retains family values and emotional connectedness, but is able to maintain friendship and intimate commitments outside the family as well.

The spouses are able to share responsibilities willingly (e.g., for child rearing). Unlike parent–child relationships, marriage is symmetrical—so there must be equitable give and take, and a balanced "ledger" of reciprocal contributions between partners. There is a high degree of "fit" between each spouse's expectations of the other (based on past experience with significant others), and his/her own earned entitlements. That is, each partner not only looks to the other for gratification, but offers consideration and support as well.

In a well-functioning marriage, each partner possesses concern for his/her own health and well-being throughout the aging process. Sexuality continues into older adulthood. There is a balance of dependencies between the spouses; that is, the "ledger" is fairly even regarding the balance of caretaking. That is, it is expected that the spouses will turn to each other for dependency needs, especially later in their life cycles, but that the nurturance and physical/emotional support must be mutual. Each partner has the capacity to be responsible for the consequences of unfair or untrustworthy behavior when it does occur, so that he/she can act to repair the relationship.

In general, according to the contextual model, lasting marriages finally succeed on the basis of their long-term resources, rather than on the basis of short-term behavioral patterns. If a marriage shows positive interactions, courtesy, clear communications, and cooperation in the short term, but does not rest on a foundation of mutual and balanced commitments and consideration, it is unlikely to survive the stress of years.

Healthy or Well-Functioning Family

In a well-functioning family, the adults can provide responsible parenting. Giving adequate care to offspring is considered a central prerequisite to healthy intergenerational functioning. At the same time, adults repay the parental care of the previous generation in three ways: acknowledgment; caretaking when necessary; and "repayment forward" by giving to their own children and investing in their future (Boszormenyi-Nagy & Krasner, 1986).

The adults in a well-functioning family also engage in the process of "exonerating their parents"; that is, they try to be fair to each parent's motivations, goals, and visions, despite ongoing conflicts. This exoneration represents an important life cycle task: the step toward "grasping a fundamental truth of relational reality"—the reality that most parents desire to show competence and good faith in rearing their children (Boszormenyi-Nagy & Krasner, 1986, p. 103).

Parents in a healthy family earn entitlement (consideration) for themselves by offering care in a number of ways to each other and to their children. These ways include humor and play; creativity; development of their own skills and abilities; productive work; maintenance of physical health; the taking of relational risks; trust in and empathy for the partner; self-assertion; and concern for the needs of the children. Family members all earn merit as well through trustworthy acts, and through attempts not to exploit or scapegoat one another (which is to some extent inevitable).

Healthy family members are accountable—that is, willing to accept the responsibility and commitment of mutual emotional connectedness. They can acknowledge the caring and consideration of others, as well as the contributions they have tried to make to their own well-being. Well-functioning families are also loyal, in the sense that they show preferential attachment to those who have merited intimate bonding. The contextual model supports Bowen's idea of the universality of triangles in intimate relationships (see Chapter 1). Family loyalties are seen in the way that an individual prefers a close family member to a third party from outside. Accountability, acknowledgment, and loyalty do not mean that healthy families do not have conflict. Conflicts between competing needs and desires are unavoidable and are considered normal.

Functional families support individual efforts at "self-delineation"— the building of an autonomous self within the "dialogue" of family life. Self-delineation (like Bowen's concept of "differentiation") only occurs in the context of two or more people, because experience of self is a resource stemming from the relational process. Self-delineation includes the formation of boundaries between self and others. A child's formative relationships determine the degree to which a self *can* be delineated.

These families also support the process of "self-validation," which is defined in a unique way in contextual theory. Self-validation is the capacity to earn credit (consideration) through actual acts of integrity, and attempts to "balance the ledger" of needs with others. It is the second part of the process of self-delineation, and is the true source of self-esteem. As efforts are made to balance the "ledger" of entitlements and debts, the resulting sense of self-worth enhances intimacy and healthy interdependency.

Trustworthiness is accrued through reliability, responsibility, and fair consideration, and is based on real actions. It must be emphasized that trustworthiness is dependent on action, not on a belief or wish that others will see one as trustworthy. It is an ethical strength earned over the long term, by balancing the forces of give and take with other family members.

Healthy families also show flexibility of functioning, in which imbalances of fairness occur but shift from one member to another. This flexibility prevents any one member from being excluded or scapegoated in a persistent way over time.

Finally, functional families can negotiate changing loyalty commitments within the framework of their past legacies. As the family moves through its life cycle, its members attempt to preserve past traditions, values, roles and mandates while modifying them to fit individual differences and current circumstances.

Theory of Family Dysfunction

General Considerations

Certain relational processes are difficult to separate into the somewhat artificial classifications of "healthy" and "dysfunctional." For example, the concept of familial loyalty is difficult to separate in this manner. Loyalty does not apply to a simple dyadic preference or attachment, but, as indicated earlier, refers to a triadic context of preferring one person over another or a potential other. Thus, loyalty and loyalty conflicts are to some extent inseparable, since several partners can compete for one's loyalty.

In the case of these normative processes, it is perhaps the extent or persistence of one particular stance, or the maintenance of an ethical stance with one or several persons only, that causes problems: "The breakdown of trustworthiness of relationship through *disengagement from multilateral caring and accountability* sets the stage for symptom development" (Boszormenyi-Nagy & Ulrich, 1981, p. 171; italics added). In this model, "pathology" refers to ethical, or emotional, stagnation in family relationships. There are three major obstacles to functional relationships:

1. Collision between internal expectations and external relational realities, creating projective identification, displacement, narcissism, and inability to adapt to loss (Boszormenyi-Nagy, 1965).
2. Rigid, repetitive feedback cycles, which obstruct negotiation on the transactional level.
3. Punitive or vengeful behavior by a person who feels entitled and has no remorse for this behavior—in other words, who clearly is rejecting interpersonal growth.

Dysfunctional Marriage

One cause of marital distress is a horizontal imbalance between two partners—that is, a unilateral quality in which one spouse exploits the other and unfairly ignores the needs of the other. There are also vertical imbalances, which result from transgenerational conflicts in either spouse. For example, a wife may feel an "invisible" loyalty to her distant family of origin, causing her to reject her husband's bids for closeness. Vertical stressors are especially a cause of early marital problems, but also contribute to distress in longer-term marriages.

A marriage will become symptomatic if there are persistent projective identifications, especially attributes of badness or blame, or an expectation that one's partner will vindicate past injuries (an idealization). This situation reflects a "revolving slate" process, stemming from responses to past hurts.

Misusing the loyalties of children by parentifying them, in order to diffuse tension from a marriage, results in their loyalties' becoming split. The marital conflicts remain unaddressed and unresolved, contributing to rigidity and chronicity of marital symptoms.

The Dysfunctional Family

One symptom of familial dysfunction is "delegation" (Stierlin, 1974). In the contextual model, delegations are defined as transgenerational expectations imposed on offspring by parents' or grandparents' emotional needs. Delegations are different from legacies, which are mandates not intensified by demands. A delegation includes a quality of sacrificing tasks of an individual's life cycle, in order to meet the needs of elders.

"Destructive entitlement" is the dysfunction related to earned entitlement. It is an escalation of normal entitlement that results from dysfunctional family patterns in the family of origin. Contributing symptoms include inadequate nurturance; exploitation of a child's needs for trust and affection; receiving mistrust or disqualification in return for loyalty; blaming; and scapegoating. Exploited children go on to see other adults as beholden to them, and may try to get compensation in a vindictive manner.

"Disjunction" is a common condition in clinical families, in which there is "disengagement from fair or due consideration of relationships" (Boszormenyi-Nagy & Krasner, 1986, p. 416). The resulting relationships are mainly based on control issues or drives for immediate gratification. Disjunction resembles the object relations concept of "basic fault" or empathy failure (see Chapter 4). It is a divergence between self-service and altruism, which depletes trust.

Another common dysfunctional symptom in families is "parentification," an adult's pressure to turn a minor into a functional caretaker in an age-inappropriate way. Parentification is not destructive if it represents a transient shift in roles, but becomes so if it depletes a child's emotional resources and trust. Parentification is especially destructive if a parent pulls for a child's innate loyalty and devotion (Boszormenyi-Nagy, 1965; Boszormenyi-Nagy & Spark, 1973). Filial loyalty tends to make *any* child somewhat parentified, in the sense of backing up an imperfect parent (Boszormenyi-Nagy & Ulrich, 1981).

The phenomenon of "split loyalty" occurs when a child is forced to choose one parent's love at the cost of seeming to betray the other parent. It can be considered one type of triangle between two parental figures and a child. The condition arises when the parents themselves are split by mutual mistrust or conflict. Generally, the more subtle and unstated the mistrust, the more severe the loyalty split. Split loyalties can develop with nonparental pairs, such as a mother and grandmother, or a birth parent and adoptive parent. Children try to create a three-way trust base, but in the dysfunctional family these attempts may be challenged by the notion that trusting one parent hurts the other. Split loyalties form the basis for destructive parentification and create severe symptoms. The contextual model holds that it is one factor that can underlie suicidality (Boszormen-yi-Nagy & Ulrich, 1981).

An indirect or unexpressed loyalty may appear as indifference, avoidance, or ambivalence, and is called an "invisible loyalty." Overtly, invisible loyalties are observed as silent obstacles to commitment in another current relationship (e.g., a marriage). The current relationship is sacrificed in a way, by directing overconcern toward the vertical involvement producing the invisible loyalty. This process can lead to the playing out of a "revolving slate," or re-enactment in the current commitment.

Family legacies, if they contain an element of coercion or demand, can cause negative patterns of behavior to be repeated from one generation to the next. If so, they become destructive and create the "revolving slate." In order to accommodate to dysfunctional patterns in the family of origin, children grow up preserving their loyalties and beliefs by showing the same patterns along with their anger and disappointment. This result of excessive and invisible loyalty is a chief factor in marital and family dysfunction.

Most of what is "pathological" or ethically stagnant in family relationships involves some form of emotional exploitation. If actions do not consider the position of other family members, they lack merit. Then there is unequal give and take, the exploitative relationship loses trustworthiness, and interactions become symptomatic. There are "asymptomatic pathologies," which are culturally accepted but distressing behaviors, such as those seen in the daughter who is raised to wait on male relatives or the husband who feels he must achieve political office to be acceptable to his father (the symbolic-experiential model also makes this point; see Chapter 2).

Finally, the phenomenon of "scapegoating" often involves one or both parents' using projective identification, moving a legacy of "badness" or perceived failure onto a child instead of re-experiencing it themselves. Scapegoating also reflects relational exploitation, in that parents are motivated to expect gratification from a scapegoated child, often because they perceive themselves as having been exploited elsewhere (Boszormen-yi-Nagy & Ulrich, 1981).

Interventions and Technique

Theory of Change

Contextual therapy strives to deal directly with invisible loyalties, which influence family members' availability to one another. The contextual therapist seeks to loosen binding loyalties, and to help couples and families explore new options for becoming stronger resources to one another in the present. Its central assumption is that "fair (due) consideration of . . . relational obligations can result in personal freedom to participate in life's activities, satisfactions, and enjoyment" (Boszormenyi-Nagy & Krasner, 1986, p. 414). Due consideration is made the major interpersonal mechanism of change, and is used as a resource for redirecting marital or family relationships from a context of obligation or conflict to one of mutual commitment.

The chief methodology in the contextual model is that of "multidirectional partiality," an examination of each family member's experience of intimate relationships. The capacity to make change is related to one's ability to examine the quality of one's family relationships, especially in asymmetrical bonds with vulnerable members such as children or elderly parents.

Change for the sake of change—that is, shifting from one family organization to another for aesthetic purposes—is considered of questionable value in the contextual model. The contextual model directs change toward life consequences in the future, especially for the welfare of children.

Goals of Change

In accordance with its emphasis on activating family resources, the cornerstone of contextual therapy is not affect, as in object relations therapy, but the invisible field of commitment. Its major goal is to allow each family member to rely on self-validation (earned entitlement), or validation built on fair consideration of the others. Self-validation and commitment are seen as self-sustaining sources of self-esteem and motivation.

Another major goal is to work toward a "balance of fairness," or relational mutuality, which is an ideal and thus never fully attainable. This goal requires periodic examination of the trustworthiness (fairness) of family relationships. Each new act of give and take rebalances the trustworthiness in the family.

Finally, contextual therapy aims to mobilize positive relational resources, rather than focusing on removing symptoms or presenting problems. This focus reflects the concept that relational resources are real and basic emotional processes between family members, by which they can aid and improve themselves and each other without therapeutic intervention in the future.

Assessment

In order to assess a family's strengths and liabilities, and to diagnose their current status, the clinician must examine several relational patterns.

They are chiefly patterns in the ethical dimension, rather than in the psychological or directly transactional dimension. The therapist utilizes multidirectional partiality to collect information about the quality of familial relationships. Early questions focus on aiding members to bring to the surface concerns about their perceived balance of fairness and unfairness. During assessment, the therapist also helps members to begin the process of delineating and validating their respective positions with one another.

The therapist also assesses the degree to which members are *reliable* for one another—how attuned they are now to one another's needs and interests, even in the presence of alienation and conflict. If family members have earned merit with one another in the past and have been reliable, they retain some trustworthiness despite severe symptoms.

Interpersonal conflicts of interest, or competing needs, are assessed in an effort to distinguish between those that are unavoidable (e.g., adolescent separation vs. parental concern), and those that may be avoidable (e.g., intolerance of differences). The clinician also looks for evidence of invisible loyalties and split loyalties. Signs include restricted psychological development, depression, self-destructive behavior, behavior problems, psychosomatic illness, and anxiety symptoms. Specific transgenerational legacies and mandates are explored, particularly the degree to which these expectations are imposed rather than retained by choice.

An early primary task of assessment is to determine remaining sources of caring and surviving attachments. The contextual model holds that relatives *always* represent potential resources to one another, no matter how distant or alienated they may be. Indications of broken-off family dialogue, or "cutoff," can provide clues for the therapist as to residual sources of family trust.

The presence of various types of relational exploitation, particularly delegation, scapegoating, and distancing, is assessed. Historical facts are recorded, such as developmental history, adverse circumstances and their impact on the couple or family, and emergencies that have required crisis intervention. The clinician also assesses life cycle events, nodal events, adjustment to current stage of the family life cycle, and coping capacity with extenuating circumstances such as chronic illness.

Individual psychological factors that are assessed include degree of a differentiated self; capacity to give up old forms of relating and to mourn them; ability to "work through" losses; presence of parentification; intense affect (an indicator of relational imbalances); and degree of maturation.

Finally, in the transactional dimension, the clinician observes "power" alignments of hierarchy; the presence of competition and alliances;

and other short-term behavior patterns. When possible, the therapist seeks to sort out the personal needs, motives and capacities behind power alignments.

Therapeutic Techniques

GENERAL GUIDELINES

Contextual therapy uses as its central method an exploration of familial legacies, invisible loyalties, and ledger balances. Generally, the clinician guides the family toward tasks that increase mutuality; that strengthen and identify resources for trustworthiness; and that encourage exoneration of previous generations, so that they are seen in a less blaming light.

SPECIFIC INTERVENTIONS

The technique of "eliciting" encourages spontaneous initiatives in family members to address their own concerns constructively. Beliefs and behaviors are considered within the framework of balancing obligations and entitlements, and any step that family members take to improve this balance is supported. The emphasis is on the balance of fairness between individuals, rather than on a systemic level.

The "moratorium" is a step that guides clients toward considering the benefits of making relational change, without demanding that they make change. The therapist waits until family members become spontaneously motivated to pursue a change, providing active therapeutic input about options while respecting their individual timing. This intervention combines a message of change in accountability, with an offer for the client to choose when he/she is ready (Boszormenyi-Nagy & Krasner, 1986).

The process of making relational change, particularly reconnecting after a long period when dialogue has been severed or restricted, is called "rejunction." It is the equivalent of "detriangling" in the natural systems model (see Chapter 1). It is an effort to rework impasses, in which family members choose to re-earn merit through increased connection with the extended family. Rejunction requires some risk-taking in acknowledging responsibility for past problems and encountering them again in a therapeutic context.

"Therapeutic crediting" is a technique that involves multidirected crediting of one family member after another, in order to create a basis for trust from outside the family. It especially includes focusing on any initiatives taken, creating the prospect of more reciprocity in the future, and building hope. It is a type of eliciting, like positive connotation, but is based on familial efforts rather than on the therapist's agenda.

Pathological symptoms are often related to unutilized or underutilized resources of support. The therapist can mobilize unutilized resources by focusing on latent sources of support and caregiving, to emphasize them.

"Siding" is an intervention in which the therapist earns trust by relating freely to each family member at different times. Siding with one member is balanced by an expectation for accountability from that person, beginning with the demand to define one's point of view. There is a demand to listen to and consider the interests of other family members as well. An inability to offer consideration is a sign that deeper siding is necessary. Siding softens intermittent confrontations, and may be used to suggest a moratorium on painful or difficult changes (Boszormenyi-Nagy & Ulrich, 1981).

The therapist may also frame the therapy as a process in which existing loyalties will be respected, and disloyalties examined; this technique is called "loyalty framing." It is based on the idea that leaving family members in unresolved antagonism is damaging, and has multigenerational implications.

Finally, "exoneration," as noted earlier, is the process of exploring parents' and grandparents' choices and behaviors in a more human, less judgmental context. The clinician reopens questions about parents, partly to dispel affects of shame, blame, and implicit negative connotation that are attached to those relationships. The goal is not insight, but rather a re-exploration and a commitment to open up new dialogue. If there is intense ambivalence, rage, guilt, or grief, this procedure takes a long time and requires repeated use of multidirectional partiality.

·4·

Object Relations Family Model

History of the Model

The object relations model of family therapy derives from psychoanalytic principles of "listening, responding to unconscious material, interpreting, developing insight, and working in the transference and countertransference toward growth" (Scharff & Scharff, 1987, p. 3). There has been considerable analytic influence in the early development of several family systems thinkers: Nathan Ackerman, Lyman Wynne, and Theodor Lidz. Norman Paul and James Framo are not analysts, but have been influenced by object relations theory. Virginia Satir borrowed heavily from self psychology from the Chicago Institute of Psychoanalysis, and used many of those concepts in her work at the Mental Research Institute and elsewhere. Donald Jackson was influenced by Harry Stack Sullivan. Murray Bowen was, and Salvador Minuchin is, qualified as an analyst. Mara Selvini Palazzoli is also an analyst, as are (or were) Helm Stierlin, Maurizio Andolfi, and Ronald D. Laing. John Byng-Hall and Robin Skynner received analytic training.

In the United States, psychoanalytic development has tended to be dominated by Freudian theory, which contains few interpersonal and interactional concepts. Derivations in the 1950s, 1960s, and 1970s (e.g., Otto Kernberg's theory of personality) have been difficult to utilize in the family interactional arena. Sullivan's theory, which was originally elaborated in 1953, was not accepted and therefore not applied widely.

The object relations model, also called "ego psychology" or "self psychology," does not draw from Freudian structuralism or the concepts of the sexual (Eros) and death (Thanatos) instincts. Instead, this derivation stresses the individual's adaptation to the environment, and also internal conflicts arising from attempts to master the environment. Wishes, fantasies, and affect do not determine family process causally, according to the model, but arise within the context of family process. Extended to family systems, the object relations model draws from John Bowlby's (1969, 1973) concepts of attachment and traumatic separation, Margaret Mahler's (Mahler, Pine, & Bergman, 1975) concept of separation–individuation, and theories of parent–infant bonding (Brazelton, Koslowski, & Main, 1974; Benedek, 1959; Fraiberg & Fraiberg, 1980).

This developmental psychoanalytic model allows room for observation and description of families because it contains transactional concepts, which Freudian theory does not. Initially, the model focused on individual behavior and symptoms, developed by W. R. D. Fairbairn (1952), Michael Balint, Donald Winnicott (the independent group), Harry Guntrip, and Melanie Klein (the English school). Fairbairn stayed fairly structural, but felt that intrapsychic structures develop in interaction between very young children and their primary caretakers. In Fairbairn's theory, infants form an "ideal object" with negative or disruptive characteristics split off. He emphasized the importance of repression (of negative interactions) in creating later symptoms of rigidity, constriction, and repetition of trauma.

Klein's (1957, 1975) concept of "projection" became the central notion that frozen, repressed ideas (beliefs) are split off onto attachment figures, in order to protect against memories of pain. Klein departed from Freud's notions of psychic structure, and theorized that individuals cope with and manage positive and negative instinctual urges in relation to the primary caretaker. She stressed the problem of managing the "death" instinct, which she felt could spoil early bonding, and which is most often accomplished by splitting interactions into "good" and "bad" objects (or others) to protect the self or the loved one from pain.

H. V. Dicks's method of treating marital couples applied the concept of the "ideal object" and the idea of projection to the selection and handling of spouses. He posited that marriage presents an opportunity to reintegrate repressed ideas, but may instead repeat them if the partner is collusive. Dicks (1963) felt that birth of children contributed to projecting repressed material out of a collusive marriage. Bion (1961) applied Klein's projection-splitting hypothesis to group function, observing that unrelated individuals appeared to perceive helplessness, anxiety, and other negative emotions in other group members, when actually the affect probably reflected their own internal state.

A number of systemic family theorists have explicitly considered this older material on idealization, projection, and splitting. Norman Paul, James Framo, and Ivan Boszormenyi-Nagy (Boszormenyi-Nagy & Spark, 1973) all mention interest in Fairbairn's object relations approach. Mara Selvini Palazzoli (1974) felt that only the concept of introjection in the object relations model could adequately explain disturbed body image.

Key Concepts

The "introject" is a psychological representation of relationships with significant others. It is essentially an internal image that influences behavior in current significant relationships and is outside awareness. Introjects are often split into "good" and "bad" objects, and may be integrated into a personal belief system or projected (attributed) to others. " . . . Active unconscious attempts are made to force and change close relationships into fitting the internal role models" (Framo, 1970/ 1972, p. 26).

An introject is considered the most basic "mental structure" (or belief system) that reflects real interpersonal relationships. The process of introjection begins early in an undifferentiated self, in a young child dependent on caretaking. Introjects are defensive in the sense that real relationships have painful as well as positive aspects. Fairbairn (1952, 1954) speculated that during introjection, the negative aspects are split off and either suppressed or modified later in light of subsequent relationships.

"Mutual attribution" (Dicks, 1963) is a process in distressed marriages, in which each spouse perceives the other to a degree as an internalized object. Accordingly, instead of responding to the real attributes of the partner, the spouse interprets his/her partner's behavior in light of earlier, childhood familial figures.

"Mutual projection" (Dicks, 1963) is another process in distressed marriages, in which each spouse's identity is preserved by splitting off internalized bad objects that have been disowned. The partners begin to conform to the roles projected onto them, in a collusive manner. The process reflects unresolved family-of-origin conflicts. Each partner hopes to regain lost introjects (internal relational memories) by "finding" them in the other.

"Unconscious contracts" (Sager, 1976) are marital bargains in which each partner accommodates to the other's perceptions and subtle demands, in exchange for the confirmatory behavior he/she wishes to receive from the other spouse.

"Parental projections" are split-off parental traits that are attributed to the offspring. Offspring tend to conform to these expected traits and to act them out behaviorally (similar to Stierlin's [1974] concept of "delegation"). Bowen, Framo, and Williamson all suggest that there are risks associated with parental projections, and counter them with explicit adult–adult renegotiation.

The "basic fault" is an empty-feeling state reflecting lack of fit or empathic connectedness between parent and child. This "basic fault" is seen in attachments that seem insecure, anxious, or needy, and in problems of social isolation or distancing. It is not regarded as a defense against negative impulses or beliefs, but rather as a deficit (Balint, 1968).

"Transitional space" refers to the boundary between self and intimate others, which is quite ambiguous in infancy. It becomes progressively defined relationally, in context, between two parties. A firm boundary separates the internal world from the other, who must be trustworthy and empathic for a developing child's true self to be expressed; otherwise, he/she may (falsely) suppress self (Winnicott, 1951/1975, 1965).

"Projective identification" and "introjective identification" are Kleinian concepts. Introjective identification involves introjecting parts of an object into the self, and identifying with part or all of it. Projective identification involves projecting parts of self into an object, and either identifying with that object or perceiving the object as like the self. Guttman (1989) adds that partners may also project onto each other aspects of significant others that they have experienced (e.g., a critical or withholding parent). Projective identification can become pathological if the parts attributed to the other are then split off (or denied) in oneself.

Theory of Healthy Functioning

The object relations family systems model is a life cycle developmental model, which focuses upon stages of internal individual development *paired with* the interactional process of bonding/attaching and separating (Scharff & Scharff, 1987). These phases include birth and physical symbiosis; an early "psychosomatic partnership" (Winnicott, 1971); psychological partnership; separation and individuation of babyhood; rapprochement; separation and individuation of adolescence; launching; marital bonding; and parental bonding (and working through of repressed material as one's children develop).

Well-Functioning Marriage

In the nondistressed marriage, both spouses have personalities largely formed of central, conscious ego, and relatively little internal conflict (similar to the natural systems concept of differentiation; see Chapter 1). They are able to perceive each other realistically rather than engaging in mutual attribution, and these perceptions are consistent and fond. Attachment is active, including sexual arousal, romance, and a sense of adventure. Each self perceives the spouse as "good enough," and accepts flaws or disappointments without finding them intolerable. The partners feel committed to the marital bond. They can accept themselves, and can access more primary-process, irrational sides within the context of marital trust.

Each partner can contain pathological (split-off) projections put on him/her by the other, accept them, modify them, and return them with trust and empathy. Each partner can take responsibility for his/her own projections. The central self (identified as "me") can access impulses and wishes to seek intimacy, work, and pleasure.

Healthy Family

In a well-functioning family, the couple has developed to the point where each spouse has experienced and understood mutual patterns and individual unresolved emotionality, thereby "clearing the field" for child rearing. The new parents can confront their own and each other's unacceptable expectations and projections, so that they are not invested into the children.

When these pathological projections occur, the family system is open enough that through parent–child interaction, the repressed fantasies can be expressed and reworked. Over time, conflicts and interactions within the family also modify the children's image of the parents and siblings, so that their perceptions can mature without becoming distorted, frozen, or projected.

Theory of Family Dysfunction

Dysfunctional Marriage

As mentioned earlier, from an object relations standpoint, a couple becomes distressed when one or both partners enter a marriage carrying a great deal of repressed, painful material that is out of awareness. This material arises from experience with significant others—grandparents, parents, siblings, peers, and influential others—which creates conflict or feels frightening or traumatic.

Because it feels intolerable to experience this anxiety or negative affect about intimates, the affect is suppressed and is discharged indirectly through various coping strategies (or "defenses"). However, as a result of this suppression, young adults may marry without revisiting unresolved relational conflicts and recognizing or coming to terms with the effects on themselves. If marriage takes place in this context of poor self-awareness and inadequate launching, the conflicted partner often goes on to project the intolerable aspects of his/her affect or memories onto the spouse.

In some very distressed marriages, the process of projection can be two-way, or mutual. In this situation, each spouse harbors significant degrees of discomfort with intimacy, based on previous problems in the family of origin. Furthermore, neither spouse has recognized or revisited these unresolved problems to create viable solutions for himself/herself or the family of origin. In order to prevent the painful memories from becoming predominant, each spouse projects unacceptable feelings and memories onto the other.

As pointed out earlier, spouses also come to accommodate to the projections onto themselves by showing the behavior expected of them. For example, a man from a physically violent home may feel great anger toward the parents who beat him. This affect is painful in that experiencing anger toward one's parents, if there has been no reconciliation or repair of trust, may seem isolative and dangerous. This man may, instead of recognizing and using his anger to create change, suppress it and deny that it exists. In his marriage, he may react quite intensely whenever his wife is dissatisfied, believing her to be furiously angry. Furthermore, his wife may over time accommodate to this projection of her husband's anger, and see herself as a hostile and rejecting partner.

The Dysfunctional Family

"The point about an object relations approach is that it is not so much a theory as it is a way of working" (Sutherland, 1985). According to the object relations family systems model, children may become used as a vehicle for their parents' repressed or unacceptable strivings, engendering battles between a parent and child rather than between spouses. This idea is echoed in Bowen's theory that one method of siphoning off marital tension that results from differentiation problems is overfocusing on the behavior of children.

From the object relations point of view, when marital partners are engaged in a projection process with each other (which may be mutual), this method of siphoning off tension is quite common and perhaps inevitable. Whereas other transgenerational models amy define this triangulation of children as one symptom, object relations theory suggests that it is impossible to remain flexible and constructive in child rearing if one cannot cope with one's past family experiences.

The concept called "return of the repressed" is a description of how a conflicted parent relives stagnant family relationships through offspring. Often applied to the stage of parenting adolescent children, "return of the repressed" refers to increased awareness of negative thoughts and feelings left over from unresolved family problems the parent experienced *at the same age*. It is a type of anniversary reaction, applied to an entire life stage rather than to one traumatic incident.

For example, a woman who left her family too early by becoming pregnant out of wedlock may have received parental disapproval and a critical lack of support in her adolescent life. She may retain strong feelings about adolescence, sexuality, and social approval. She may experience difficulty in sexual intimacy with her husband (e.g., orgasmic dysfunction). As her children mature, she may have difficulty accepting her own teenage daughter's sexuality, show disapproval of normal dating behavior, and view her daughter as oversexualized, withdrawing her own emotional support as a consequence.

Other types of familial dysfunction involve failures of bonding and failures of empathy from parent to child. An adult who was abused or neglected as a child, or who suffered a traumatic loss, may be able to maintain an emotional connection with a nurturant spouse, but may be unable to provide nurturance to children. This symptom reflects a deficit that has been earlier defined as a "basic fault." Since empathy is a relational process that is learned by observing and internalizing, if it is not observed or is lost with one's parent(s) it cannot be learned. Such individuals often seek out supportive partners to replace the empathic parents they have lost (or did not experience), but have not learned to show empathy themselves. After the birth of children, the parent with an empathic deficit often appears unable to bond intimately with offspring, or to feel confident about how the children feel and perceive the world.

Finally, there is a category of family dysfunctions that has to do with repetition of destructive behavior over generations. A mother who was battered as a child may batter her own child when emotionally aroused. A father who was molested may engage in incest with his daughter. This repetition of behavior is explained, in the object relations view, as a type of emotional overconnection with the destructive elders. It is called "identification with the aggressor." These individuals have not suppressed their memories of unresolved family problems, nor projected these memories onto the spouse; instead, they have chosen to see themselves deliberately as "like" the symptomatic elders. In an effort to preserve an emotional connection with the elders, the adult children essentially agree to behave as they behaved. (The contextual model refers to this pattern as one of "invisible loyalties"; see Chapter 3.)

Interventions and Technique

Goals

Generally, the object relations family model seeks " . . . to expand the family's capacity to perform the holding functions for its members and their capacities to offer holding of each other" (Scharff & Scharff, 1987, p. 62). This includes improving the family's ability to master life cycle transitions via maintenance of an envelope of protection for each member; and to offer empathic communication and behavior to members as they develop.

Specific subgoals include the following: to recognize and rework defensive projective identifications; to provide "holding" (nurturance) for attachment and growth; to aid in the construction of healthy dyadic relationships within the family; to maintain a developmental level appropriate to tasks of life stage and family preferences; to clarify individual needs and to provide later individual therapy as necessary; and to enable family autonomy, including separation and individuation within the family and between members and outside groups.

Assessment

The process of assessment includes six tasks. It begins with the provision of a therapeutic space that can accommodate all age levels (including toys for children), and that will permit the therapist to assess familial life stage and developmental level. The therapist wants to obtain an enactment *in the room* of defensive functioning; that is, he/she wants to determine what place the symptoms have in the belief system of the family (values, needs, fears, etc.). Next, unconscious assumptions and anxieties underlying the symptoms are explored—the unwritten contracts and expectations that underlie marital and parenting decisions. These include transference responses to the therapist's initiatives in the evaluation sessions.

The family's response to the assessment format is tested, as well as their reactions to interpretation. The clinician is especially interested in the family's ability to tolerate frustration, psychological-mindedness, commitment to therapy, insight orientation, and presence of individual symptoms (Scharff & Scharff, 1987).

Therapeutic Techniques

Family systems therapy within the object relations model may include individual, marital, and family sessions, or may employ a combined strategy that is designed to fit the needs and motivations of each particular family.

GENERAL GUIDELINES

One of the central techniques of the approach is analysis of resistance by use of interpretation. Analysis of resistance includes a formulation of covert alliances that have formed among family members around the resistance. For example, one person may be the spokesperson for familial discomfort; one may offer only agreement; one may passively support the resistance; and so on.

Another general technique is enlarging the field of participation. This involves inclusion of multiple perspectives and observations from within the family, increasing the complexity of interactions by adding more members, and linking symptomatic behavior to other familial conflicts and family-wide patterns.

Finally, the therapist positions himself/herself to direct "core affective exchange" (Scharff & Scharff, 1987, p. 179) into the here and now, which increases immediacy, credibility, and understanding of a problem pattern. Use of past or peripheral information is not discouraged, but is shifted to in-the-room events whenever possible. "Conveying specifically (in the room) how these [interactions] involve the hurt and longing of the family members enables each of them to feel understood. . . . The change in the external object modifies the internal object" (Scharff & Scharff, 1987, p. 179).

SPECIFIC INTERVENTIONS

There are four levels of specific intervention that can be utilized. All levels are used repeatedly until the family members begin to provide these functions for themselves, later in therapy.

First, there are comments aimed at organizing the session. These include giving individuals room to talk; calming explosiveness; containing affect; gathering transgenerational information; and facilitating empathy and understanding.

Second, there are comments aimed at giving support or advice. These include explicit or implicit encouragement; validation; interpretation; exploration of material; advice (didactic education) limited to child development; and eliciting alternatives from families in a less authoritative mode.

On a third level are comments showing understanding. These include descriptive comments (such as review of events), as well as more interpretive comments; joining statements that increase therapeutic alliance; nonverbal role modeling; and incorporating family modifications into previous comments. This level of commentary is mostly directed at affective tone and underlying beliefs, and uses family metaphors (similar to the structural family therapy technique of "tracking"). Also included are metacommunications from the therapist. Interpretations are put as often as possible in either a normalizing or an exploratory mode.

Finally, there are comments aimed at examining transference behavior and countertransference behavior. Families are seen for prolonged periods in this model (as long as 1 to 2 years), and evidence of dysfunctional relating often shows up in attitudes toward the therapist.

Alternative forms of commentary include "facilitating communications" (asking family members to voice their opinions and reactions directly); strategically using silence; and utilizing play with children and adolescents.

James Framo has adapted many of the techniques of object relations family systems therapy to couples groups. Although his interventions are eclectic (Framo, 1976/1982, 1980, 1981/1982), he shares the therapeutic goal discussed earlier of empowering individual spouses to think about and rework family relationships that have been problematic. He utilizes family-of-origin sessions late in the therapeutic contract, for two purposes: (1) to provide diagnostic information about how past family problems are enacted in the present; and (2) to create a source of change. Change occurs in this arena in several ways: discovering previously unknown information about the family; clarifying old misunderstandings based on childhood perceptions; demystifying "magical" symbolic meanings that members carry for one another; becoming acquainted with one's parents as real people; and developing adult–adult relationships with aging parents. The resulting differentiation allows married clients to respond to spouses and children without projecting disowned parts of themselves out.

Therapeutic Parameters

Families are usually seen for 1 to 2 years, to maximize "depth" and accommodate severe dysfunction. Brief interventions are made when the family insists on limited goals, when family members are stuck in transition, when the family cannot continue for practical reasons, or when the therapist's agency will not support lengthy therapy.

Cotherapy is often used in order to mediate very conflicted families, and also to encourage multiple transferences for analysis. It is also used for training purposes, and in sex therapy; however, it is not an extensively used mode of therapy.

Limitations

Scharff and Scharff (1987) consider inner-city families, multiproblem families, and those with substance abuse "difficult to treat," rather than faulting the object relations model. This approach requires an intact capacity for symbolic thinking, and few rather than multiple deprivations. Rigidity (an unwillingness to tolerate too much challenge) also impairs results. However, many family therapy trainers agree that analytic training is useful for understanding internal aspects of family functioning, even if specific techniques are not applied in a treatment case.

Termination

This model of therapy typically involves a lengthy (months-long) process of work in preparation for termination. The termination phase consists of learning new strategies through repetitions over time. Repetitions of new solutions supposedly represent higher levels of maturation and self-awareness each time. Ideally, termination occurs when the family can adequately provide resources, manage boundaries, and provide nurturance, without input from the therapist.

Termination may also be imposed by the therapist when no gains are being made. It may also occur prematurely in families that do not have enough parental limit setting and structure. For premature terminations or those imposed by external changes (e.g., relocation), late-stage sessions address the obstacles and help the family plan for the future. Some terminations are planned as a transfer to individual therapy, or other modalities.

The termination phase focuses more on working through previous material, and avoids dramatically new or discordant material. It also attends to the mourning process inherent in ending an intimate, long-term relationship between therapist and family.

·5·

The Transgenerational Lens: Functional Family Process

Each transgenerational model of family functioning has a theory of "normal" or "healthy" functioning, even if that theory is not well articulated. Functional family process includes multiple levels of experience: patterns of interaction, emotional dynamics, and internal structures. We say that a family is functional, or healthy, if events on all these levels contribute to the following:

1. Completion of important life cycle tasks.
2. Acceptance and nurturance of individual members' needs, especially those of children being reared.
3. A degree of individuation and autonomy for each member and each subsystem (e.g., the parental marriage).
4. Capacity to tolerate conflict and to adapt to adverse circumstances without long-term dysfunction or disintegration of family cohesion.

All of the four major transgenerational models have at least these basic aspects of healthy functioning in common. Specific aspects of healthy functioning can most easily be discussed by examining each level of family functioning separately: interactional patterns, emotional dynamics, and internal structure. In this chapter, I examine each level of healthy functioning as it applies to three specific family subsystems: the parental marriage, the parent–child subsystem, and the sibling subsystem.

The Parental Marriage

Major transgenerational models agree on the importance of a strong, functional marriage to maintenance of family health. However, each model tends to focus on different aspects of marital functioning. The object relations model focuses on emotional dynamics in couples. This model considers a functional marriage to require two partners who have a relatively nonambivalent attachment to each other; few expectations and motives projected onto the other; commitment to the marriage; and belief that the partner is "good enough" despite problems and disappointments (Scharff & Scharff, 1987).

In the marriage, from the analytic viewpoint, both spouses have well-differentiated selves, and can experience self-acceptance even of their irrational sides. This requires that each partner has developed a strong identity, with a well-articulated set of internal self-representations, and ability to maintain self-esteem even in the face of stressful events or loss. Self-acceptance includes awareness of their own needs and impulses, so that emotional needs are not diverted in self-destructive ways, or chronically suppressed (which leads, in analytic theory, to negative projections).

Although spouses in functional couples show some degree of self-awareness, it is still inevitable that extremely painful or anxiety-provoking thoughts and feelings are at times suppressed. Over time, if these reactions are not faced and resolved, they are projected onto the partner, creating negative expectations. The partner becomes viewed as the one suffering from these painful feelings. For example, a wife who has difficulty accepting her own desire for achievement and meaningful work may perceive her husband as too invested in his own career ambitions. In a functional marriage, when such projections become persistent, the spouses are able to tolerate each other's unrealistic expectations until they can be modified or corrected (Scharff & Scharff, 1987).

The natural systems model of Murray Bowen focuses less on the interplay of spousal fantasies and projections. However, this model also focuses on emotional dynamics in marital couples. It looks intensively into the impact of differentiation of self on the quality of marital functioning. From the natural systems viewpoint, spouses with well-differentiated selves can maintain decisiveness or goal direction, hold clear personal values, are flexible in accepting individual differences, have a sense of security in the marriage, can tolerate autonomy in the partner, and can tolerate conflict (Bowen, 1966/1988).

These characteristics create interactional patterns that are relatively conflict-free, open to new information, and self-aware. The natural systems model complements the object relations view that on a fantasy level, irrational expectations are at a minimum; that is, because the two married individuals are well differentiated, they are less likely to project intolerable feelings and beliefs onto one another. Projections that cause tension and stress are negotiated until each spouse becomes more realistic about the other. Both models agree that developmental failure, or poor differentiation, creates the most severe obstacles to flexible marital functioning.

The natural systems model also examines the role of internal structure in functional marriages. As noted in Chapter 1, Bowenian theory was the first to speculate that the smallest stable relational unit is not a dyad, but a triad. This hypothesis stemmed from the observation that dyads frequently become overloaded with intense emotionality during periods of familial stress. During these stressful periods, a third, "outsider" party is triangulated into the dyad, usually in an alliance with one partner. As a result, the level of tension between the individuals in the dyad decreases. This process is considered normative, as long as it is transient and flexible (involving different parties at different times).

The contextual model is unique in that, of all the transgenerational models, it explicitly addresses the emotional dynamics of ethics: mutuality, empathy, and "due consideration" or respect (Boszormenyi-Nagy & Krasner, 1986). Its proponents hold that in order for these important elements to be present in marriage, that they must be present in each spouse's family of origin. If two generations of a family are unable, because of trauma, adverse circumstance, or dysfunction, to provide empathy and nurturance to the young, then when those offspring marry they will be unable to advance this consideration to their own spouses and children. We have seen how, in the contextual model, deficits in empathy are transmitted by a process of parentifying children who grow up to feel exploited and self-involved.

In this area of theory, all of the transgenerational models of healthy marital functioning agree, if only implicitly. The degree to which a parental marriage functions well reflects the degree to which each spouse has experienced and can offer empathy, receptivity, and *quid pro quo* to the other.

The symbolic-experiential model agrees that a well-functioning marriage depends on spousal differentiation and empathy. However, there is much more emphasis on interactional patterns, as well as on the quality of emotional dynamics between spouses. Spouses attend to the needs of the marriage before those of their families of origin, but in times of crisis each can focus on the family of origin without producing feelings of rejection or anxiety in the other partner (Roberto, 1991). There is flexibility in the roles each partner occupies, so that as each spouse changes beliefs or behavior over time, the marital expectations can be renegotiated and adapted. This flexibility includes gender role flexibility, so that the couple possesses resources to resist the pressure of our masculine-oriented culture. In this way, a functional marriage is flexible enough to allow the wife to focus on her own developmental needs, as well as on marital and family demands.

On the more implicit level of beliefs, the symbolic-experiential model holds that healthy marriages construct creative ways to incorporate transgenerational traditions, values, and mandates from the families of origin. Although spouses need not reproduce earlier marital patterns from one or two generations before, this model posits that the values of past generations must to *some extent* be considered and adapted into the current marriage, in order to achieve meaningful separation from families of origin.

Symbolic-experiential theory resembles the contextual model, in its attention to the influence of family myths and customs on roles taken and options pursued by their offspring. Both models posit that in addition to separating psychologically from their families of origin, and bringing the capacity for empathy and mutual consideration to the marriage, spouses must incorporate and modify family-of-origin mandates in some useful way in order to function in adult married life.

The Parent–Child Subsystem

From an object relations standpoint, emotional dynamics between parents and children reveal healthy functioning. Object relations theory maintains that an optimally functioning family provides a "holding environment" for its members, which provides a context of security, trust, and nurturance to underpin individual maturation (Scharff & Scharff, 1987; Winnicott, 1965). Within the context of this holding environment, children pass through stages of psychological separation and individual self-awareness, intermittently turning to the parents for confirmation of their competence, and for emotional reassurance (the process termed "rapprochement").

From this standpoint, the well-functioning parent–child subsystem allows for shifts between attachment and separation, so that children can experiment gradually and with confidence. Object relations theorists have pointed out that parents need not be perfectly accessible and encouraging in order to promote healthy functioning. Winnicott (1965) referred to the well-functioning caretaker as the "good enough mother."

In terms of parental responses in families with several children, optimal parenting allows each child to be encouraged in his/her own individuality. Also, although children are believed to project many idealized expectations onto parents in the infancy stage, the object relations model states that by the time of adolescence any idealizations of the parents should be modified into a more realistic, balanced view.

James Framo (1970/1972, 1980), in his transgenerational work, has adapted the object relations model extensively to the study of parents with adult children. Framo states that in adulthood, offspring need again to rework childhood perceptions of the parents; to demystify "magical" expectations once held of elders; to access previously hidden information; and to increase intimate interchange about the parents' lives, thereby increasing knowledge of the parents as "real people."

The natural systems model considers "the 'triangle' (three-person system) the 'molecule' of any emotional system, whether it exists in the family or in a larger social system" (Bowen, 1972/1988, p. 469). Because of the somewhat geometrical or mathematical properties of this concept, the natural systems model applies certain structural criteria when looking at parent–child relationships. Since the triangle is the smallest stable relationship system in Bowenian theory, it is inevitable that in functional families a child may occupy one point in a parental triangle.

As noted in Chapter 1, triangles form when a dyad becomes stressed because dyads are unstable (Bowen, 1972/1988). In periods of calm, the triangle is occupied by a dyad (e.g., two parents) and an "outsider" who is less intimate (e.g., a selected child). Proponents of this model believe that when the "outsider" or third party in a triangle becomes stressed, he/she pulls one member of the dyad toward him/her, and the ally becomes more peripheral. Or the stressed members of the dyad may involve the third party in their conflict (Bowen, 1966/1988). Under severe stress, the favored position is that of the outsider, since that position is less pressured and emotionally laden. If the outsider cannot be pulled in, another third party is pulled in. Triangles have two "positive" sides and one "negative" side; that is, one member of the dyad usually feels quite negative toward the outsider. However, even in the most fixed and invariant triangles, positive and negative forces shift back and forth continually (Bowen, 1972/1988).

It can be seen that this normative process occurs and recurs within intimate relationships, in functional as well as dysfunctional families. However, functional parent–child subsystems differ from dysfunctional ones in several areas: (1) the resiliency and transience of these triangles; and (2) the absence of severe family projection onto the selected child or children; leading to (3) an attenuated multigenerational transmission process.

In functional families, triangles that form around highly stressed dyads are situational and relatively fluid. Although one or more children may become involved in a parental triangle, the same child is not always involved. The membership of emotional triangles is not fixed, but fluctuates as unresolved family disputes arise. Moreover, in healthy families the parent–child subsystem does not require triangles to persist, so that the child or children are not delegated to assist on a chronic basis. As a conflict is addressed directly, with a strong "I" position for all the parties involved, the triangle surrounding it can dissolve. As a consequence, pressures within the marital dyad, or between a spouse and the family of origin, need not be transmitted to the children.

According to the contextual model, it is not so much the structural characteristics of a parent–child relationship that determine health, but rather the trustworthiness that a parent demonstrates and his/her ability to exonerate others (a dynamic, ethical level of analysis). It is true that a parent who is severely burdened with marital or unresolved family-of-origin stress cannot devote much emotional energy to a child. For example, a parent who has major depressive symptoms following loss of an ambivalently loved father may not be able to show attention to the needs of small children in the home. However, even in a family with such an overburdened parent, it is still possible for that parent to demonstrate trustworthiness to his/her children.

Trustworthiness is built up through active consideration of a child's feelings and views, even if the parent cannot always grant the child's wishes. In a well-functioning parent–child relationship, the parent is sufficiently oriented toward respecting the child so that he/she can acknowledge the child's point of view even in the midst of a difficult family problem.

Exoneration, according to the contextual model, is the process of examining and understanding the efforts of one's own parents. Adults who are willing to rework their relationships with their own parents to enhance and strengthen their mutual attachment teach children the value of remaining connected. Children in these families, in turn, have a strong sense of identification with the family and a sense of cohesion. Perhaps in a sense, this contextual concept provides one ingredient in the "holding environment" prescribed within the object relations model.

The symbolic-experiential model focuses on structure as well as emotional dynamics, unlike the object relations and contextual models, which take a more process-oriented view of parent–child relationships. Its attention to structure is also on a more "macro" level than that of the natural systems model, which restricts its structural considerations to the interpersonal triangle. From the symbolic-experiential perspective, there should be permeable boundaries between generations (grandparent, parent, and child subgroups). Permeable boundaries also surround the nuclear family, so that children may have access to friends and outside interests without being perceived as disloyal or threatening (Roberto, 1991). There is also an invisible boundary around the three-generational extended family, such that its members have a family identity that separates relatives from friends and acquaintances.

Alliances and three-person coalitions (triangles) form around specific symptoms or problems until they are resolved. As in the natural systems view, however, these alliances and triangles are seen as functional *if they are transient in time and membership.* The symbolic-experiential model holds that the most enduring alliances function best within parental and sibling groups, rather than across generational lines.

In another parallel with the natural systems model, the symbolic-experiential view holds that in well-functioning families, no one family member receives all the family projections of "problem patient." Whitaker (1985) has described the functional family as having transient and "rotating scapegoat(s)," with no one child selected for transmission of all the multigenerational pressures (Whitaker & Keith, 1981).

On the more implicit level of beliefs and values, each family does have transgenerational mandates based on past events, losses, and belief systems, which combine to create expectancies and preferred roles for each family member (Roberto, 1987; Whitaker & Keith, 1981). In well-functioning families, as children develop and mature, they can examine and negotiate these mandates and can modify them.

On a process level, from the symbolic-experiential point of view, considerable bonding and intimacy must be present between parent and child as well as within the parental dyad. Although attachment is not necessarily expressed verbally, offspring need a sense of trust that the parents can be emotionally responsive. This concept is similar to the contextual concept of trustworthiness, and to the object relations concept of the "good enough parent." These demonstrations of attachment and parental availability may be precursors to the optimal "holding environment" that healthy families provide for growing children. Symbolic-experiential theory posits that the sense of belonging that results from mutual trust and bonding is essential to healthy family functioning.

Symbolic-experiential theory also states that in healthy families, children are encouraged to show individual differences, and can express their perceptions without being "spoken for" (Roberto, 1991). As in the natural systems model, this encouragement of differentiation requires *as a precondition* that the parents have separated, to some degree, from their own families of origin. In this area, the object relations model also attests to the importance of encouraging individual separation and development of self-awareness. In a well-functioning family, growing autonomy is balanced by the sense of identification with, and commitment to, the family group.

The Sibling Subsystem

Until recently, family systems models did not generate a great deal of theory regarding how siblings relate in families and how to distinguish between functional and dysfunctional sibling subsystems. The transgenerational models shared in this general deficiency, although the symbolic-experiential model did contain several generalized concepts regarding how sibling groups function. Recently, there has been more attention to sibling groups as one of the three pivotal "organelles" within the "cell" of the family. However, much of our current transgenerational theory regarding siblings is not well formalized and is therefore somewhat inferential. In particular, theorists within the object relations and natural systems models have made recent conceptual contributions to our understanding of sibling bonding.

Object relations proponents believe that within a family system, siblings provide specialized functions for one another where the parents may not. One specialized function is that of the "selfobject." "Selfobjects" are important others who mirror, or reflect aspects of ourselves, which we seek to understand better during the process of emotional maturation. This mirroring needs to be provided with empathy and mutual trust, in order for developing individuals to build or enhance their self-esteem (Kahn, 1988).

In mutual selfobject relationships, children can safely experience a number of complex emotional responses: needs for love; hope and excitement; anger and hate; envy and jealousy; merger; mirroring; idealization; devaluation and disappointment; and identification. However, although sibling relationships can thus be deeply involving, the participants are immature. Therefore, their relationships can appear to adults to be disruptive, conflictual, and discontinuous, despite the deep emotional interp lay between them.

Siblings tend to carry "frozen" historic images of each other throughout adult life. From an object relations point of view, these images are maintained partly out of the ongoing need to maintain object constancy (a sense of secure connectedness) in a social world that is frequently inconsistent and fragmented. Children partly define themselves by virtue of the images they carry of their siblings.

Modifying these "frozen" images, since they serve a self-defining function, then entails children's modifying their own internal self-definitions. For example, a brother who recognizes that his sister is more competent than he formerly believed, may conclude that his own achievements are less stellar than he believed. For this reason, theorists believe that siblings carry unmodified, psychologically youthful images of each other until they reach a life stage when further self-examination and self-definition occur.

Siblings may also provide for each other a sense of continuity and connectedness, particularly during periods when disruptive events or permanent familial changes take place (e.g., parental divorce). It is important to reiterate that the siblings' interactions may not necessarily be loving, and they may even interact in tense or even combative ways. Nevertheless, in either case, the intensification of a sibling relationship can create a sense of continuity to bridge episodes of family disengagement or stress.

The natural systems model, consistent with its less affective and more structural focus, draws on theories of birth order and sibling constellation. One example of this theoretical work is found in the writings of Walter Toman, at the University of Erlangen-Nürnberg in Germany. The object relations view links sibling bonding to the quality of the parent–child "holding environment," and to the presence or absence of parental nurturance and early mirroring for the children. Toman's "ordinal theory" focuses on the way in which chronological birth order and gender balance affect sibling bonding.

No matter what kind of emotional "atmosphere" that a particular family possesses, its children are likely to share certain characteristics in common with other children in the same ordinal position (Perlmutter, 1988; Toman, 1988). For example, a firstborn child is likely to have a role of responsibility and guidance with younger siblings, and to be encouraged in this by the parents. Toman, reviewing several sociological studies, concludes:

> Sibling position characteristics tend to account for some 10 to 20% of the variance in a person's longterm . . . behavior . . . and preferences. If [the person] occupies an identical or similar sibling position as his same-sex parent, the characteristics of that sibling position can sometimes account for up to 50% of [the variance]. (Toman, 1988, p. 49)

Toman points out that sibling ordinal position, including sibling gender, also exerts influence on later intimate relationships. For example, in a sample of 32 couples at Brandeis University, matched for age, educational background, and socioeconomic status, there were 9 complementary pairs in 16 intact couples but only 1 complementary pair in 16 divorced couples (Toman, 1988). "Complementarity" in sibling position refers to an older brother (of sisters) marrying a younger sister (of brothers), or vice-versa.

Another way in which ordinal positions of children affect the way they bond with each other involves the degree to which those positions resemble those of the adults in the family. For example, if siblings' relative positions duplicate those of their parents, they have a pattern for interrelating that is less experimental and more familiar. An older brother may watch to see how his father treats his young stepmother, and may do likewise with his little sister.

Perlmutter (1988) points out that "The internal logic of the sibling group is essentially that of accommodation to the linearity of birth order and to individual characteristics, while the internal logic of the family system is . . . synchronous functioning" (p. 31). Despite their individual and ordinal differences, however, "The formation of alliances excluding and often opposing the parents affords siblings different relationship patterns than those found in the total family context" (p. 32).

Birth order effects actually create a different family context for each child. Each successive child's birth changes the family's structure, which then influences each child's "map" of the family. For example, the birth of a first child necessitates the making of explicit rules to be communicated from parent to child. The second child may observe some of the rules without so much explication, while a youngest child may learn parental rules by observing interactions between parents and older siblings (Zimmerman, Collins, & Bach, 1986). In turn, each child is to some extent viewed according to his/her characteristic way of perceiving the family.

As another example of the way in which birth order, individuation, and sibling bonds tend to interact, we can observe differences in older and younger siblings' processing of familial events. The responsibility and adult orientation of firstborns tends to promote a rational, parental way of relating to siblings. Along with this orientation, there may be difficulty in appreciating relational patterns (cycles). This kind of awareness is more available to younger siblings. Youngest children, who are in the position of observing multiple interactional patterns that preceded them, have a comparatively strong understanding of the complexity of family relational patterns.

Observations of ordinal position in sibling groups have been most extensively utilized by the natural systems model. Other transgenerational models have tended to overlook offerings from this literature. To be sure, the unique characteristics of each extended family must transcend any generalizations about the privileges and pressures that accompany different sibling positions. For example, in some families, the eldest child will report that he/she deliberately avoided familial responsibilities, which were taken on by the second child. In many families, an eldest son has abdicated the position of parental aide in their advanced age, while a younger sister has taken this burden instead. The other transgenerational models have tended to examine each family individually for its distribution of roles and expectations. However, the sociological literature on ordinality has advanced enough to warrent consideration by other transgenerational theorists.

In summary, familial function and dysfunction can be discussed in terms of the family's three major subsystems: marital (parental), parent–

child, and sibling groups. In describing each of these smaller systems of relationships, the four transgenerational models interweave with one another, but differ in their conceptual focus—in their way of understanding how relationships function. The object relations model examines the quality and nature of emotional dynamics underlying intimate bonding and differentiation. The various concepts utilized to describe functional families are well represented in the ideas of the "holding environment" and the "good enough" parent.

The contextual model, although it shares in primary use of emotional dynamics, emphasizes relational ethics as opposed to more basic dynamics such as attachment, separation, and individuation. Although the natural systems model also st resses the dynamics of adequate differentiation in preserving intimacy and adaptation, it adds a secondary structural focus on the presence of triangles in functional families.

The symbolic-experiential model is the most interaction-oriented of the transgenerational models, and focuses on functional family processes such as alliances and coalitions, triangulation and detriangulation, negotiation and conflict resolution, and affection and sexuality. However, it shares a secondary focus on emotional dynamics, such as generational identifications, autonomy and individual development, parent–child bonding, intimacy, and self-disclosure. It may be said that all of these models reveal a dynamic underpinning, which is overlaid with concern for either adequate family structure, effective interactional patterns, or mutual balancing of ethical commitments.

·6·

The Transgenerational Lens: ~~Dysfunctional~~ Family Process

Dysfunctional families can be described at several different levels of observation. We can consider dysfunction, family distress, and the emergence of clinical symptoms with attention to the same three foci employed in Chapter 5: patterns of interaction, emotional dynamics, and internal family structures. Using these levels of observation, we can contrast dysfunctional families with functional ones if events on any of the three levels create the following:

1. Obstacles to negotiating, or failure to negotiate, important life cycle transitions.
2. Rejection of, neglect of, or negativity toward individual members' needs, especially those of children being reared.
3. Poor differentiation and lack of autonomy for each member and each subsystem (e.g., the parental marriage).
4. Intolerance of conflict, difficulty in adapting to change, and disintegration of family cohesion during periods of severe stress.

Each of the major transgenerational models recognizes symptoms in these four areas as critical indicators of family dysfunction. As in Chapter 5's discussion of healthy families, these four symptom areas can best be examined as they arise in specific family subsystems: the parental marriage, the parent–child subsystem, and the sibling group.

The Parental Marriage

Dysfunction in distressed couples can be described in terms of structural problems, destructive emotional dynamics, or symptomatic cycles of interaction. As in the case of healthy families, each transgenerational model tends to focus on a different level of observation in its diagnostic

80

formulations. The object relations model emphasizes the role of destructive emotional dynamics in distressed couples. From the psychoanalytic view, one or both spouses have failed to master critical life cycle tasks, particularly during childhood stages of psychological separation and individuation. Developmental delays or failures reflect problems in the family of origin in the area of encouraging individual differences and autonomy in growing children.

Unable to maintain self-esteem individually, troubled spouses tend to look to important others to confirm their self-worth and bolster important decisions. Thus, they are dependent on supportive responses from intimate partners, and require mirroring or confirmation frequently (Slipp, 1984). Such individuals are poorly differentiated from their intimate partners, and tend to show the destructive defense behaviors described in Chapter 4. Object relations theorists believe that these unmet developmental needs influence marital intimacy, and even contribute to selection of a marital partner.

If one spouse has experienced developmental failure of this kind, then the other spouse must be in either a symmetrical or a complementary position. In a symmetrical marriage, the partner is likely to show similar problems, turning toward the other in turn for mirroring and support. In a complementary marriage, the partner accommodates to the unmet needs of the poorly differentiated mate, in order to satisfy his/her own doubts about self-worth. By definition, a marital commitment can only be sustained under these conditions by mutual dependency or an overfunctioning–underfunctioning arrangement between the partners.

Essentially, in a distressed marriage each spouse needs and wants the projections and projective identifications of the partner. The mutual expectations, however unrealistic, are fulfilling each spouse's beliefs about who he/she must be in order to be loved. The mutual identifications, based on misunderstandings about what each spouse is really like, are comforting and reassuring even though they are mistaken. For example, a wife who sees herself as incompetent may value her husband's caretaking, believing it to be based on the devotion that she experienced with her overprotective father. The husband may resent the caretaking, but may enjoy the adoration shown by his wife.

According to the object relations model, over the course of time a dysfunctional marriage also experiences further shaping because each spouse responds to chronic projective expectations in predictable ways. An ongoing "balance" or equilibrium is achieved, whereby each spouse misreads the other and in turn experiences the response he/she continually expects on the basis of this misunderstanding. "Thus the external marital relationship that develops serves to reinforce the internalized object world of both partners. Old conflictual relationships stemming from childhood become resurrected, recapitulated, and acted out in the marital family" (Slipp, 1984, p. 69). For example, the wife who believes that she is incompetent expects that when she acts helpless, her husband will respond with guidance and reassurance the way that her over-protective father did. When the husband, gratified by his deferential wife, reassures her, he reinforces her view that her husband wishes to protect her and that she is incompetent.

The natural systems model clearly duplicates many of the ideas regarding marital dysfunction that are found in the object relations literature. Bowen (1972/1988) specifically posited, for example, that selection of marital partner is one reflection of individual level of differentiation. He stated that individuals tend to marry others at the same level of differentiation, which mirrors the analytic viewpoint that if one spouse is developmentally delayed (undifferentiated), the other either is delayed too or has a complementary set of unmet needs that "fit" with those of the poorly differentiated spouse. The lower the level of differentiation in a nuclear family, the more intense the marital conflicts will be.

From the natural systems standpoint, one spouse in a fused or poorly differentiated couple often appears to take care of the other, compromising personal needs and wishes in the face of the other's symptoms. For example, the wife of a psychotic husband may reorganize much of her life to care for him, accompany him and structure his day, or make important family decisions. He may appear needy and demanding, while she appears giving and accommodating.

Yet this model posits, as does the object relations model, that the accommodating spouse is also meeting implicit needs by being "the strong one." On the level of emotional dynamics, the more functional spouse is gaining a sense of self as the partner loses it (Kerr, 1985). The linear appearance of the marital problem—that is, one partner's appearing more symptomatic—is really a product of the way in which *both* partners are playing out their needs.

The contextual model complements these two systems of ideas with its attention to the emotional dynamics of ethics. Its view of dysfunctional marriages highlights the role of "split loyalties," in which one or both spouses cannot respond to the requests and wishes of the other because of impasses with the family of origin. Split loyalty can be seen as one type of differentiation failure, and is a more specific concept than that of "undifferentiation."

A second mechanism of marital dysfunction specified by the contextual model is that of the "revolving slate" (see Chapter 3). This concept resembles that of "mutual projection" in object relations theory. The revolving slate is a metaphor for attributions of familial motives or behavior to one's partner, based on past hurts. The "slate" of perceived obligations, unmet needs, and negative expectations "revolves," or passes, from a single adult's relationship with his/her parents to that with his/her spouse. As in the case of split loyalty, the contextual model provides a more specific relational explanation for how spousal exploitation, conflict, and tensions are transmitted across generations.

The symbolic-experiential model holds that dysfunctional structures, distorted emotional processes, and unadaptive familial beliefs all contribute to marital dysfunction. In terms of process, there is much less emphasis on the intrapsychic attribute of differentiation than there is in both object relations and contextual theory. However, symbolic-experiential theory agrees that a symptomatic spouse is often the identified client in his/her own family of origin, the conduit of emotional tensions. In this sense, we can infer that a symptomatic spouse has not had the opportunity to separate emotionally from family-of-origin pressures.

Chapter 2 has reviewed how marriages commonly become dysfunctional in three areas, according to symbolic-experiential theory. In the area of attachment, some marriages are too distant and are affectively void. Partners in this type of marriage seem uninvested in each other emotionally, and seem to live parallel lives under the same roof without engaging each other. Other problem marriages lack resources for coping with conflict, and remain rigid and closed to new dialogue or problem-solving. Instead, the spouses occupy rigid, invariant roles in the marriage that are re-enacted during every disagreement, such as "the hothead," "the crier," or "the cold fish." There are also overly complementary marriages, in which one spouse appears persistently symptomatic while the other overfunctions. The symbolic-experiential model does not analyze the hypothetical basis to these latter two interactional problems, but tends to treat them as dysfunctional structures that need to be altered. The first pattern, the "affectless" marriage, is considered a problem of emotional process, reflecting overinvestment outside the marriage (usually in families of origin).

These three dysfunctional marital patterns are also identified as common clinical problems by the other transgenerational models. Lack of deep mutual attachment is particularly recognized by the symbolic-experiential and natural systems models, which consider interpersonal distancing as a severe symptom. The structural problem of poor conflict resolution and rigidity is most clearly addressed in symbolic-experiential theory, but is echoed in the contextual model, which emphasizes lack of *quid pro quo*, revolving slates, and invisible loyalties in dysfunctional marriages.

The third dysfunctional marital pattern, extreme complementarity, is addressed extensively by all four transgenerational models. The natural systems model ascribes the pattern to one spouse's gaining "self" at the expense of the other, who forfeits it and appears ill. Object relations theory explains this complementarity in terms of mutual projections that are idealizing and devaluing, respectively. The contextual model suggests that severe complementarity represents exploitation of the needs of one spouse (who nurtures) by the other spouse (who feels entitled to aid and comfort). The natural systems model and contextual model appear somewhat at odds here, probably because each model focuses on the contribution of only one spouse (the "strong" one or the "weak" one) to the problem.

Finally, symbolic-experiential theory identifies a separate level of dysfunction, which involves beliefs, mandates, and binding legacies. When one or both spouses come from families of origin in which there are burdensome expectations, it is inevitable that there will be distress over how to carry out the expectations and whether to change or modify them. This distress emerges in the marriage in two ways: through symptoms in the distressed spouse(s) , and through one spouse's pressure on the other to help fulfill the binding legacies. For example, a man who has married out of the faith of his hyperreligious family may pressure his wife to run the household in ways that his parents could still approve of. The contextual model, with its focus on delegation, also puts heavy emphasis on the role of binding family legacies in marital dysfunction.

The Parent–Child Subsystem

According to object relations theory, when one or both marital partners do not have a well-integrated sense of self, they are likely to experience recurrent anxiety in intimate relationships. As we have seen, this anxiety must be suppressed a good deal of the time in order to function, and as a result is frequently "split off" from individual awareness and projected onto the partner (see Chapter 4).

Under these conditions, a third family member is triangulated into the anxiety-ridden marriage (Slipp, 1984). From the analytic standpoint, when a child is triangulated into a dysfunctional marriage, he/she fulfills the role of "part object"—the set of memories, beliefs, and feelings that is being suppressed. A child may be pressured or delegated to represent either very positive memories and feelings that seem dangerous for the parent to recall in the marriage, or very painful unresolved issues that are intolerable to recall.

Stierlin, in particular, has written a great deal about children who are "delegated" to act on the suppressed needs and beliefs of their parents (Stierlin & Ravenscroft, 1972; Stierlin, 1974, 1977). His Heidelberg model, which incorporates many theoretical concepts from the object relations literature, specifies a number of ways in which triangulated children are either "bound" (retained) or "expelled" (rejected) by their families when they have been delegated to represent parts of their parents that have been emotionally denied. As discussed earlier, the mechanism by which this triangulation occurs is thought to be the use of splitting, projection, and projective identification by the distressed parent(s).

> Thus, symptomatology in the identified [child] patient can be viewed as arising out of an induced countertransference reaction. The patient has accepted and identified with the projective identification of a part self or object placed into him or her, and acts out this acceptance behaviorally. (Slipp, 1984, p. 70)

Essentially, the distressed parental dyad and triangulated child or children become trapped in an overly interconnected relationship, functioning together as if they each make up different parts of one another. The impact on triangulated children is to interfere with their own individual growth, autonomy, and social competence. In addition, as Slipp has pointed out, the distress or symptoms of a burdened child confirm the parents' view of him/her, increasing the rigidity and chronicity of the triangle.

As in the case of the dysfunctional marriage, the natural systems model shares some focus with the object relations model on emotional dynamics. Bowen's definition of "undifferentiated family ego mass" is exactly that of parents and children fused through a process of family projection, leading to multigenerational transmission of anxiety downward. However, Bowenian theory emphasizes structural problems by emphasizing pathological triangles in the genesis of family dysfunction. Parent–child triangles become pathological through a projective process from parent to child(ren). In the language of the natural systems model, pathological triangles differ from normative triangles in that (1) pathological triangles are rigid and unchanging over long periods of time; and (2) there is a high level of family projection (of needs, values, and emotionally charged feelings) onto the selected child or children, leading to (3) increased multigenerational transmission of symptoms (for a comparison with normative triangulation, see Chapter 5).

As discussed in Chapter 1, the natural systems model agrees with object relations theory that one precursor to the parent–child (or grandparent–parent–child) triangle is poor differentiation of one or both parents from their families of origin. Unresolved emotional attachment (Bowen, 1974/1988) is not negotiated between spouses or between parents and grandparents, because the distressed adults do not have sufficient self-knowledge. As unresolved issues become more chronic in the parental families of origin and/or the marriage, the parents' high level of anxiety can only be channeled into triangulation of children.

The contextual model closely resembles both the object relations and natural systems literature in its treatment of the concept of family projection. It examines Stierlin's (1974) idea that children are delegated by virtue of their role in a dysfunctional family, and go on to express issues and attitudes that other family members cannot explicitly acknowledge. As noted in Chapter 3, the contextual definition of delegation is that transgenerational expectations are imposed on offspring by the emotional needs of parents and grandparents.

The contextual model adds to the overarching concept of projection by specifying symptoms that arise in parent–child relationships where severe, persistent delegation has occurred. Previously, I discussed problems that arise through exploitation of children, destructive parentification, and scapegoating, and the resulting symptoms of destructive entitlement (narcissism), disjunction (disengagement), and invisible loyalty. For example, a woman who feels disappointed and rejected by her own mother may marry a husband who also has high expectations of her. In her loneliness and resentment, she may fault her own daughter in the same areas important to her mother (such as her weight or appearance), and pressure the daughter to achieve the elegant and pleasing appearance that she has not achieved. She thus scapegoats her daughter, who feels the burden of this delegation and does not appear or look happy and well. The daughter may resent her mother's pressure and distance herself from trying to understand her mother's motives and feelings, resulting in a critical disjunction between them.

As in the case of dysfunctional marriage, symbolic-experiential theory defines dysfunctional families in terms of structure, process, and implicit beliefs. Structural dysfunction includes overly rigid or diffuse boundaries inside and outside the nuclear family. Symbolic-experiential theory emphasizes the particular problem of weak generational boundaries, in which the needs of children are not recognized as separate from the needs of parents and grandparents. Other transgenerational models do not directly address the importance of boundaries. The contextual model indirectly addresses this point in its discussion of children who are inappropriately burdened with the expectations of their parents.

A separate structural problem in parent–child relationships is the coalition, frequently depicted as triadic. *All* transgenerational models consider pervasive parent–child triangles to lead to severe family dysfunction. The symbolic-experiential model does not dwell on the "pathological triad" (Hoffman, 1981) as extensively as does natural systems theory. Finally, the structural problem of overly rigid prescribed roles (including sex stereotyping) receives much attention. As in the case of dysfunctional marriage, symbolic-experiential theory discusses the problem of role rigidity most clearly, although contextual family therapy also examines the way in which "delegated" sons and daughters have difficulty altering their own behavior.

Dysfunctional parent–child *processes*, according to symbolic-experiential theory, may consist of fusion or enmeshment between parents and children, or extreme distance and lack of empathy. These disturbances of parent–child intimacy are recognized by all of the transgenerational models as critical problems. Poor conflict resolution, another dysfunctional process, is also recognized by all of these models. There is some disagreement among schools of thought in defining conflict problems. Symbolic-experiential theory views conflict as inevitable and normal, even in its explosive or chronic forms. Contextual theory specifically separates one category of disagreement, "unavoidable existential conflicts," from family conflicts that reflect deeper emotional tensions.

In contrast, the natural systems model views severe parent–child conflict as one symptom of poor parental differentiation from the grandparents. As noted in Chapter 1, Bowen posited that unresolved anxiety in fused families of origin emerges in one of these arenas: chronic marital conflict; parent–child conflict; or dysfunction in one spouse. This idea negatively connotes parent–child conflict, as opposed to Whitaker's position that even intense, emotionally laden generational conflict is inevitable. Whitaker's contention is that only when one participant in the conflict (either child or parent) is unable to advocate for his/her own views is the family conflict dysfunctional. Object relations theory, like natural systems theory, takes a less compromising stance; it tends to view parent–child conflict as the result of parent's projections and projective identifications of parts of themselves (or significant others) that are unacceptable. Therefore, conflict is defined as pathological per se, reflecting inadequate self-awareness and individuation in the parents. Symbolic-experiential theory emerges as unique in its view of parent–child conflict as inevitable, and in its position that dysfunctional families need help to fight better, not necessarily less.

The Sibling Subsystem

As in other family subsystems, the object relations model emphasizes the role of emotional dynamics in dysfunctional sibling groups. This model suggests that in families where children are neglected, scapegoated, or physically/emotionally abused, they may bond together emotionally to seek nurturance from each other. This process is not as likely to occur in sibling groups where a child has been delegated as "the bad one" or "the good one," since in such cases the siblings tend to "deidentify" with one another, becoming alienated and competitive (Schachter, 1982).

When children lacking parental attachment turn to each other, they can come to experience each other as the most important persons in their respective emotional worlds. Increasingly, the siblings may look to each other for attention and affection, becoming "selfobjects" to each other (see Chapter 5).

If the children in a distressed family do not have a consistent empathic relationship with the parent(s), a secondary pattern is to protect themselves from pain by either withdrawing emotionally, or aggressively demanding attention and responsivity. Withdrawn children are experienced by close siblings as abandoning. Aggressive children may appear to the siblings to wish to "smother" or dominate the others entirely (Kahn, 1988).

Children raised in families that continue to be overly distant or chaotic over long periods of time do not have an opportunity to modify their perceptions of their siblings with the more sophisticated understanding that comes with age. As a result, offspring from chronically disengaged or chaotically engaged families tend to carry rigid images of each other through adulthood. These images can interfere with establishing functional adult relationships with each other, and even with other people. For example, persistently negative characterizations of a sibling will create chronic dislike, producing the complete avoidance of de-identification. A persistently idealized image of a sibling can create a preferential, unrealistic love which interferes with forming other peer bonds.

If bonding between two siblings has been need-driven by family dysfunction and is too intense, it can become sexualized and lead to sibling incest. Kahn (1988) has termed this type of incest "nurturance-oriented" (as opposed to sadistically abusive) incest. He notes that it usually involves a mutual search for caring, rather than use of exploitation or force by one sibling against another. Kahn speculates that sibling incest reflects the processes of merging, or fusion, and idealization. Typically, an idealized and loved brother fuses sexually with a supportive, mirroring sister.

Sibling violence is another symptom of chronically dysfunctional families, often families where parents and/or grandparents are abusive. Physical or sexual sibling violence involves the transformation of one child into a persistent aggressor and the other into a repeated victim. From an object relations standpoint, such repeated violence may be the children's only form of emotional attachment, painful though it is. This form of attachment can reflect a displacement of anger toward neglectful parents, mixed with the need for emotional response, in order to increase a child's sense of importance or self-awareness. Or it can represent identification with a violent elder, stemming from the need to suppress fear and resentment in order to preserve a sense of attachment to that adult.

The natural systems model deviates from its close association with object relations theory in the area of sibling relationships. Although it shares the assumption that sibling conflict often reflects parental dysfunction, natural systems theory limits its focus to the consequences of family projection process and to multigenerational transmission.

Symbolic-experiential theory has not explicitly contributed to the growing literature on sibling relationships and symptoms. However, there is repeated reference in symbolic-experiential case studies to problems in sibling relationships, particularly noting the effects of parent–child (or grandparent–parent–child) dysfunction on the quality of sibling relationships. Although symbolic-experiential writers have not yet formalized their views about how sibling bonds fail, we can infer several ideas from these case studies and papers.

The symbolic-experiential model attaches great importance to maintaining a firm generational boundary within a family, so that the concerns and priorities of offspring are separated from those of the parents. We have seen that when this boundary is too permeable or inconsistent, one or more children tend to acquire the role of peer, confidant, or partner to the parent(s). In dysfunctional families, this process of "parentification" effectively removes any such children from peer status with their siblings, and puts them in peer status with the parents.

Furthermore, to the extent that a child becomes more emotionally connected with the needs and viewpoints of a parent, the child is that much less emotionally available to initiatives and concerns of siblings. The symbolic-experiential literature is full of references to dysfunctional families in which the children do not ally with each other to support mutual interests, or confide in each other when stressed. Another often-cited problem is that of the isolated symptomatic sibling, who wars with a parent and is alienated from brothers and sisters. The implication behind these two types of sibling problems, is that when a child has been co-opted into the position of parental confidant, sibling relationships are stunted, and the siblings fail to develop their own "peer culture."

Natural systems theory echoes this viewpoint with its focus on parent–child triangles. However, it does not examine the effects of chronic parent–child triangles on the quality of sibling bonds. The object relations model does not discuss the idea of a "peer culture," or the importance of sibling cohesion, but looks closely at the problem of sibling alienation ("deidentification") when a child is targeted by a needy parent.

Symbolic-experiential theory also considers the sibling group as the laboratory for learning and practicing socialization, and appropriate romantic/sexual behavior. Older siblings are viewed as role models and teachers to younger children. In turn, the younger children afford the older ones the opportunity to learn how to teach and nurture dependents. In a severely distressed family, if a child is symptomatic or the environment is not supportive, older siblings may actually "teach" the younger ones symptomatic behavior. For example, in an alcoholic household, the elder son may avoid the family and distance himself. By observing that their brother does not confide in their parents, younger children may be influenced to see their parents as unapproachable.

Aggressive behavior by a troubled older sibling teaches younger ones to view themselves as victims, and to fear tension and conflict. Regardless of age, when one child is symptomatic, the other siblings are often neglected on behalf of their brother or sister. "Invisible," nonsymptomatic siblings often react with depression, anger, or withdrawal (see, e.g., Roberto, 1988).

In sibling groups that lack mutual trust and cohesion, the siblings also have difficulty helping one another through life transitions such as peer friendships/dating, advancement in school, launching from family of origin, and engagement/marriage. Symbolic-experiential theory, with its emphasis on the educational resources of sibling groups, emerges as unique in its concern with strengthening sibling bonds.

In family psychotherapy, the symbolic-experiential model has encouraged the use of sibling sessions for the purpose of increasing sibling cohesion, developing boundaries between generations, diffusing scapegoat roles, and counteracting pressures on one or several delegated children. Symbolic-experiential theory considers sibling relationships to be a key resource in freeing offspring of distressed families to renew individual development.

·II·

TRANSGENERATIONAL FAMILY THERAPY

·7·

Plotting a Course: Goals of Change

Transgenerational therapies differ from strategic or solution-based therapies, and from behaviorally oriented therapies, in that they set goals of change *beyond relief of immediate symptoms.* Transgenerational therapists conceive of change more broadly as expanding the abilities of family members to do the following:

1. To achieve greater relational competence.
2. To enhance self-confidence and self-esteem.
3. To complete important tasks in the individual and family life cycles.
4. To care for and provide parental guidance to children and young adults.

Restoration versus Symptom Control

These broadly defined goals resemble the basic characteristics of the healthy or functional marriage and family, as discussed in earlier chapters. If we believe that these characteristics are necessary (if not sufficient) in order for a family to function, then it follows that in treating a dysfunctional family, the therapist must work to help restore or strengthen its members in those areas. In contrast, family therapy models that are solution-based often conceptualize change as if an asymptomatic family is a functional family.

Interestingly, few strategic therapists or behavior therapists articulate clearly what a truly healthy marriage or family "looks" like. When an explicit description is given, it is usually confined to the third point listed above, completion of important life cycle tasks. Emphasis may be placed on the ability to make executive decisions, maintain parental hierarchy, preserve marital or family boundaries, or "make transitions" from one life cycle stage to another. It is as if absence of crisis is equivalent to positive emotional health, and as if removal of critical symptoms is equivalent to enhanced quality of life. This equation of symptom absence with competence is not logically sound.

Furthermore, couples and families rarely request therapy confined to a completely discrete symptom. Often, a disturbing symptom (e.g., anorexia nervosa, alcoholism, or school failure) is accompanied by unhappy mood, family dissatisfaction, marital disturbance, and other dysphoric events. Symptom-based therapies are too frequently based on the position that a major portion of therapeutic change *"consists of getting them to agree on a problem"* (P. Watzlawick, personal communication, 1985; italics added). Then, once family members have compliantly limited their complaints, progress is defined as improvement in the complaints! Moreover, these therapies prescribe that new complaints in the future be dealt with in future (additional) therapies (Watzlawick, personal communication, 1984).

Defining goals of change in such a reductionistic manner may be workable with families who tolerate this procedure. However, I believe that many legitimate complaints and therapeutic goals are bypassed in the process—for some clients, perhaps the most legitimate complaints. For example, using the reductionism of strategic theory, Watzlawick has stated that a marital complaint in which a wife wishes to conceive a child while the husband opposes it "is not a therapy problem" (personal communication, 1984). Perhaps if the therapist's conceptualization of the problem is systemically expanded to examine the four elements of healthy functioning, this complaint could be brought into the province of relational problem solving.

Symptom-focused therapists tend to cope with multiple or vague complaints by forming a systemic hypothesis in which one distressing symptom is linked to another, which is seen as more basic. For example, an anorexic daughter is reframed as responding defiantly to a failure of parental guidance, brought about by maternal overconcern and paternal uninvolvement. Another way of stating this is to say that in the process of examining each family member's contribution, symptoms are often prioritized. Maternal overconcern is frequently highlighted in the family therapy literature, with symptoms such as anorexia given second priority and paternal uninvolvement tertiary priority. The solutions recommended by the therapist then focus on whichever symptom has been given highest priority. For example, the overconcerned mother may be instructed to attend to her husband by planning a weekend vacation, leaving unattended the starving daughter, who will *ipso facto* have to debate by herself whether to eat.

It is possible—and, furthermore, necessary and possibly more efficient—to go beyond controlling a single presenting symptom in plotting a course of change. Restoring or strengthening a family's ability to function in the four areas listed earlier incorporates work on discrete symptoms in any one area. For example, a family whose father and son are physically combative with each other requires intervention to stop the violence. In addition, it seems necessary (in order to control further tensions) to improve their relational competence as males, and to build mutual cooperation in their father–son relationship (perhaps including grandfather and uncles as well). Adding such broader goals should, in theory, ease chronic father–son tensions and prevent further outbreaks of stress, such as a stormy launching from the home, emotional cutoff when the son has achieved adulthood, or emotional distancing between the son and his own future children. By broadening our goals of change beyond symptom control, we add therapeutic efficiency in the sense of practicing preventive care. The process of restoring a family's capacity to care for its members is not antithetical to symptom control, but it exceeds symptom control.

Again, broadening therapeutic goals beyond symptom control is not only possible, but necessary. The fact that a familial complaint is not specific enough, or emergent, does not mean that it does not require attention. For example, a family with an isolative teenage daughter may present for therapy with complaints that she has a hand-washing compulsion. The therapist will intervene in family interactional patterns that heighten her anxiety and impulses to wash her hands—possibly parental fights that precede each episode. She, as well as the parents, may be taught alternatives that are more functional, such as joining the arguments overtly or leaving the scene. However, at some point, the isolative behavior and social withdrawal must also be addressed even if it is not of concern to the family, because it is dysfunctional for an adolescent to be withdrawn.

This point evokes considerable controversy in the family therapy field, because it may be seen as imposing the values of an outsider (the therapist) on a family. However, I submit that it is impossible to deliver a value-free therapy. A symptom-focused therapist who chooses to ignore the implicit problem of the social withdrawal conveys actively to the family that it is not important to attend to one another's emotional state or well-being but only to behavior (or, more drastically, to critically self-destructive behavior). Transgenerational family therapies, with their emphases on strengthening familial resources for nurturance and competence over time, cannot afford to convey this message. Quality of life—that elusive concept having to do with self-esteem, personal growth, relational resources, and caring for needs of others—becomes an important concept when we are concerned with three to four generations of family evolution.

One way to label this broader perspective would be "restoration of family resources." Transgenerational therapists assume that each family, in its own history, has periods in which some members have been able to provide for developmental needs (intimacy, support, empathy, problem solving, constructive conflict); to enhance personal dignity; to make decisions during life stage transitions; and to protect children. Transgenerational family therapy, which considers levels of family functioning over three to four generations, seeks to maximize a family's strengths by restoring its skills in whichever areas are fragile (or damaged by circumstance). "Restoration" conveys the intention to ameliorate, to help repair, and to heal, but also *to put back that which is out of place*—in other words, to put it back into a proper (and receptive) environment. This kind of goal clearly implies more than repairing a discrete area of distress and then disengaging from the context that gave rise to the distress. Transgenerational family therapy is palliative, but also restorative.

The Presenting Symptom

Couples and families request consultation when members' attempts to correct a problem or to provide for one another emotionally have failed. Transgenerational family therapists look for signs of dysfunction in a family's structure (its membership, groups, and subgroups), its emotional process (the quality of its relationships), and its implicit belief systems (including its traditions, values, prior legacies, and unspoken mandates).

Families themselves do not necessarily experience these disturbances firsthand (Roberto, 1986). As Dell (1986) has stated, causality may be circular (systemic), but experience is linear. In saying that experience is linear, Dell means that couples and families often observe and respond to behaviors and relational patterns by locating them in one person. For example, spouses who have become distant from each other may not frame the distance as a conscious problem, but they do notice that their 4-year-old child acts "clingy" and attention-seeking. In such cases, the husband and wife do not usually formulate an interactional concept of the problem, but instead attribute the problem to their child. The family members' definition of their chief problem becomes their "presenting symptom" when they visit the therapist's office. The individual to whom they attribute the presenting symptom is the "identified patient."

As stated earlier, transgenerational therapists do not in practice or in theory oppose focusing on the presenting symptom. It is true that the founders of several transgenerational models took an extreme stand at times regarding this focus. Bowen, for example, indicated on a consistent basis that in the case of child symptoms, he preferred to perform marital therapy, with the expectation that the child symptoms would resolve when dysfunctional parent–child triangles were diffused. However, other transgenerationally based models, specifically the object relations and contextual models, have not shown this extreme bias.

Furthermore, in the past two generations of practice and training, this bias has shifted somewhat. Many transgenerational therapists are quite willing to begin assessment and treatment with a focus on the couple's or family's presenting symptom, proceeding to broaden their mutual definition of the problem over time. There is no reason in theory to contradict this practice, and no evidence that initial work on symptom control is harmful per se. In contrast, I have already discussed the possible consequences of restricting therapy to symptom control; this is also an extreme position, which is problematic and even potentially harmful when it is an incomplete response to emotional distress.

A young family sought psychotherapy because of the spouses' concern for the wife's 8-year-old son, Stephen. Stephen seemed listless and depressed, was markedly underweight, and had failed second grade. The timid mother, in her 30s, suspected that his depression was linked to painful incidents in the past, including the sudden death of his biological father in a motorcycle accident. The stepfather, also in his 30s, had known the mother during her bereavement and married her subsequently. However, he held himself aloof from the family, stating that the mother had already left him once because he (abused in his own childhood) had been a harsh disciplinarian to Stephen after the remarriage.

It was clear that this mother's timidity, and her earlier marriage to a biker, reflected long-term problems in her family of origin. Her own mother was bulimic, her father was distant, and she and her sisters had been molested by an elder brother. The stepfather had been severely traumatized by constant beatings by his own mother's multiple partners. His alcoholic father had abandoned the family when he was 10 years of age.

However, the mother and stepfather entered therapy quite emotionally cut off from their families of origin, and completely focused on the "presenting symptoms" of the malnourished, demoralized child. Accordingly, the therapist accepted this initial problem definition, and focused the first 2 months of family psychotherapy on encouraging the spouses to actively feed Stephen and to develop a plan of special education within his school. Only later did the therapist move to expand the problem definition by mapping and examining multigenerational legacies from the spouses' families of origin.

The structural, strategic, and systemic family therapy literatures have argued for some time that the most proper focus for psychotherapy is the presenting symptom. This argument is often made from three specific positions. The first position is that since the presenting symptom is the source of a family's immediate distress, a focus on this problem is the only therapeutic focus that shows respect to the family. The second position states that to consumers, insurers, and fiscal intermediaries, therapeutic accountability lies in effectively treating the presenting problem. The third position holds that families, not therapists, should be the arbiters in goal setting. No matter what values and norms the therapist holds about a family's interrelationships, the family members should have the authority to define the problem in the context of their own beliefs and values.

Transgenerational family therapists take the stance that it is important not to "throw out the baby with the bathwater" (Slipp, 1989, p. 13). Although it is true that a family's immediate distress focuses on their perceptions of a specific symptom, addressing critical conflicts or deficits in their relationships *as the therapist perceives them* can raise individuals' self-esteem, improve confidence in facing adversity, promote familial cohesion for future problem solving, and prevent the outbreak of further symptoms at other points in the family life cycle.

Although therapeutic accountability is measured by the business community and third-party payers in terms of the presenting symptom, this does not mean that the mental health professions should adopt a reductionistic attitude in setting goals for marital and family therapy. Again, transgenerational therapists advocate a stance of broadening therapeutic goals beyond presenting symptoms, not neglecting presenting symptoms.

Finally, from an ethical standpoint, it seems clear that a couple or family in distress should ultimately have the authority to define the therapeutic problem. However, for epistemological reasons described earlier, family members do not directly observe and experience the effects of their own belief systems and emotional processes. One cannot observe oneself, as Freud commented nearly 100 years ago. In order for family members to experience these effects, implicit dysfunctional rules and expectations must first become explicit in interaction with an observer. Since dysfunctional patterns usually become explicit in the process of family therapy, it is important for the therapist to provide a broader problem definition over time for the family's consideration. In my experience, once family members are aware of the interactional rules surrounding a presenting symptom, they frequently choose to address the dysfunctional rules and expectations in therapy, creating their own initiative.

Setting Goals: Transgenerational Marital Therapy

Consideration of the characteristics of well-functioning couples should guide the therapist in setting goals for marital therapy. Are the spouses in treatment romantically bonded to each other? If not, does the lack of emotional attachment reflect structural inconsistencies, dysfunctional interactions, or maladaptive beliefs? For example, has the couple experienced a courtship? In some distressed couples, the courtship phase has not occurred. The partners may have decided to marry impulsively in order to relocate from their parental homes, or may have responded to outside pressure to marry, as in the case of some early pregnancies. Lack of courtship is a structural problem, since such a couple has essentially skipped an important transition stage. In such cases, one relevant goal for marital therapy will be to create a courtship phase, or courtship activity, to strengthen the couple's affective bond.

Is there a problem in the spouses' interactive, relational patterns? Many distressed couples fall into this category. The contextual model specifically describes how marital partners withhold meaningful emotional commitment from each other when their affective energies are tied up in relationships with families of origin, in the process known as "split" and "invisible" loyalties (see Chapter 3).

Natural systems theory directs us to look for specific intergenerational triangles involving a distant marital partner, which command his/her initiative away from marital intimacy (see Chapter 1). The object relations model points out that some marital partners, deprived of a nurturant and predictable parental environment in childhood, have difficulty learning or internalizing the empathy and emotional receptivity required in marriage (see Chapter 4). Contextual therapists consider this deficit one source of "invisible loyalty": If one's father was unwilling to show consideration for one's mother, then perhaps it is disloyal to show consideration to one's wife. When interactional problems reflect triangulation into families of origin, or invisible loyalties, marital therapy will require focus on achieving a constructive separation from families of origin by addressing the conflictual relationships that bar the way to greater investment in the marriage.

Are there dysfunctional beliefs about marriage, familial legacies that interfere with marital intimacy, or mandates that forbid marital intimacy or cooperation? Symbolic-experiential theory directs us to look for patterns in spousal families of origin that might influence offspring to spurn deep emotional attachment to a partner. For example, the son of a family in which a parent divorced and remarried four times may believe that marital commitment is illusory or unattainable. A daughter whose mother was chronically unhappy in a long-term dysfunctional marriage may carry a message from her mother's family never to allow herself to grow close to, or depend upon, a husband. When distressed spouses show evidence of beliefs about their marriage or the institution of marriage that prevent them from investing in mutual problem solving or attempting change, one goal of marital therapy will be to create a dialogue concerning these implicit beliefs and familial mandates in order to make them explicit and amenable to re-examination.

Does the distressed couple have difficulty with chronic or severe conflict? Chronic conflict can reflect dysfunctional structure, process, or implicit beliefs. For example, some marital conflicts do not reach resolution because the couple has in adequate private time to sustain disagreements and to clarify respective positions and wishes. The presence of parents or children in the home, excessive work commitments, and disorganized homes all create structural or boundary problems, which can interfere with setting aside time for constructive marital conflict.

Chronic marital conflict frequently reflects a severe problem in a couple's interactive, relational process. Natural systems theory in particular describes how unresolved, emotionally laden issues in married spouses are touched off under stress. Under the pressures of family tasks and demands of the life cycle, especially in adverse circumstances, each spouse becomes more vulnerable in those areas where his or her own family tended to have conflict. Increased feelings of vulnerability lead the stressed spouse to seek validation or aid from his/her partner, often in ways that are demanding and oppressive. For example, a man who is denied a promotion may begin to feel that he has shamed his successful family, and to seek admiration and comfort from his wife. The wife, expending considerable energy to reassure her preoccupied husband, may grow depressed. The growing intensity of affect during periods of personal vulnerability tends to create tension between the troubled spouse and his/her partner. The tension readily emerges in persistent conflict, often focused on inconsequential matters. In situations where both spouses have never achieved much emotional autonomy from their birth families, conflict can be chronic.

Other transgenerational models, as noted in earlier chapters, focus on different aspects of marital conflict and offer further description. For example, the object relations model examines in detail the way in which an agitated man, experiencing intense and intolerable anxiety, tends to misinterpret his partner's behavior by assuming that she is too anxious also (the process called "projection"). It is easy to see how a vulnerable husband, faced with decisions or problems that were painful for his family of origin, would look to his wife to manage his distress and even scan her behavior to see if her level of concern matches his own.

In some cases, chronic marital conflict reflects deep divisions between the belief systems of the two spouses. Frequently, during courtship, the compatibility of underlying beliefs about marriage and about family life partly determines whether a given couple will make its commitment permanent. Although few premarital pairs explicitly discuss and compare their own family legacies, when great differences emerge they are likely to culminate in an end to the courtship before marriage.

However, in some marriages, it appears as if the spouses have decided to marry despite an awareness, on some level, that their beliefs about marriage are extremely opposed. For example, in a couple where each partner has previously been divorced, the woman may be determined to have an "ours" child because she believes that the two families can only blend if they share children, whereas the man believes that having an "ours" child would betray his children from his former marriage. Yet the couple decides to marry anyway. Such diametrically opposed beliefs about the nature of parent–child commitment, belonging, and loyalty can later create severe, sometimes irreconcilable, conflicts.

When the presenting problem in a distressed couple involves chronic conflict, it is important for the clinician to assess whether the conflict is taking place in a poorly structured marriage, a marriage with dysfunctional interaction, or a marriage with severely opposing belief systems. Where the couple is poorly structured, a major goal of marital therapy is to create boundaries around the marriage that will allow sustained disagreement and conflict resolution. Significant others will have to be consulted to create the space for a new marital boundary. Typically, the couple will need to negotiate with parents and with children to increase their awareness of the needs of the marital dyad.

Chronic conflict that involves problems of poor differentiation, persistent emotional intensity, and dysfunctional interaction requires that each member of a couple disengage emotionally. One goal of marital therapy will be to examine, for each spouse, which family problems create anxiety. Incidents and tensions within each family of origin that contribute to these anxieties will need to be clarified. The focus will have to be moved from pressured interchanges between spouses aimed at *managing* the anxiety, to more individual examination of the past incidents *maintaining* anxiety. The spouses can then choose alternative strategies for coping with their own family tasks—strategies that have more "fit" for them. Common family issues that can trigger chronic marital conflict include sexuality; achievement problems in a spouse or children; caretaking pressures, particularly for wives; and autonomy problems, particularly when children are launched.

When chronic conflict mirrors deeply divisive belief systems in husband and wife, a central goal of marital psychotherapy is to make each spouse's values and beliefs as explicit as possible. Although clarification of these differences will not necessarily lead to agreement, one outcome is a decrease in the emotional intensity of the marital fighting. As each spouse's unique history, experiences, and familial traditions become manifest, there is greater potential for dialogue rather than mutual criticism and attack. The therapist will then have the option to encourage each spouse to examine whether his/her family's assumptions about marriage and family life were productive and accurate. It is possible that in the light of re-examination, one or both spouses will modify their beliefs in light of their own marriage and adult experience. Of course, this is not always the case; widely divergent familial values and mandates can be quite powerful obstacles to marital cohesion.

Setting Goals: Transgenerational Family Therapy

Achieving restoration of strengths to a symptomatic family with children requires a different set of goals than does marital psychotherapy. The locus of symptoms in these cases is frequently a child, and the attachment between child and parents is a biological one rather than the voluntary commitment of marriage. The contextual model in particular emphasizes that this biological attachment is profoundly different from that in any other type of human relationship, because children incorporate our plans and goals for our future lives, as well as the future security and integrity of our communities and kinship networks (Boszormenyi-Nagy & Krasner, 1986). Therefore, the expectations, emotional bonds, and family structures surrounding children involve biological imperatives and ethical stakes that are completely different from those in a marriage.

The symbolic-experiential model recognizes this basic difference through its insistence that family therapy must "diffuse the scapegoat" early, by taking pressures to change off the vulnerable young, and moving more toward parental options for change. However, symbolic-experiential theory is not explicit about the future-oriented dimension in parent–child relations and the significant weight that this lends to preserving children's well-being. One rather metaphorical reference is the statement that "you can divorce your spouse but you can never divorce your children(/parents)" (C. A. Whitaker, personal communication, 1978).

Natural systems theory is explicit about the unique biological dimension of parent–child problems, chiefly through the concepts of "family projection process" and "multigenerational transmission of symptoms" (see Chapter 1). However, again, the chronological element of the future, or the "feedforward" effect of child symptoms, is not addressed. Of all transgenerational models, the object relations model is by far the most deficient in recognizing the biological pressures present in parent–child conflict, and in setting goals that provide special consideration to protection of the young.

This principle that children represent a special, biologically necessary responsibility in family therapy suggests that the first goal for *any* dysfunctional family is the goal of providing guidance and protection for the children. This means that regardless of the type of presenting symptoms shown, or the level of symptoms (structural, interactional, or implicit belief), family stress must be managed in such a way as to relieve pressure on children living in the home. A clinician who puts this principle first will set goals differently for the family therapy than for marital therapy, where exploration of the tensions and their source frequently means pursuing emotionally laden issues early in therapy.

A family of four requested consultation for the 16-year-old daughter, Lauren, who had stopped eating and weighed only 85 pounds. Her 12-year-old brother, Mark, was considered disrespectful, but otherwise was not in distress. During the initial interview, the parents, in their 40s, stated that they were contented with their marriage and home life, despite an obvious polite distance between them and an inactive sex life.

However, the father was quite depressed and anxious about work problems; a salesman, he had felt for a year that he could not adequately support the family and had been told that he was no longer performing competently. He had many depressive symptoms and an active ulcer. The parents were quite angry at Lauren, who had always been a compliant and hard-working schoolgirl. They felt that she was interfering with the family's attempts to support and bolster up the father.

The therapist set his primary goal as intervention and therapeutic/medical support of Lauren's failing health, as opposed to addressing the father's depression first. Lauren's position in the family as a developing child, who represented the family's continuation in the future, was considered of paramount importance.

When a family shows attachment problems between a parent and child, the attachment problems sometimes reflect inadequate bonding between child and adult. In contrast to marital pairs, in which bonding deficits often stem from lack of a courtship phase in their lives, bonding between a parent and child is biologically based. If there is not a deep empathic connection, therefore, the clinician must speculate that a disorder of interactional process is present.

However, there are some cases in which attachment deficits represent parental absence during early periods in the young family's life cycle. Family researchers have suggested that the father's absence during the first hours after the birth of a child, a possible "critical period" in the development of human attachment, may hinder him from forming a deep sense of empathic connectedness with his child. In the psychoanalytic literature, there are many case studies in which the psychological absence of the primary caretaker (e.g., preoccupation in a depressed mother) appears to have led to lack of emotional connectedness between parent and child. Addictionologists now believe that when one or both parents are periodically in an altered cognitive state from alcohol or drug abuse, the altered state can be considered psychological absence. In military families, where men are deployed on exercises for months out of each year, fathers often state that they "feel closer" to children who were born when the fathers were physically present as opposed to physically unavailable (Roberto & Mintle, 1989). A parent's actual or psychological absence at the time when a child is born precludes the family's ability to reorganize for nurturance and parenting. Therefore, it is actually a form of structural problem. It is possible that the common problem in adoptive families where a symptomatic child is seen as a "bad seed" is an example of disordered attachment following lack of early bonding.

A second form of structural problem found in families with little parent–child connection is lack of a functional boundary around the parent–child unit (either a dyad, for a single-parent family, or a triad, for a two-parent household). Poor boundaries stem from many different life events, such as a chronic illness that requires the presence of caretakers; situational stressors, such as homelessness; or long-term interactional dysfunction, such as a parent's failure to separate from his or her family of origin.

In either type of structural problem, a major goal of family therapy will be to intensify the emotional connection between parent(s) and child, in order to redress as much as possible the family's lost early bonding. This goal will entail increasing contact time between parent and child, reframing the problem in order to emphasize the special importance of parents in the child's life, and creating new ways in which a parent and child can attend to family tasks together. If boundaries around the parent–child unit are poor, the therapist will need to encourage behavior that will make a psychological "space." For example, a mother and child living at close quarters with many extended family members may be encouraged to come together during the early morning, when other family members are sleeping.

Transgenerational family therapy also considers whether attachments can be strengthened with grandparents and/or extended family members as resources for children. There are many families in which the grandparental role has become constricted and peripheral, but the children could benefit from increased emotional attachment with these important elders. Symbolic-experiential family therapy, in particular, stresses the potentially beneficial role of grandparents in maintaining family cohesion and bonding.

Dysfunctional emotional processes between parents and child include overly rich intimate involvement at one extreme, and at the other extreme too much distance or a "generation gap" between parents and child (or even between older and younger siblings). In families where there is severe distance or emotional disengagement, and parents and child are attached, the clinician must look for the presence of unresolved triangles in the extended families, much as he/she does in marital therapy. In cases where there is overly rich interconnectedness between parent and child, so that they are quite emotionally reactive to each other, the parent and child are likely to be part of a triangle with a third family member. A major goal of family therapy will be to address the hidden conflicts with extended family members, in order to free parent and child to approach each other at more appropriate times and in more constructive ways.

Differences in the values and important beliefs between children and parents have very different implications than they do in dysfunctional marriages. In marriage, the goal with divergent belief systems is to find ways to integrate some important values, so that the spouses can express common beliefs in their family decision making while maintaining individual differences. In parent–child relationships, children are forming the individual differences that they will later take into their own marriages and family experiences. Yet the continuity of transgenerational family bonds creates pressure to maintain sameness, or loyalty to important family traditions, which is not present in marriage. Therefore, where differences in values exist, parents and children must balance the need for self-definition and the need for responsibility to family tradition. There is a great deal of tension in this process, which commonly occurs in families with older adolescent and young adult children. For example, such families will request consultation because a son or daughter is converting to another religion, or marrying into a family of which the parents cannot approve. The major goal of therapy will be to find any paths of commonality that can be explicated and strengthened, while supporting the need for the offspring to modify family roles and traditions so that they are personally acceptable.

Parent–child conflicts and child symptoms may represent a problem of interactional process. Interactional problems include projective processes between a parent and child, in which the child acts in ways that cause the parent special anxiety (e.g., as extremely sexualized behavior in an adolescent whose father feels he himself is sexually incompetent). Projective processes require, as a goal, each family member's ability to take positions on controversial issues and to acknowledge his/her own anxiety and ambivalence.

Other problems involve poor conflict management, such as avoidance of direct conflict, explosive conflict, or premature closure of important conflicts. In these situations, the goal of therapy must be to expand the family's capacity for sustained, direct conflict, while maintaining enough mutual trust to remain engaged until resolution is achieved. Like severe marital conflict, parent–child conflict can reflect persistent structural disorders, interactional dysfunction, or incompatibility of deeply held beliefs. The therapist must consider subgoals that will address the level of disorder producing the chronic conflict. For example, in a disorganized family in which the busy father is consistently in conflict with a young daughter, one potential (structural) subgoal would entail creating dyadic father–daughter time in which the two can express their disagreements directly. In a family where an adolescent battles parental wishes for academic achievement by flagrantly remaining truant, a subgoal for this interactional dysfunction might involve constructing open dialogue between the teen and parent(s) (and perhaps also grandparents) concerning acceptable vocational choices, over and above good grades.

It must be noted that many of the goals of transgenerational marital and family therapy may resemble early or intermediate goals in problem-focused, behavioral, or strategic psychotherapies. However, as noted earlier, the goals selected must fit into a treatment plan that eventually exceeds symptom relief, and that emphasizes restoring familial resources for growth and strength to cope with future stresses. Thus, whether in setting goals for an uncommitted marriage or for a combative adolescent family, the therapist will convey to the spouses or family members that after mastering initial tensions, they will explore opportunities for self-expression and for enhancing their self-definition within the context of their marital and family work.

·8·

Genograms: Systemic Maps

The "genogram" is essentially a visual graph that depicts a family genealogy or family tree; it records information about members of a nuclear and extended family and their interrelationships. The central advantage of the genogram lies in its display of an individual family's biological, kinship, and psychosocial makeup. It has become a much-used device not only among health professionals, but also among families who wish to study their own histories within the context of their church, synagogue, cultural community, or academic environments.

Genograms were pioneered by Murray Bowen and colleagues (Bowen, 1980; Carter & McGoldrick, 1980; Guerin & Pendagast, 1976), and are now used by clinicians in both social and biological sciences. Their format is completely atheoretical, and can be used by clinicians from diverse theoretical orientations (e.g., Wachtel, 1982). This makes the genogram probably the only assessment instrument available that is truly universal in its application. In contrast, genogram relational symbols vary widely and may include symbols that are unique to specific schools of family therapy (e.g., relational symbols in structural family therapy). Most recently, there has been an effort to standardize the genogram's format, although whether this standardization will unite different schools of practice is still unclear (McGoldrick & Gerson, 1985).

Genograms allow the transgenerational family therapist to create a chronological "map" of a family's structure and interrelationships over generations. It also allows the clinician to modify and update information about a family as it emerges in therapy. The genogram stimulates the therapist and family members to think about extended family patterns over time, contributing to formation of systemic hypotheses about behavior, beliefs, values, and legacies inherent in a family's functioning. Genograms are also used as a therapeutic tool in the conduct of transgenerational therapy, enabling family members to learn a "metaperspective" about their organization and emotionally laden history.

Genogramming for the Transgenerational Clinician

Genograms must cover at least three generations of family information in order to yield enough data for the transgenerational clinician. Construction proceeds backward in time, from the present generation and its members to those in the parental, grandparental, and great-grandparental generations. Initially, during assessment interviews, the symptom bearer and his/her intimates are documented, and presenting symptoms are noted. All members of a household are recorded, as well as relatives who have resided with the nuclear family grouping or who are important to them. Relevant relational, behavioral, environmental, vocational, and medical information is listed alongside each member's symbol (see Figure 8.1). Critical life cycle events, also called "nodal events," are listed by date.

The identified client can subsequently be viewed on such a graph in his/her context—in the various subgroups to which he/she belongs (i.e., sibling group, maternal family lineage, paternal family lineage, important nuclear family triangles, and extended family alliances and coalitions). An individual's context is also assessed in terms of his/her place in a family's adaptation to *stressors*. Carter and McGoldrick (1980) have pointed out that families transmit anxiety or stress along two axes. There is a "vertical" flow of stress, which has to do with relational and behavioral patterns that are handed down through generations of a family. There is also a "horizontal" flow of stress, which refers to a family's

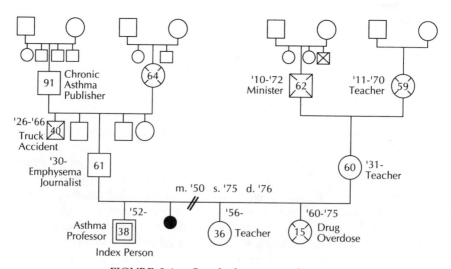

FIGURE 8.1. Standard genogram format.

difficulties in negotiating life cycle transitions and circumstantial mis-fortune. Genograms contain information about stressors on both horizon-tal and vertical axes (life cycle and generational) surrounding a symptom bearer. A number of symbols have been standardized for use in genograms to date (see Figure 8.2).

As information is recorded about the third, or grandparental, gener-ation of a family, the clinician begins to view the larger family context that surrounds and underlies current family symptoms. This larger family context is utilized by clinicians from most schools of family systems therapy, but often is viewed mainly as an additional clue to existing alliances, coalitions, and subsystems at work in current relationships. For example, a symptomatic child may show behavior that shifts in relation-ship to tensions between the mother and father, who have a dysfunctional marriage. In collecting family history, the therapist may become aware that there is a strong connection between the parental couple's tension level and stressful contacts between the father and his father. Strategic therapists, as compared with transgenerational therapists, would view this father–grandfather stress as a secondary contributor to a poorly negotiated hierarchy between the parents and the symptomatic child. Perhaps the grandfather undermines his son's confidence in marital problem solving. Perhaps the grandfather attempts to solve the problems with his son while excluding the mother. In either case, the presence of parent–grandparent stress would be given secondary consideration as a potentiating factor instead of being seen as an integral part of this family's symptomatic status.

However, transgenerational therapists realize that the third, and all additional, generations of family members contribute to a historical, evolutionary process that has a direct impact on the quality of current marriage and family life. Boszormenyi-Nagy has termed this evolutionary factor in families "feedforward"—a process of change that is linear over time rather than circular (Boszormenyi-Nagy & Krasner, 1986). Repeti-tive patterns of marital and family behavior, as well as prescribed roles, values, religious and personal beliefs, and other "unwritten rules" of a family, evolve via the experience of generations into the family's charac-teristics today.

For example, a family that appears to value education highly may contain a generation of teachers, built upon previous generations of intellectually gifted individuals who were prevented from obtaining edu-cation for political or financial reasons. The "feedforward" of values from several lifetimes of deprivation might thus produce a present-day family that holds higher education as an outstandingly important life goal.

Viewing a multigenerational genogram allows the therapist and family members to note confluences of events within one nuclear family's

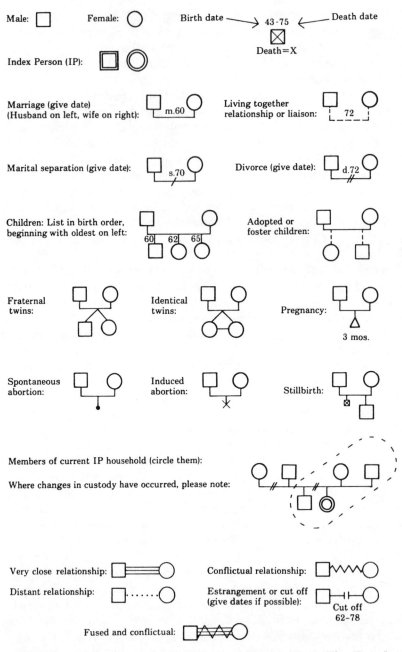

FIGURE 8.2. Symbols used in standard genograms. From "The Time-Line Genogram: Highlighting Temporal Aspects of Family Relationships" (p. 295) by H. Friedman, M. Rohrbaugh, and S. Krakauer, *Family Process*, 27, 293–303. Copyright 1988 by H. Friedman. Reprinted by permission.

life experience. I have already mentioned that horizontal stressors, or life cycle transitions, carry their own measure of disruptiveness and can be associated with the emergence of symptoms. This type of coincidence of events is readily discerned with a genogram. For example, one may see that a young adult daughter has been starving herself for approximately 1 year, and that the mother became depressed at the start of that year when the eldest son left for college.

A second type of confluence involves vertical stressors' coming to bear on a nuclear family at a time when its members are vulnerable to symptoms (McGoldrick & Gerson, 1985). For example, one may find that a maternal grandmother took ill when her alcoholic husband quit his job, so that he had to care for her, and that now a wife is having severe anxiety symptoms just when her husband is considering early retirement. This type of confluence reflects systemic patterns of behavior over generations that reflect attempts to address a problem in the past, but now have a poor "fit" with the needs of current family members.

In summary, three-generational genogramming gives behavioral, biomedical, psychological, and epidemiological information about all the members of an extended family. For the transgenerational therapist, this information has special meaning beyond relationship patterns in the here and now. Aside from noting alliances, conflicts, coalitions, and functional subgroups among the nuclear and extended family members, the clinician can also examine the long-term familial patterns that surround distressed clients. Adaptational changes in response to crises; belief systems reflecting generations of life experience; and relational rules evolving between parents and children and married couples all "feed forward" through time to bias the solutions that the family uses currently for its problems in living.

Three Dimensions of Genogram Analysis

The three-generational genogram yields information calling for different levels of analysis. In transgenerational family therapy models, no one level of analysis is considered to be of central importance, as is the case with other family therapy models. For example, in structural family therapy, structural information concerning household composition is considered key. This reflects the structural therapist's unique interest in alliances, coalitions, and hierarchies within groups living together. For the transgenerational family therapist, multiple levels of analysis are necessary, to examine the effect of past family structures and dynamic processes that have developed over very long periods of time.

Family Structure

The lowest level of analysis concerns structural information—that is, how a family household is comprised and organized. Transgenerational clinicians utilize information about household composition and structure from the outset of therapy. It is *not* a bias of all the transgenerational schools that all members of the household attend therapy sessions; for example, Bowenian therapists may treat a marital couple when children are symptomatic. However, the therapist certainly maps for himself/herself each member's place in the family organization, and also includes extended family members. Furthermore, a family's structure will influence the plan of treatment if there are significant singularities in the way it is organized. For example, in a family where a divorced mother lives with her children and her younger brother, and the divorced father lives alone in the next town, the clinician may speculate that the father is becoming peripheral or being replaced and may also plan to include him in family therapy sessions.

In terms of household composition, the transgenerational genogram also includes parental remarriages or partnerships, and the degree of inclusion of any children in new households. The presence of extended family members, such as elderly parents, in the home is also noted. All residents in a home are joined with a dashed circle to denote cohabitation (see Figure 8.2). It is important to note age differences within a family household, particularly within generational groupings such as the sibling group or the parental pair. If there is a large age difference, the older members often function as a separate generation from the younger members. For example, in a family with seven children, the oldest child may be 10 or more years older than the youngest. In this situation, the younger siblings may relate to the elder as parent surrogates. This can also be the case when one spouse or partner is much older than the other, as in a May–December or December–May marriage.

As McGoldrick (1982) has pointed out, the clinician must recall that ethnicity and culture affect which individuals are defined as extended family members. For example, in some Polynesian cultures, the father's brother has parental obligations toward the father's children. In an observant Roman Catholic family, the godparent serves important functions in the religious education of a child. Information about these selected individuals is also included in the transgenerational genogram.

Consider the genogram in Figure 8.3, depicting a remarried binuclear household in which four children rotate homes in a joint custody arrangement. On the structural level, one can assess and formulate hypotheses regarding problems in functioning subgroups, such as this family's remarried parental subgroup. Perhaps the single parent is not able

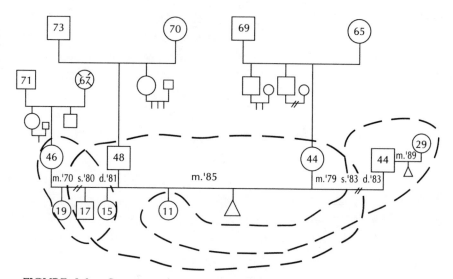

FIGURE 8.3. Genogram for a remarried binuclear household with a joint custody arrangement.

to discuss child rearing in an open and constructive way with the remarried parent and new stepparent. One can also see the quality of alliances, such as the dyad of the divorced biological mother and her own father, and assess for coalitions. Perhaps in this group of parents, the single mother and one or more of the children have become pitted against the remarried father and stepmother. Finally, one can assess the presence of dysfunctional hierarchies in the family. One of the children, often the eldest in a postdivorce family, may not be held appropriately accountable to the parents; or one parent (e.g., the mother) may supersede the others and be overburdened.

Family Life Cycle

The second level of analysis concerns the family's stage in its life cycle and the life cycle stages of its individual members. Each member's stage in the life cycle, and the configuration of all the members together, determine the strengths and vulnerabilities in each member's emotional development in predictable ways. There are no symbols to depict a nuclear family's life cycle stage. It must be inferred from the relative ages of its members, and from the social and emotional tasks that face them in their relationship to the community and the wider society (e.g., sending the first child to public school). Figure 8.4 shows how the relative ages in one family create its life cycle stage, and are even forcing the family to

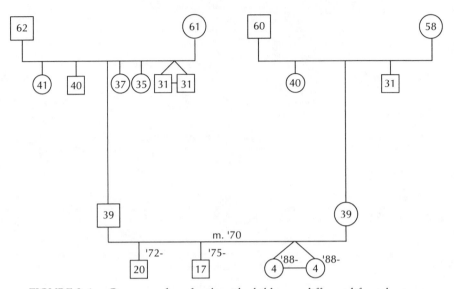

FIGURE 8.4. Genogram for a family with children at different life cycle stages.

encounter two different life cycle stages at once. There is wide disparity in this family within one generation: The ages of children show that there is a large gap of 13 years between the two elder sons and the younger twin daughters. The parents in this family must relate to the little daughters in a closely bound, secure, and child-focused way appropriate to preschool-age families. Yet, at the same time, they must have the skills to launch one adult son and prepare the second son for departure from the home in the near future. Complex life cycle statuses create an unusual amount of stress and conflict in family functioning.

Multigenerational Patterns

The third level of analysis concerns relational patterns and behaviors through three or more generations. These patterns include marital dyadic patterns (complementary or symmetrical, distant or close, hierarchical or egalitarian, fused or separate etc.), parent–child patterns (e.g., parentifying, well-structured, fused, disengaged, consistent, chaotic, abusive, nurturant), and also symptomatic triangles. One may examine the genogram for relational patterns that are repeated over generations. These patterns are, to some extent, defined by one's theoretical orientation. For example, in the natural systems model, "fusion" is delineated as one relational pattern (reflecting poor differentiation of individuals). In the object relations model, "projective identification" is delineated as a specific pattern (in which members of a dyad perceive in each other frightening aspects of their own belief systems). However, researchers and clinicians generally agree that relationships can be rated along dimensions of intimacy (close or distant), control (accommodating or dominant), autonomy (fused or separate), and conflict (high or low). Not coincidentally, two of these dimensions have been translated into pictorial symbols— intimacy and autonomy. The dimension of control has no graphic symbols, and tends to be described in a genogram in words (e.g., "abusive," "critical," "enabling/accommodating," "overpermissive").

The relational analysis of a genogram involves examining repetitions of these or other specific patterns of interrelating. For example, one may observe that in one family, demonstrative women tend to marry distant husbands. Or, it may appear that there is a recurring problem of fathers' criticizing or abusing their sons. In a more complex fashion, triangular patterns can be repeated over generations—for example, in the case of a mother in a distant marriage whose daughter turns to her rather than to her own husband (the son-in-law).

Figure 8.5 shows a family with repeating, unvarying relational triangles—triangles that dictate patterns of distance and intimacy between husbands and wives. Both the husband and wife in Figure 8.5 have surviving parents, but very different patterns of relationship with them. The husband is cut off from meaningful contact or dialogue with his parents and sibling, while the wife enjoys an engaging and supportive relationship with her parents. In this family, we see that the connection

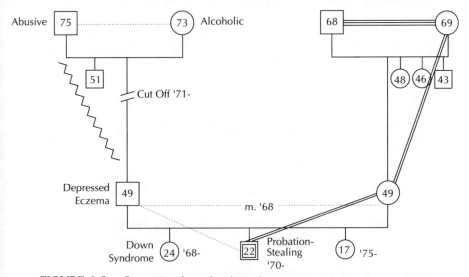

FIGURE 8.5. Genogram for a family with repeating relational triangles.

between the husband and his adult son mirrors his alienation from his own father, while the wife is able to engage the son in a manner characteristic of her relationship with her own family of origin. This bilateral replication is balanced by a somewhat distant marriage, so that the wife frequently reaches out to her parents or son while the husband may be closed off, depressed, irritable, or physically symptomatic.

Relational patterns over generations are not bounded by household composition, and can involve repetitions of symptoms, of vocations, and of beliefs. For example, a family may show three or four generations engaging in drug addiction. Or there may be a pattern of divorces af-ter the birth of children. It has been found that severe forms of dysfunc-tion, such as physical abuse, severe depression, and suicide, frequently become transgenerational patterns. A family may produce five pastors within two generations, indicating a strong transgenerational religious faith and world view. In terms of vocational patterns, many physicians come from families in which there are physicians in previous genera-tions. This is often true for other sciences, and, to some extent, the arts.

Certain adverse life events, such as natural disasters, environmental trauma, or critical dysfunction, can produce transgenerational adjustment patterns. The clinician can scan the genogram for information regarding these "vertical" stressors to analyze their possible connection with pre-sent-day dysfunction. For example, many American families still bear emotional scars from the Nazi Holocaust, World War II, and the refugee experiences of survivors and immigrants. Likewise, adults who are now in their 60s and 70s were young children during the Great Depression, with its attendant hardships and deprivation. One example of a transgener-ational response to trauma is the "anniversary reaction." A man whose parents' friend jumped to his death on the day that Wall Street crashed may experience panic attacks or depression as he nears the age of the parents' deceased friend.

Symptoms and Three-Dimensional Stressors

These three levels of analysis are all important in formulating a systemic picture of a family's emotional resources, as well as of the members' capacity to cope constructively with adverse situations or developmental problems, given their particular history. We can infer that a family experiencing rapid change in its organizational structure, along with transitions in the life cycle of one or more of its members (e.g., terminal illness) and strong repeating generational patterns of relating, will appear greatly symptomatic. Another family whose organization has been disrupted (e.g., by marriage or divorce), but whose members do not experience stressors in other dimensions, will be less symptomatic and for a shorter period of time.

Of course, significant intergenerational mandates and prescriptions for handling all three dimensions of family functioning will echo through every family's problem-solving process, coloring members' definition of their individual roles and their view of marriage, parenting, and friendship. These mandates have a strength of their own, which can exert great force and create emotional and even spiritual distress over the course of a lifetime; they are "invisible" contributors to the relational lines drawn on the genogram.

Alternative Maps: The Time-Line Genogram

The standard genogram, as described earlier, is an adequate assessment tool for studying family members and their relationships across generations. The standard genogram format is limited, however, because it cannot directly show changes in relationships over the passage of time. Because of this deficit, the clinician loses information regarding a family's temporal shifts, reorganizations, and patterns. Dates are displayed, but certain interpretive patterns are missing (Friedman, Rohrbaugh, & Krakauer, 1988). Missing information includes coincidences of life events (e.g., school failure following family relocation); relational consequences of loss (e.g., divorce shortly after the death of a parent); and problems with life cycle "fit" (e.g., a teenage pregnancy). The standard format restricts temporal information to recording dates of important life cycle events next to the relevant family members. Margin notes are often added, to show chronology. Although this information can then be used to compare dates and behavioral changes, the numerical information is not as easy to use as a *graphic* presentation. The graphic spread of family events on the axis of time yields a more complex picture, but one that is more readily apparent.

A more recent alternative is the time-line genogram (TLG; Friedman et al., 1988). The TLG is essentially a standard genogram to which a vertical axis for plotting time is added. Temporal points of interest, such as life events and relational changes, can thus be noted *when they actually occurred*. For example, the actual timing of births, deaths, separations, marriages, and adoptions can be plotted. In this way, the TLG highlights temporal aspects of family history in a way that is often obscured by the standard format.

In Figure 8.6, a TLG is used to diagram the remarried family of Figure 8.3. Significant issues in the timing of the parental divorces and

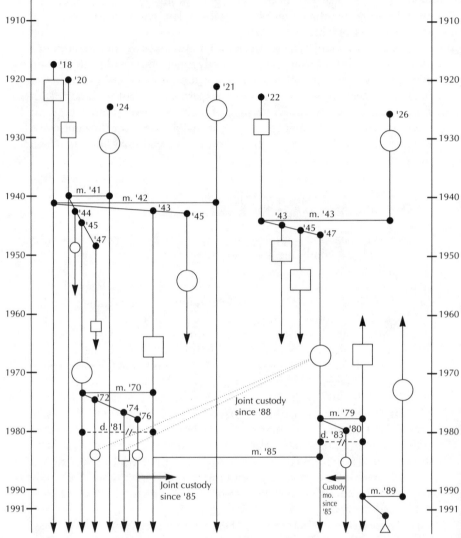

FIGURE 8.6.   A time-line genogram for the remarried binuclear family depicted in the standard format in Figure 8.3.

remarriages, and even some shifts in frequency of visitation and assignment of custody, can be seen.

For example, we can see that although all four children currently move back and forth biweekly from home to home, the two eldest children (who were in middle childhood at the time of the parental separation) did not wish joint custody until after the younger children had successfully made the transition. Although the TLG is more difficult to read, it can add crucial treatment information when one is planning for complex families or for families that have experienced political, geographical, or cultural changes.

In summary, the use of the classic genogram and the TLG can be compared in the following ways. The standard format includes three categories of information:

1. Basic family structure. This includes biological, kinship, and psychosocial ties.
2. Individual information. This refers to demographic data, and emotional, behavioral, as well as medical information.
3. Relational patterns. Dynamic aspects of familial relationships are denoted, especially degrees of intimacy, conflict, hierarchy, alliances, and coalitions.

Constructing a TLG is quite similar to constructing a standard genogram, save that there is a vertical axis on which one can create a time scale of up to 100 years (Friedman et al., 1988). Symbols and notation are similar to those in the standard format. In addition, each individual receives a "life line" that extends down from birth, along which important life events are recorded. In doing so, it adds information in a way similar to that of the "chronological chart" (Duhl, 1981). The chronological chart was designed as a grid for recording experiences and reactions of family members over time. Other theorists have advised the use of a "critical events" listing, to supplement the standard genogram. Yet the TLG synthesizes both sources of data, keeping its pictorial format and extending it.

The TLG in its present form does have several disadvantages. Because there is vastly more chronological information depicted in it, the diagram is more complex to read. Nodal events in the family life cycle also tend to produce myriad changes of relational patterns in tiny blocks of time, creating dense sections in the TLG. One research team recommends use of boldface type for critical items (Friedman et al., 1988). An alternative involves the use of "windows" of information for clarification.

Genograms as Assessment Tools

It is clear from the vast amount of information depicted in a single family genogram that this device serves as a valuable building block for formulating diagnoses and planning the direction of marital and family therapy. As a record of family development and history, its visual appeal and accessibility make the genogram a powerful tool as well as a clinically rich resource.

However, the transgenerational models of family therapy place heavy emphasis on examining ongoing behavioral and emotional processes within a family in the present as an important source of information in understanding the nature of the family's problems. This emphasis reflects the evolution of transgenerational models from their roots in the investigation of psychotic and severely disturbed family communication processes. Accordingly, from the transgenerational viewpoint, one cannot rely completely on "objective" factual information recorded on a genogram in order to assess the meaning of a client's symptoms or the familial consequences of his/her behavior and choices.

Furthermore, three of the four major transgenerational family therapy models place special emphasis on the necessity for clinicians to examine their own emotional reactions, associations, and values as an additional source of diagnostic information. An experienced therapist's "use of self" to assess the impact of family interactional patterns (as if he/she were a member of that family system) adds a subjective, affective dimension to family assessment techniques, which cannot be explored with only the more factual data of the genogram.

In sum, the standard genogram and especially the TLG offer incomparable resources to transgenerational clinicians, providing a wealth of information in a highly accessible visual diagram. However, genogramming can only be one element in three-generational assessment, because the data recorded are static, self-reported, and rational rather than interactional in nature. In the next chapter, other basic components of three-generational assessment are explored in terms of their contribution to transgenerational family therapy.

·9·

Transgenerational Assessment

From a transgenerational viewpoint, families are defined or "punctuated" by including all members within three generations or more. Although the "nuclear family," or parents and children, may be the ones present for a therapy session, the therapist organizes his/her hypotheses about family functioning by using information about the three-generational extended family. This use of extended family data naturally follows from the principle that the relational processes that underlie symptoms, and that build family belief systems, unfold over the course of many years. In other words, therapy will apply a comparatively "wide lens" to examine family behavior and beliefs, and to plan points of intervention.

Thus, if transgenerational therapy were to focus only on treating symptoms within the nuclear family, the therapist would overlook important transactions between generations that are contributing to the nuclear family's structure and methods of solving problems. Not every transgenerational model has applied equally well the wide lens necessary to create this extended family perspective.

For example, object relations models do not focus in therapy on interrelationships with extended family members. An entire course of family therapy may be held without once inviting in these important influences. The family participating in sessions typically consists of two generations, or parents and children. In contrast, symbolic-experiential therapists are most likely to adhere to the three-generational focus, frequently holding extended family sessions even from the outset of therapy. The natural systems and contextual models tend in practice to exclude direct work with extended family members, although innovators such as Donald Williamson and James Framo have encouraged the use of extended family visits for the clients of natural systems therapists.

This is not to say that change is impossible without the ongoing participation of extended families. Family systems theory, with its idea that behavior is influenced in a circular fashion rather than a linear cause–effect fashion, also implies that as one individual shifts his/her

121

position regarding intimates, the intimates' behavior will shift in tandem. As Michael Kerr, a natural systems therapist, has remarked:

> The consistent goal has been designing a technique that would most likely permit the emergence of some increase in the level of differentiation of self in at least one family member. It is a kind of reverse domino theory, in that if one domino begins to stand up again, this will trigger off the process in the other dominos as well, regardless of whether the other dominos happen to be symptomatic or not. . . . Experience has proven that seeing the couple or whole family together can, at times, work against a family member's working towards a better level of self. (1981, p. 255)

Kerr's comments focus on the therapeutic goal of differentiation, in line with the emphasis that natural systems theory places on this aspect of healthy functioning. However, his point regarding "reverse domino theory" is an important one. There are many advantages to including extended family members in marital and family therapy sessions, but it is not necessary to have them present to create change in a nuclear family. Because family members are bound together, and in fact define themselves over time through a set of relational rules, the relational rules begin to shift as soon as one member begins to alter his/her expectations, values, and behavior. As in a set of dominos lined up closely together, shifts produced in the interpersonal field create movement in significant others. Carl Whitaker has commented on the power of this process:

> If causation is circular, change is circular. Everybody in the family is altered by any change at any level. A cross-generational group carries the most power for change. Grandparents have amazing symbolic power and it is amplified when they remain separate from the treatment process. By bringing them into the interview, the grandparent homeostatic power may be modified or adapted to catalyze change in the family system. (Whitaker & Keith, 1981, p. 205)

A Wide Therapeutic Lens

If behavior changes in a nuclear family can be created without inclusion of extended family in psychotherapy sessions, what advantages accrue in using a wide therapeutic lens at all? Why define a family as a three-generational unit when it can be altered as a one- or two-generational unit? There are several reasons why inclusion of former generations adds power to transgenerational therapy:

1. During assessment, observation of three generations reveals to the therapist implicit belief structures, roles, and familial mandates before they can be voiced by the index client.
2. In creating a treatment plan, the therapist is more likely to succeed in selecting workable goals of change if he/she understands an extended family's existing conflicts and triangles.
3. During the process of therapy, the therapist will be able to predict and plan for disruptive reactions in families of origin if he/she has firsthand knowledge of the positions of extended family members.
4. Individuals in therapy derive self-respect and a sense of merit from the knowledge that they have been willing to meet with members of their extended families, to hear them out, and to attempt to offer their own views in return.

In other words, marital and family therapy certainly *can* succeed in the absence of firsthand information regarding extended family members. However, including them, particularly early in therapy, can add information to the therapist's working hypotheses, power to his/her interventions, and a sense of accomplishment for the identified client(s).

Julie, a 33-year-old woman, appeared suddenly in the therapist's office—disheveled, highly anxious, and cognitively disorganized. She stated that she lived out of town and was visiting her parents and brother because her husband had announced that he wished for a marital separation. There were no children. Four days after returning to her parents' home, Julie had been eating compulsively and was suicidal. She stated that her husband was unwilling to fly into town to help her, saying that he "could not take any more emotional pressure from her" and that life during their 13-year marriage had been "an emotional roller coaster."

Since Julie insisted that she needed to return to her town of residence in 2 weeks to resume her job, it was necessary to treat her on a brief, crisis-oriented basis. Rather than taking steps to bring the husband in, the therapist chose to bring in Julie's family of origin, in order to gather the information necessary to make a systemic hypothesis and create a plan.

In the first family interview, the information that emerged was as follows: Julie's parents, in their 70s, were religious fundamentalists who had never accepted her marriage to a man from another faith. Julie's brother, who had also married out of their religion, had divorced many years earlier and would not remarry. Julie's mother was considered unimportant by her own ultrareligious parents, who preferred their male children; the mother had been ridiculed and abused in her parents' home. Julie's father was also raised in an ultrareligious family, but his parents felt that his marriage was beneath him. The marriage of Julie's parents was highly symptomatic, since the mother was chronically explosive and the father avoidant. Julie's older brother was adored by the parents, and had achieved high status as police chief in their city. Julie had been hospitalized three times for depression, had moved to a poor rural city, and worked at a low-status job.

From this transgenerational information, the therapist was able to formulate the following hypothesis: Julie was in the position of the family scapegoat, mirroring a long religiously based tradition in the mother's family of rejecting female children. Julie had been exposed to recurrent explosions of maternal anger, but observed her father being passive and avoidant; in turn, Julie had married an avoidant husband. She believed that husbands were worthy of respect, but not wives like herself. Moreover, Julie believed herself to be hopeless and unimportant.

The therapist's formulation opened the way to prescribing a course of marital psychotherapy (to be undertaken in Julie's town of residence), in order to examine the nature of each spouse's contributions to the marital breakup. Julie was told that her requests for help in the face of long-term family unhappiness was evidence of great personal strength, all the more so since her family felt strongly about not focusing on female children. The elderly parents, whose own lives were devoid of encouragement and support, were commended on their attempt to tolerate a grown daughter's decision to work on her marriage, despite their religious reservations.

The central activity in an extended family assessment is the evocation of multiple perspectives on the presenting problem. As in other systemic psychotherapies, the more divergent the views that emerge, the more potential alternatives may evolve for later problem solving. In other words, as a dialogue develops among family members across generations regarding the problems, the dialogue itself suggests possible solutions within that family's unique structure and history. This multiple perspective helps the therapist to formulate his/her systemic hypotheses and plan of intervention. However, two other dynamics that operate in these meetings are also of particular interest to the transgenerational therapist.

Holding extended family assessments elicits evidence of the implicit values, traditions, and world views that each family possesses but cannot necessarily articulate. As Whitaker has commented:

> The healthy family is a subculture established over several generations. The power of this subculture is well structured and the struggle between that subculture filtering down from the mother's family of origin is gradually integrated with the power of the subculture handed down from the father's family of origin. (Whitaker & Keith, 1981, p. 193)

Although Whitaker ascribes this "culturalness" only to healthy families, it is inescapable that every family—symptomatic or not—possesses its own culture. As mentioned earlier, a second chief value of extended family assessment is the resulting demonstration of familial beliefs surrounding the members' relational histories and behavior.

A 31-year-old woman requested consultation for chronic problems with self-starvation and depression. Although her husband was supportive and receptive to her concerns, the couple's joint efforts to encourage Blanche to eat had failed totally. At 80 pounds, she was infertile, exhausted, withdrawn, and unable to leave her home for errands or recreation.

When Blanche was hospitalized for medical care, a meeting was called for herself, her husband, and her parents, who resided in a distant state (Blanche was an only child). In the first meeting, her mother commented that she and the father considered Blanche's long-term illness the result of spiritual failure on their part, leading to lack of self-confidence in their daughter. Blanche noted somewhat angrily that, in fact, she and her husband followed the born-again Christian beliefs of her parents, and she did not feel they had failed her spiritually in any way. It became evident that in the family's concern with accountability, Blanche's self-destructiveness had never been addressed; in fact, it had been enhanced by the parents' self-blame.

The third benefit of extended family assessment is a therapeutic benefit for the self-esteem of the symptom bearer (and perhaps other family members as well). Whether or not emotion-laden issues are resolved within these early sessions, the distressed individual earns self-regard through the process of extending consideration to his/her family and attempting to negotiate personal concerns openly with them. This self-regard, according to contextual theory, stems from a universal need to relate, together with the inevitable loss of self-respect that accompanies cutoff of those who parented and preceded us. The act of inclusion inherent in an extended family meeting, in and of itself, begins to address the self-doubt, mystification, and isolation of symptomatic individuals by reconnecting them with their intimate context.

Extended Family Interviews

Clients often report—and tend to believe—that if they request that members of their families of origin attend sessions, they will be refused. This idea is all too frequently mirrored in the therapist's assumption that conflictual families will view psychotherapy meetings defensively or even with hostility. Alternatively, some clients describe their families in one- or two-dimensional terms that make it difficult to justify a joint meeting, as if the extended kinship group has no tensions or sensitivities of any kind. One variant of this position is that the extended family is never anything rather than extremely close, loving, supportive, and so on. These resistances frequently put the therapist in the position of seeming to argue with a client that his/her extended family needs therapy. However, if the therapist assumes from the outset that he/she cannot assess a client's symptoms except in a multigenerational context, there is an immediate basis for mutual cooperation rather than conflict. Extended family members can initially be put in the position of *consultants to* the therapy, rather than *unwilling participants in* the therapy. Although this position actually shifts once other members hear and discuss family problems, an assessment framework removes a sense of obligation and pressure within symptomatic families.

Extended family interviews may be conducted at several different intervals. As noted earlier, the symbolic-experiential model so strongly emphasizes implicit beliefs and values that family members are invited to attend meetings from the initial interview on throughout early-stage therapy. The natural systems model does not utilize this information as much as it does data concerning differentiation of family members. Extended family members are more likely to be invited on a consultation basis in middle-stage therapy, in order to examine the effects of therapy-induced differentiation on the larger family.

Object relations family models have not thus far commented on when, and how often, extended family interviews are considered. Case studies suggest that, by and large, they are not utilized; the therapist uses genogram information exclusively in order to gather important family data. However, the contextual model, which uses many of the concepts central to object relations theory, does include participation by extended family members when it will aid the symptomatic member to strengthen relational ties ("rejunction") or to test new self-definitions against their perceptions of him/her ("self-delineation") (see Chapter 3).

These different uses of extended family interviews are not mutually exclusive. Rather, they represent discrete methods that have received exploration within separate schools of transgenerational theory, so that the methods have not been compared and contrasted as techniques in their own right. It is possible to hold three-generational family meetings during initial assessment; to reconvene them during the midphase of therapy in order to help reorganize familial roles; and in late therapy to invite in specific extended family members (such as a significant uncle or sister-in-law) if it will help to build relational resources. When extended family interviews are held intermittently in this way, members often come to perceive the therapist as a family advocate, and are more willing to take initiatives and risks with one another.

Early-Stage Family-of-Origin Consultations: Diagnostic Uses

Issuing the invitation to participate early in family therapy often means that the symptom bearer is making a personal request for the first time in a long interval. Because family tension is frequently dealt with through chronic conflict, avoidance, or distancing, parents and grandparents may have little prior knowledge of the symptom bearer's decision to enter therapy. In these situations, an alliance is more likely to take place if these relatives are informed that the client is distressed and would appreciate their viewpoints as to the nature of his/her problems and history.

Therefore, in its early stages, extended family participation should not be framed as exploring mutual contributions to emotional problems. This frame demands that family elders (who often have not been approached or consulted by the symptom bearer) trust in his/her loyalty and good regard, and reveal intimate and often anxiety-provoking information. A therapist who takes this stance, or allows a symptom bearer to take this stance, is asking more than he/she is willing to give. In contextual terms, the therapist has not yet demonstrated the "trustworthiness" necessary to earn that much risk taking in return from the extended family. In order to merit trust, the therapist needs to extend consideration and fairness first. Given that the family members may not have been approached for help, or may have been approached in a conflictual or distressing way by the symptomatic member, they are often most open to the idea that the therapist and client are interested in their views. It is a sadly common problem to find that relatives have been called in to a family member's psychotherapy before, only to find themselves confronted or even attacked, and expected to offer comfort and cooperation in return.

When one is interviewing an extended family during the assessment phase of therapy, it is frequently necessary to schedule a 2-hour block of time, rather than the more common 1-hour or 1½-hour block. If members have traveled a long distance, it is most productive to hold two of these meetings over 2 days, so that travel plans can be made efficiently. When a family of origin resides in a distant location, the therapist must consider whether to simplify planning and invite one segment of the family, in contrast to planning more elaborately for participation by parties from diverse areas.

When families have fragmented in this fashion, it often makes more sense to delay family assessment until most members can arrive together, rather than meeting with different segments that do not have regular contact with one another. The reason for this is that a large family meeting will yield more complex information. In some cases, the absence of an important family member represents a form of resistance, intended to diffuse a severe conflict by excluding one of the parties involved. This has been called the "absent-member maneuver" (Sonne, Speck, & Jungreis, 1962). In general, although smaller meetings are easier to arrange, they yield less information while still demanding extensive planning and consideration.

A 25-year-old handicapped man requested psychotherapy for severe agoraphobia, social withdrawal, and suicidality. Although Martin's mild brain damage (from a surgical accident) meant that he walked with braces, he had still been able to finish school and work at a challenging job until his parents' divorce required that he move into his own apartment. Since Martin's divorced parents lived in different states, and formulating a treatment plan appeared urgent, the therapist agreed when the parents informed him that their schedules required that they come into town at different times.

Martin's mother arrived with his maternal grandmother and 20-year-old brother, who resided in the same city. Extended family meetings held with that group revealed that Martin resented his parents' breakup, depended on his mother completely for emotional support, and neglected his brother unless he offered Martin favors. The sessions focused on how Martin's mother and grandmother tended to "baby" their spouses and children, while at the same time expecting (and receiving) little in return from their own parents or husbands.

Subsequently, a family meeting held with Martin's father showed that Martin held great anger toward his father and refused to consult him for advice regarding social and financial problems. His father appeared highly supportive, and reported many incidents in which he had given Martin physical and financial (but not emotional) aid. Martin's anger at his father appeared, in this context, to suggest a problem of distancing between father and son, leading to a lack of social skills and self-confidence in Martin's adulthood to help him weather the stresses of his handicap.

One month later, all family members stated that they were able to convene for a large family session (despite the mother's reluctance to "sit in the room with" her ex-husband). The high level of tension between the parents, Martin's sudden protective hovering over his mother, and the grandmother's veiled statements that the father had "left" the family clarified that a chronic coalition of mothers and sons against the father was contributing greatly to Martin's alienation from his father.

Process of the Interview

As mentioned earlier, one purpose of extended family assessment is to elicit multiple perspectives on the presenting problem from different generations and members. This multiple perspective becomes the source of alternative strategies for change in any systemic family therapy. However, the *process* of the assessment interview differs when a transgenerational framework is used.

Systemic interviewing focuses on the methods of circular questioning, neutrality, and hypothesizing, to elicit and highlight differences from a distant position so as to observe them. Instead of neutrality, transgenerational interviewing tends to utilize the posture of "multidirectional partiality" (Boszormenyi-Nagy & Krasner, 1986), in which the therapist is affectively more responsive and proximal to each family member. The method of circular questioning, in which members are asked to comment on the relationship between two or more others, is replaced with direct questioning of each member's understanding of family history and relational patterns. Hypotheses are constructed about the relational dysfunctions in the family by putting together these multiple perspectives.

Each model tends to emphasize certain domains of information over others in the interview process. Wachtel (1982) has commented, for example, that in constructing family genograms, natural systems therapists emphasize descriptive information such as evidence of triangles and fusing–distancing patterns. In contrast, object relations models are "very much concerned with feelings and idiosyncratic interpretations of reality, as well as the 'hard data' " (p. 336). Symbolic-experiential therapists, like object relations therapists, tend to utilize questioning to further emotional expressiveness. The purpose of eliciting emotional reactions is to alert the therapist to family members' interpretations of important events. As Wachtel states,

> Such a focus enables the therapist to learn more about what the client values than he could disclose consciously. . . . It is not just the words which convey unrecognized implicit meanings. The affective tone can also reveal unconscious longings which, with the therapist's help, can be used to establish new goals and directions. . . . Just as family stories help uncover unarticulated wishes, so, too, do they reveal fears, taboos and family "object lessons." (1982, pp. 340–341)

I believe that *both* traditional means of information gathering are valid and necessary components of extended family consultation. It is important, in these first few meetings with relatives, to assess the presence of structural and process problems in the larger family system. Members need to be asked their perceptions regarding which individuals are allied in the family; which ones are in conflict or peripheral; which members are called upon in decision-making situations; which relationships are close and which are distant; and which life events have contributed especially to their distress.

However, they also need to be observed carefully for their affective tone, which gives clues regarding their unspoken wishes and values. For example, a grandmother who calmly describes her grown son as "self-sufficient" may be praising him for a highly valued family role. The same woman speaking angrily about his "self-sufficiency" may be connoting that he is violating a family value of interdependency. If the therapist is trying to assess why this grown son is not close to his children, these contextual differences are crucial. The first statement might suggest that the father is recreating a generational boundary that has a long tradition in his family of origin. The second statement might suggests that the father is reacting to an unresolved conflict in his family of origin regarding dependency—possibly a triangle with his own parents, which created a loyalty bind for him. Although it is a common understanding among family therapists of all persuasions that nonverbal behavior gives important contextual information, this point is frequently minimized in discussions of technique.

In addition to observing affective tone in the extended family interview, the therapist can feed back his/her observations to other family members and request their reaction. In the example just given, the therapist might turn to the son's wife and ask her whether her mother-in-law sounded angry to her, and whether her husband has ever commented on this anger to her. The affect shown by such a deliberately triangulated "third party" will reveal his/her position on the issue in question. For example, if the wife responds sympathetically that her husband does not notice his mother or her anger, this would suggest that the wife is allied with the mother (and perhaps the children) to form a coalition against the husband. Or possibly the wife is frustrated by a "revolving slate" situation in which the husband has cut off his mother because of past injury, and now cuts off his wife and children as well. If the wife responds empathically with her husband, the therapist might infer that the marital alliance is strong but that the husband remains peripheral because of severe family-of-origin pressures.

In extended family interviewing, the goal of interviewing is not to achieve resolution of familial conflicts or correction of deficiencies. Therefore, the position of the therapist is like that of a fact-finding team, which will report back its findings but give no immediate advice or conclusions. The extended family members can be told this during the interview, and can be invited to ask questions of their own as well for the purpose of future discussion. The therapist has reached his/her goal for the interviews when he/she can do the following:

1. Explicate some of the central beliefs and values underlying a family's unique structure.
2. Describe the various positions of important family members in regard to conflictual issues and symptoms.
3. Predict how these positions may shift if the identified client becomes more self-controlled and less symptomatic.
4. Help the symptom bearer to credit himself/herself for having joined with family members to examine the problem.

The Negative Therapeutic Reaction

In the psychoanalytic literature, writers have commented extensively on a phenomenon in which a symptom bearer experiences extremely negative effects from the process of discussing material with the therapist. Called the "negative therapeutic reaction" (Freud, 1937/1964, p. 243), this phenomenon is considered by object relations theorists to reflect the projection of split-off, negative affects and beliefs about the self onto the therapist. Interacting with the therapist then activates a re-experiencing of these projected affects and beliefs, leading to great anxiety about the self and increased symptoms.

It is quite possible for extended families to have a "negative therapeutic reaction" in interviews. Under the pressure of severe dysfunction, or a marital or family crisis, families are apt to experience great apprehension, guilt, fear, or anger regarding the breakdown of one or more members. During such periods, the feelings of responsibility, failure, confusion, hurt, and disappointment are easily transferred onto the therapist. For example, members of a family whose child is hospitalized with suicidal symptoms may project their feelings of inadequacy onto the therapist, who is seen as incompetent or incapable of helping the child and family. The process of opening up painful areas of disagreement or distress then becomes intolerable. It is as if the basic structure of the psychotherapy relationship, involving extension of trust and voluntary self-exposure, is not secure.

In some families, the negative therapeutic experience centers more on a sense of embarrassment or humiliation than on one of mistrust or anger. Such feelings will escalate in these families after an extended family meeting, unless the embarrassment is discussed and acknowledged by the therapist at the time of the meeting. The sense of humiliation is a derivative of a family's shame over the symptomatic member, and over an expectation that outsiders or the community at large will view the family's information with contempt. This problem is especially common in families where domestic violence, incest, or substance abuse has occurred. It most probably reflects experiences between family members and the community in which blame, disapproval, social sanctions, or legal punishments have been meted out. The therapist is then viewed as one more instrument of social control, and the shame that family members feel is moved onto the therapist, who is seen as contemptuous or judgmental. Early intervention is crucial to establishing an alliance with these families, especially the use of multidirectional partiality toward all members.

Later-Stage Family-of-Origin Consultations: Diagnostic Uses

It has been noted earlier that at times it is most constructive, as well as logistically practical, to hold extended family meetings in later stages of marital or family therapy. The best example of this method is that developed by James Framo (1980). In summarizing the rationale for this method, Framo states:

> Current family and marital difficulties largely stem from attempts to master earlier conflicts from the original family; these conflicts and transference distortions from the past are being lived anachronistically through the spouse and children (Framo, 1965, 1970[/1972]). When these adults are able to go back to deal directly with their parents and brothers and sisters about the previously avoided hard issues that have existed between them, an opportunity exists for reconstructive changes to come about. . . . The great resistances of adult clients toward bringing in family of origin testifies [sic] to the great power of this approach. . . . This procedure has general applicability and serves diagnostic as well as therapeutic purposes. Not only can clients discover what from the original family is being worked out through the spouse and children, but these adults are being given the chance to come to terms with parents before the parents die. (1980, p. 192)

Framo's method of incorporating later-phase family-of-origin consultations has, as he states, both diagnostic and therapeutic utility. Although its therapeutic uses are discussed in a later chapter (see Chapter 11), its diagnostic uses are relevant here. Framo notes:

> The adult, by having sessions with his or her family of origin, takes the problems back to their original sources, thereby making available a direct route to etiological factors. These sessions serve diagnostic purposes . . . in that both the old and new families [of origin and of procreation] can be cross-referenced for similar patterns. (1980, p. 197)

Framo's method includes only one spouse with his/her family of origin; the partner is excluded from the meetings. His rationale is that many families balk at opening up anxiety-laden dilemmas in front of an in-law, or at directing their focus on the marriage of the son or daughter rather than on their own family process. However, he discusses exceptions in which the in-law relationship is so infused with tension that it is necessary to address it in the meetings.

I believe that there is diagnostic value in including the partner (if there is one) in extended family consultations. Although these late-stage consultations serve to clarify the linkages between a symptomatic spouse and family-of-origin dysfunctions, I feel that it is important to both the adult son/daughter and the extended family to acknowledge the reality that he/she is married in the here and now. It is a useful connection to present family structures, and a valuable "container" for family anxiety, when all can recognize that the unresolved issues stem from the past and not a current desire to regress back into the lap of the parents. Furthermore, when a family is in therapy for chronic or severe marital conflict, both spouses have usually noticed and even verbalized that at least one partner's difficulties are related to earlier experiences in growing up. Sometimes a spouse even attempts periodically to help the partner examine these formative experiences, although the efforts are not necessarily successful. It seems appropriate to relieve the spouse of this "helper" role, as well as to satisfy his/her curiosity and concern, by allowing him/her to sit in, observe, and even comment on the extended family consultations.

The unique advantage of deferring extended family meetings to late-stage therapy, rather than holding them at the outset, is that the symptom bearer is in a different position for the meetings. As an individual, he/she is now cognizant that reworking unsatisfactory connections with parents, siblings, and others is possible and beneficial. He/she also is now aware that present marital or parent–child conflict reflects lessons learned from the family of origin over several generations, and is not merely symptom-focused as in early psychotherapy. Ideally, disruptive behavioral, physiological, or affective disturbances are now controlled and do not require constant attention. There is now an emotional "space" in which an adult son/daughter can research and re-examine the antecedents of his/her distress and achieve a greater sense of mastery. As Framo states,

> It is fascinating to observe how the marital [or family] conflicts, which totally preoccupied the client several weeks earlier, fade away and are replaced by the dawning realization that maybe something can be done about that longstanding guilty overcloseness or alienation from a mother, father, or sibling. (1980, p. 214)

In order to appreciate the relative advantages and disadvantages of early- versus late-stage extended family meetings, it is important to bear in mind that "assessment" is not a procedure but a process. That is, assessment yields different kinds of information to the observer, depending on the position of the observer in the family system. This great truth, which has revolutionized our physical and social sciences, implies that observing a family of origin at different stages of psychotherapy reveals different data. For instance, a wife with psychosomatic symptoms may use a family-of-origin meeting to discuss her illness, and this may give rise to a family discussion of illness patterns in the parents and grandparents. The therapist will be able to observe how important family stresses have been handled covertly through the emergence of physical symptoms in the most vulnerable members. The family may emerge with a greater understanding that there are key relational problems underlying those illnesses, which need to be addressed.

In contrast, in later-stage therapy, when the wife's symptoms are no longer active, a family consultation is more likely to focus on how the wife's earlier behavior served to mask specific dissatisfactions. The therapist will probably see the family react to learning of her specific concerns, rather than a more preliminary conversation regarding illness. This difference will partly reflect the fact that the wife has already linked these personal issues with her symptoms, and no longer uses the metaphor of illness to explain herself. In turn, the family members are likely to develop a group exploration of these key relational problems during the consultation; perhaps, for instance, they may look at how the problems influenced different members in their own marriages and families.

This distinction between "kinds" of information to be garnered is a subtle one. However, as the therapist experiments with holding extended family meetings at different stages in therapy, it becomes evident that as the position of the symptom bearer changes vis-à-vis spouse and family, the very definition of key family issues changes and is refined.

·10·

Techniques I:
Creating a Transgenerational Frame

In transgenerational theory, the family is seen as an entity that has survived for many decades of life, and therefore has possessed adaptive mechanisms for meeting at least some of the needs of its members in the past. Thus the role of the therapist is most a ppropriately defined not as an agent of *change*, in a generic sense, but as an agent of *restoration*, in a more specific sense. Rather than assuming a simple deficit model of marital or family functioning, this approach places current dysfunction in the context of the family's past ability to provide nurturance, guidance, support, problem solving, and necessary skills. The unique strength of transgenerational theory is this larger perspective on previous relational patterns and solutions to life problems.

In a relevant paper, "The All-Too-Short Trip from Positive to Negative Connotation," Anderson (1986) makes the point that one of the other predominant family systems models—the systemic model—possesses certain weaknesses that allow it to pathologize families even with its emphasis on circular causation. I believe that, similarly, many strategic variants allow therapists to see families primarily in terms of pathology. Their ahistorical nature leads the clinician to overlook the past forces and events that have shaped current family patterns, in favor of identifying and modifying "dysfunctional interaction cycles." Of all the ahistorical family therapy models, the structural model comes closest to affirming that the organization of a family reflects adaptation to past needs if not present ones. In fact, the structural model contains a great deal of attention to transgenerational family behavior patterns, without acknowledging the importance of this attention. A reading of many classic structural family case studies reveals close attention to parental, grandparental, and long-term sociocultural mandates in family life, both in assessment and in therapy.

I have found a transgenerational frame to possess great power in helping families to *demystify themselves*—to identify for themselves the sources of "horizontal" (chronological) stress (see Chapter 2) and of their important beliefs and values for living. This process of self-study can be quite effective in combating guilt, shame, or self-blame in symptomatic families. Once such a frame is established, family members can begin to explore how to mobilize dormant resources within the extended family, or to restore important relationships that have become restrictive or unhelpful. There are a number of ways to create a transgenerational frame within the context of therapy.

The Position of the Therapist

Much of the work of creating a transgenerational frame in therapy is accomplished in the attitude of the family therapist. From the time of initial interviewing to establish the nature of the family's complaint, the therapist follows two tracks of reasoning simultaneously: (1) the track of the presenting problem, and the interactional cycles that surround symptoms; and (2) the track of probable relational antecedents for these interactional cycles. In order to follow these two tracks of information, the therapist must cultivate a consistent observational stance while he/she relates to the family.

Tracking the Presenting Problem

The therapist's position with a presenting problem is discussed extensively in the next chapter, which focuses on goal setting and the concept of family restoration. Essentially, the transgenerational therapist views presenting problems as systemic escalations, reflecting inadaquate solutions applied by family members. This stance is identical to that of structural, strategic, and systemic therapists. Observing behavioral interactions centering around the troublesome symptoms, the therapist watches for who intervenes and who refrains; the sequence of interventions by family members; and how interventions affect the presenting symptoms. He/she asks for information regarding each member's beliefs and intentions regarding the problem, as well as past efforts to intervene.

The position of the therapist is one of experimentation, openness, interest, warmth, and curiosity. Elsewhere in this book, I have discussed my preference for cultivating "multidirectional partiality" rather than "neutrality" in order to build a therapeutic alliance. In contrast to Stierlin and Weber (1989), who recommend that the therapist side clearly with *no* family member, I prefer Boszormenyi-Nagy's recommendation that *all* family members feel sure that the therapist is considering their own individual views (Boszormenyi-Nagy & Krasner, 1986). This preference follows from the transgenerational principle that each member's familial history and unique position in his/her family of origin determine that person's role in current dysfunctional behavior cycles. Therefore, rather than remaining "neutral" to each contribution and distant from each individual view, the therapist is "partial" to each contribution and actively responsive to each individual view.

A chronically dysfunctional family requested consultation on behalf of the eldest child, Alicia, who was depressed and unable to attend classes at college in a consistent way. The family consisted of the father, Alicia, and two younger sons; the children were 21, 18, and 14 years of age. The mother had left the family 2 years previously, after which the parents had divorced; she now resided in Europe. The father and children were mutually enraged with one another; physically combative during arguments; and discouraged by the father's continual "shelling out" of money while the children felt too angry and mistrustful to work and earn their own.

In the first session, the therapist worked hard to promote discussion of Alicia's depression while staving off accusations and escalations in the room. All the children felt that their mood and productivity problems stemmed from their father's constant threats to disown them, verbal explosions, and distance. Each child provoked the other in order to elicit some kind of personal recognition.

The therapist questioned each family member in turn for information regarding his/her role in the chronic disputes and threats. At the same time, he showed particular interest in the unique difficulties of each member's tasks in this grieving family, pointing out specific needs and problems facing each member at this point in the family's development. Regarding the father, he further pointed out the especial problems facing him in raising three children without female assistance or aid from his own neglectful parents (the children's grandparents).

Regarding Alicia, with whom all the others were enraged, the therapist pointed out that she could hardly be happy about falling behind in her studies while her peers prepared for graduation. When the 14-year-old son objected that she frequently frightened him by leaving home in the middle of the night when their father was out of town, the therapist questioned whether he felt that anyone was "mothering" him enough.

The therapist's role is partly to help the couple or family demystify the nature and source of the stressors, in order to combat the anxiety and blaming that often accompany chronic symptoms. In order to achieve this while tracking the presenting problem, it is necessary for him/her to be personally "transparent" as opposed to mysterious and distant. In this model of therapy, a key element in achieving "transparency" is use of self. "Use of self" has been written about widely in the symbolic-experiential literature (Roberto et al., 1987; Whitaker, 1976a; Whitaker & Keith, 1981). Essentially, the therapist seeks to share aspects of his/her own life experiences where relevant, thus giving the family information that makes his/her own individual personality more visible. These shared stories are selected from previous familial events in the therapist's life that have been well resolved and have yielded helpful information to the therapist about how to approach relational problems in the present. For example, the therapist may share with the family of a school truant how his/her own cousin shocked the therapist's family by flirting with the idea of running away.

In sum, we can say that the transgenerational therapist tracks presenting symptoms just as all systemic therapists do. However, in this model, this tracking procedure includes two unique aspects in the therapist's *position* vis-à-vis the family: establishing multidirectional partiality, and using the self of the therapist. These two positioning behaviors will create an atmosphere of egalitarianism, self-examination, and mutual disclosure to support later discussion of long-term familial patterns that are emotionally stressful.

Tracking Relational Antecedents

In addition to tracking the presenting problem and the interactional cycles surrounding it (a procedure typical of all systemic therapies), the transgenerational therapist simultaneously formulates hypotheses regarding possible relational events that might explain or account for their current interactions. These hypotheses guide the therapist's questions regarding each spouse's family of origin and important extended family dynamics. In turn, answers to questions about relational problems in the two families of origin aid the therapist in predicting and planning for the kind of interactional conflicts that are likely to arise in the process of therapy.

> Fourteen-year-old Sean was hospitalized after he took a bottle of his mother's antidepressant medication and lost consciousness on his bed. Depressed, angry, and hopeless, Sean appeared in the first family meeting to be extremely reactive to his mother's every statement about the family. At the same time, his mother spoke hesitantly and shyly, as if she were not sure her opinion was important. Her self-effacing way of speaking belied the fact that it was she who had competently and quickly found care for him and requested his admission.

Adam, Sean's new stepfather (who had found him unconscious), agreed with most of the hopeless and angry statements that Sean made, stating that his own teenage years were painful and discouraging as well. Overall, however, he appeared withdrawn from the meeting. Of course, from an interactional standpoint, this configuration left Sean in the position of a peer to a seemingly incompetent mother and a self-absorbed stepfather who also was quite new to the family.

The therapist noted the complementary "fit" of the mother's self-doubt and Sean's anger, and also the anger and discomfort of the stepfather. From these observations, he hypothesized that Sean had been subjected to painful life events in which his mother had perhaps not felt comfortable demonstrating authority. Furthermore, he speculated that the mother, who was self-effacing, had herself probably experienced punishment or ridicule from elders in her own development. Such a shy individual is likely to marry a more forceful and even aggressive mate, unless she has had the opportunity to re-examine her own self-critical stance and to balance it with approval. Could Sean's biological father have been such a spouse? Finally, the initial statements by the stepfather that he himself had not enjoyed a pleasant adolescence suggested that he had himself felt overwhelmed by adversity.

Using these relational hunches, the therapist referred to the genogram provided on admission, and directed his questions toward issues of possible violence, abuse, and psychological maltreatment in the mother's first marriage and in her family of origin. It quickly emerged that she was the product of a violent home, had been molested by her own father, and had married a violent first husband who beat Sean. Moreover, her new husband was from an alcoholic home. In fact, the mother then reflected that her request for admission for her son was the first time in her adult life that she had taken on authority.

In order to track relational antecedents that could account for interactional cycles observed in a session, the therapist must be very familiar with functional and dysfunctional parent–child and marital dynamics (see Chapters 5 and 6). The amount and intensity of affect within a parent–child dyad, for example, suggest information about their degree of comfort with intimate relating, apart from how they interact in regard to their presenting problem. In the case example just given, the immediate problem was that the mother could not take authority to intervene in her son's depression but rather acted like a self-conscious peer, while the stepfather was peripheral and agreed with the son's extreme hopelessness. However, a more basic element in the case (which would of course influence the family's responses to intervention) was that the mother was not comfortable in general being directive with her child, preferring to defer to men and to blame herself under stress. In order to track this level of the problem, the therapist would need to be familiar with the principle that functional parenting includes guidance and directiveness with adolescents.

A number of transgenerational patterns can underlie dysfunctional interaction (although not all are necessarily operating in every case). These patterns arise from the kinds of dysfunctional emotional processes noted in Chapter 6. Several of these patterns are as follows:

1. Parent–child violence, which creates in the child perceptions of victimization and negative identification with the violent parent. The negative identification springs from the belief that the child, who looks up to the adult, must "deserve" the violence; this leads to a sense of either worthlessness and depression, or grandiosity and rage.

2. Spousal violence, which creates in children perceptions of adult frailty and abandonment (the battering spouse is seen as out of control, while the battered spouse is seen as weak, unreliable, and unable to protect herself or the children). Often, children in such a family develop a parallel contempt for the battered spouse (usually the wife); they come to view women as frail and incompetent. Male children can become aggressive, like battered children, while female children often develop a sense of personal worthlessness and fear of loss (abandonment).

3. Parent–child maltreatment or ridicule, in which the child is made to feel ashamed of momentary errors or situational problems. Because the maltreatment is not obviously inappropriate, children easily internalize severe ideals for their own performance. They are highly sensitive to criticism as a reflection of their relational worth, and ashamed or angry during periods of conflict. Male children are commonly exposed to ridicule by their fathers when they show anxiety or fear—one major source of affective suppression in adult men.

4. Environmental trauma, which subjects entire families to periods in which their physical survival or emotional security is threatened. Family members embroiled in catastrophic events such as war, epidemic illness, famine, or severe poverty respond to outside threat by developing an unusually high degree of internal cohesion to try to protect one another emotionally. For example, in a family where a grandparent was murdered during the Holocaust, adult grandchildren may experience a type of personal anxiety that is termed "survivor guilt." For these third-generation survivors, it is as if they have been forcibly separated from this grandparent, whom they never even knew.

Of course, the descriptions of these four patterns of transgenerational dysfunction are quite cursory and incomplete; nor do these by any means represent the full range of possible patterns. They are provided to illustrate the idea that interactional problems observed in a session are often superimposed on longer-term relational disorders, which can be tracked via close attention to the positions family members take with one another. For example, if the therapist observes that a young girl seems oversolicitous of an elderly grandmother and reluctant to separate from her family, he/she should track information concerning whether the family has been subjected to environmental trauma such as immigration, economic deprivation, or traumatic loss.

A family requested consultation for their bulimic teenager who lived at home with her parents and attended a local college. Despite numerous interventions to increase her autonomy and self-care, and to create greater attachment within the parents' marriage, the daughter still preferred to spend her time with her father and to struggle along in a major she could not master (international banking). It emerged in the third month of family therapy that the uncle's best friend had committed suicide during the Depression by leaping from his office building. The now-adult daughter believed strongly that if she did not carefully follow her own father's steps in business, she too would "lose everything" and experience calamity. If the therapist had carefully observed her devoted attachment, and questioned for a history of family trauma, this information might have emerged quite early in therapy.

Creating Self-Study in Family Therapy

In a lovely paper titled "Study Your Own Family," Philip Guerin (1976) laid out elementary principles of natural systems theory for practitioners and laypersons who wished to begin examining transgenerational patterns in their own families. The message of this paper is that through deliberate examination of one's family's past, one can increase self-understanding and add a dimension to one's feeling of connectedness to others. This message can be quite potent as a means of empowering families in distress, especially in our current society, which isolates and divides families in order to maximize achievement and productivity in the economic world.

Although it is true that every family in therapy undergoes a type of self-study when providing a genogram, many therapists use the genogram primarily for personal reference in formulating a plan of treatment (or in hypothesis formation). However, genogram information can alternatively be used to create an atmosphere of exploration within a couple or family regarding the members' own relational endowments (Wachtel, 1982).

A lawyer and his wife of 3 years requested consultation for problems of chronic, intense verbal fights and inability to negotiate and decide even the smallest household matters. The 40-year-old husband, in his second marriage, was concerned that this marriage too might end in alienation and divorce. His wife, a health care professional, felt that she loved her husband but was being drained and exhausted by the demands of job, household, and sole responsibility for their 2-year-old son.

In the gathering of genogram information, it immediately became apparent that this hard-working and stressed young mother had little or no connection with the members of her own family (despite the fact that they lived locally). In contrast, the husband's large, extremely close Irish family commanded his daily attention, especially his mother and older sister, who had recurrent psychosomatic symptoms. The husband reflected that his tie with his family was the most important relationship in his life, and, coincidentally, that his wife repeatedly complained that he paid more attention to his mother than to her. It also emerged that the husband's family looked to him as family leader, never inquiring as to his welfare or personal difficulties, and that since the remarriage they had treated his wife in a similar fashion. The spouses rapidly ceased arguing about household decisions and began to examine their expectations for familial support, especially whether the husband would be willing to ask for more consideration for his needs and the needs of his wife.

Transgenerational family therapists draw on genogram information in order to enhance each family's ability to identify and recognize its own unique heritage of cultural, historical, and emotional mandates and traditions. This ability is a central ingredient in rebuilding mutual trust and cohesion between members, in families where these qualities have been disrupted by stress and dysfunction. To the extent that the therapist can encourage self-study in a family, aiding the members in this reflexive work rather than formulating the problem for them, he/she positions them to respect their own "story." Spouses and family members can then initiate the process of questioning, examining, and modifying or reworking outmoded roles and options that do not fit current life circumstances or immediate needs.

The therapist can ask a number of questions in early marital or family sessions to position participants for self-study. Some of these positioning questions are as follows:

1. How would you describe your own rearing? Was your family of origin close or distant? Quiet or emotionally expressive? Well-organized or chaotic? Have these patterns changed since your own launching? If so, how? Did you notice these patterns in your grandparents' household? In the households of your uncles and aunts?

2. Which parent have you been closer to over time? Has this changed at different periods in your life? Which grandparent(s) have you

been closer to? Has this been true of your parent(s) as well? How do you explain these differences? Have these differences (or any other tensions) been discussed openly between yourself and other family members?

3. At the time of your marriage (or relational commitment, if the adults are unmarried), how much contact were you having with your own parent(s) and siblings? With your partner's? How would you describe your own courtship? How did the two families of origin respond to the court-ship and the decision to make a commitment?

4. To which members of the extended family have you confided your current distress? If you were to inform someone of how the situation is progressing, whom would you choose first? Whom would your partner choose first? What makes this individual (or these individuals) seem most trustworthy at the current time? Is this a change from individuals who were confidants in the past?

5. With which members of your family of origin is there the greatest emotional intensity (tension)? How do you account for this? How do you keep the intensity (tension) "cooled down"? Have you ever addressed this point in the family? Is there similar intensity (tension) with your partner, or have you chosen a partner with whom you felt things would be different?

6. Are unresolved family problems or events in the past avoided or discussed? If there has been significant avoidance, what was the pur-pose of doing so? Has there been a cost involved in doing so? In your marriage and family of procreation, are painful differences addressed directly or skirted? Is this a change from the pattern in your family of origin?

7. What, in your opinion, were the preferred roles, values, and lifestyle advocated in your upbringing? Have you realized these pre-scriptions, or modified them in some way? How have your intimates responded to your modifications? Is it difficult for you to make modifica-tions, or to allow your partner to make modifications, in previous marital expectations? Do you allow your children to make significant modifica-tions, or does this cause great concern or distress?

8. What roles do you fulfill in your marriage and family of procrea-tion? Are they the positions you wished to occupy in your plans for your own life? If change requires taking a new position with your partner or children in order to eliminate symptoms, do you feel able to take on this challenge now? If not now, when?

9. Has your family of origin, or your partner's family, ever re-quested psychotherapy for distressing symptoms? Were you a participant? Do you feel that the views and concerns of each participant were re-spected and taken into account? Did family members and therapist ex-change their views candidly and with good faith? If not, do you trust that

your views will be given consideration? Are you concerned about the possibility of encountering failure or punishment for offering your views?

10. To what extent, in your family belief system, is importance attached to individual happiness and development? Is there greater emphasis on serving the needs of others? Are you willing to examine your own needs and goals as part of therapy, or do you feel that your participation must be limited to aiding another distressed member? Do you accept that your own well-being (or lack of it) affects your partner and children, or do you insist that they pursue their own life tasks without your wholehearted backing and participation?

Using Extended Family Consultations

The next chapter discusses various specific techniques in the transgenerational lexicon that are used for bringing about systemic change. Among those techniques are a number of forms of extended family meetings, which are planned and composed both for purposes of assessment (as described in Chapter 9) and for purposes of inducing relational change. For detailed descriptions of these procedures, and discussion of their use in therapy, the reader is referred to Chapter 11. Here, I wish to point out that early-phase extended family meetings are particularly useful in helping a couple or family to initiate self-study and in creating a transgenerational frame.

It is common, but by no means universal, that transgenerational therapies include as many members of an extended family as possible in every session. For example, in a family with an oppositional adolescent boy, the family sessions will frequently include not only his divorced mother and her fiancé, and his sisters, but also the paternal grandmother who resides in town and participates in his care. Family meetings commonly draw in divorced parents, involved aunts and uncles, cousins who are social peers to a child, older siblings who reside at college or nearby, and significantly close friends of the family who participate in the life of the household (e.g., an important pastor).

However, the postindustrial communities of the 1990s no longer allow members of extended families to reside within close range, or even to travel easily in order to gather together. Branches of the U.S. service military reassign their families every 2 to 3 years to all parts of America, as well as to Europe and the Caribbean. Large corporatons can assign their executives and engineers and their families to the Middle East and Latin America for 3 years or more. Advancement for families of academics may mean relocating far from their hometowns to larger universities across the country. Therefore, transgenerational therapies have evolved to use the extended family consultation for time-limited periods that may range from 2 days to 2 weeks during the course of treatment. Most useful among these consultations is the early-phase consultation, for it not only clarifies many family dynamics to the observer, but also immediately brings to life a three-generation (or more) frame of reference for its participants.

An early-phase family consultation is arranged by telephone with the referring family member before the initial session, or at the latest by the end of the initial session. The therapist informs the referring family member that he/she will be gathering a great deal of history, and that it will ease the process of evaluation considerably if certain family members can be present. These members typically include all those residing at home, any grandparents residing within traveling distance, and siblings of the identified client who may live separately. If a noncustodial parent has divorced and remarried, the noncustodial parent is asked to attend as well initially. The new stepparent is invited if the adults have attained a cooperative division of responsibilities at the time that therapy is initiated. If not, his/her participation should be deferred until the biological parents have broached the problem as a pair and begun discussing their respective roles in therapy.

If the referring member states that the problem is too volatile to discuss openly, or that one or more family members constitute a danger or a threat in some way to the process of disclosure, the consultation is arranged after the initial interview so that the danger can be assessed. For example, a mother may state that her divorced husband is addicted to cocaine and behaves in a quite unpredictable or explosive way with their children. Or a grandmother may have been physically abusive to the father in the family, so that he feels unable to meet the therapist for the first time with his mother present in the room. There are also times in which the member requesting consultation states that the problem is severe and chronic—so much so that he/she cannot speak about it in front of certain others, because of anxiety. For example, an adult daughter who has participated in two trials of family therapy with an explosive father may feel that she does not have the emotional resources any longer to face him in the first session. In all these cases, the therapist may elect to restrict the participation of some extended family members until it is discussed in the initial interview.

When early-phase family consultation is utilized, one of its primary functions is to bring three generations of interaction into the therapy session. The purpose of permitting this "three-tiered" interchange is to redefine the context of the problem from an ahistorical, cyclical-appearing symptom to a relational context in which players can alter their positions and responses. Participants begin to experience their distress as embedded in a field of relational tensions that includes significant others from different eras in their life cycles. In fact, members are actually re-experiencing the interpersonal field that gave rise to, and enabled, the emergence of the distressed individual's symptoms before the symptoms became self-perpetuating and separate from relational tensions. In the next chapter, I describe the use of early-phase family consultation, as well as other forms of extended family meetings and other transgenerationally based techniques.

·11·

Techniques II:
Restoring Familial Resources

Once a couple or family in therapy can describe and experience its current and long-term relational patterns in a therapy session, there is a shared language for creating change. The therapist is interested in how each spouse, and each significant party in each family of origin, would solve the current problem if it were his/her own choice. The therapist will also create a series of steps by which the couple or family member(s) in distress can examine each option in light of family traditions and values, and can begin to negotiate these options with intimates. As specific steps in this process are created and unfold, the therapist will work with a distressed individual when he/she becomes apprehensive, ambivalent, or confused about taking action to make change. Motivating an ambivalent individual to change his/her position in family relationships involves a set of "nonspecific" therapeutic techniques, which are also discussed in this chapter.

Because a marriage or family can become dysfunctional in either its structure, its process, or both, a variety of transgenerational interventions address both areas of dysfunction. Although they are not classified this way in the family therapy literature, the reader can consider them in separate groupings for greater conceptual ease. Some of these technical interventions have not been well linked to theory, and have been recommended in either concretely pragmatic or, conversely, extremely global ways without specification of the symptoms for which they are most effective. I hope that classifying different techniques for use with specific dysfunctions or populations will help the practitioner to let theory guide his/her interventions.

Techniques for Structural Dysfunctions

Creating Boundaries: Addressing Obligation

In families where there is emotional fusion between parents and young children, or parents and grown offspring who have married, the task of therapy is to create rules and boundaries that will promote separation between generations and individuation between members. Whitaker's frequent comment that there is a "generation gap" in well-functioning families refers to the damaging consequences of intergenerational enmeshment. As contextual theory has pointed out, persistence of enmeshment creates a context of obligation in which later commitments (e.g., marriage) must compete in a contest of mixed loyalties. Therefore, in these families, therapeutic tasks are directed toward creating a tolerable intergenerational separation.

The therapist must address a distressed family member's sense of obligation in order to encourage him/her to focus away from the fused parental relationship(s). When parents are fused with children, the enmeshed relationship may be primarily dyadic (as in an alliance with one parent) or triadic (in which the child belongs to a coalition—the Bowenian triangle). For example, a son may be overly involved with his widowed mother, with whom he spent his life alone, or with two parents who have an unhappy marriage. The long-term effects of parent–child collaboration and overinvolvement include an ongoing sense of obligation to continue being available at all times. It is difficult for enmeshed family members to allow themselves, or each other, to change (i.e., to distance themselves).

It is best to intervene in enmeshed families by calling their attention to the ways in which members are actually impeding each other's functioning rather than helping. This move directly assails the feelings of obligation, commitment, and guilt, and reframes the fusion as an abandoning or inconsiderate relationship rather than a helpful one. For example, a teenager who stays home with his divorced father after school and weekends can be told that he is keeping his father from taking risks with friends and social contacts. A wife who assists her elderly mother overly often can be told that she is aging her mother prematurely by letting her neglect her independence skills. Since obligation is the glue that continues the fused interactions in these families, the obligation can be mobilized in the service of relational separation. As family members begin to shift their positions to allow for individual initiative, the therapist can support and encourage them by pointing out how they must make space for one another. This does not mean, of course, that the distancing members will get appreciation and thanks from their intimates. In fact, it is helpful to let the members in therapy know that there may be considerable conflict or even recriminations for a period of time. However, this behavior can be framed as others' "not knowing what is good for them because they have never examined their own needs individually." The symptom bearer can be encouraged to show loyalty in a new way by helping the others change, despite their confusion or upset.

Diffusing Boundaries: Family-of-Origin Visits

Transgenerational theory has an extensive and well-developed literature on the use of visits to the family of origin. Structured visitation for a grown son or daughter has many potential uses, but perhaps the most fundamental of these is the resulting increase in emotional connectedness that can result. For adult clients whose families contain rigid and impenetrable boundaries between parents and offspring, the use of visitation can serve as a direct intervention to increase productive interchange. As noted in earlier chapters, in families where there has not been sufficient parental consideration or involvement over a long period of time, a number of dysfunctions can appear after the sons or daughters leave home. Boszormenyi-Nagy discusses the phenomenon of the "revolving slate," in which an injured individual directs chronic disappointment and resentment toward his/her spouse or children. Natural systems theorists point out how unresolved emotional triangles proliferate into marriages and families of procreation through the participants' inability to disengage. Object relations theorists have observed how, from an internal individual standpoint, perceptions of uninvolved or rejecting elders are stored out of awareness and later applied to a partner or children through the use of projection.

These symptoms are common in the offspring of families where the emotional boundaries between elders and children (and even between father and mother, parents and grandparents, etc.) are overly rigid. One of the most efficient modes of intervention for these symptoms, therefore, is to render the boundaries more permeable, allowing for increased interchange. In other words, in families where there is a rule that children and parents (and/or grandparents) do not share personal needs and goals with one another, that rule can best be challenged when a grown son or daughter voluntarily seeks contact with the parents. Now at a more self-sufficient life stage, the grown offspring has the capacity to experiment with parental interchange that is free from the risks associated with childhood dependency.

Nevertheless, even for men and women who have long since left their family homes to establish their own, there can be a great deal of anxiety associated with diffusing parent–child boundaries. Framo, in a classic paper on this subject (1976/1982), describes considerable resistance in his clinical couples to confronting rigid familial boundaries:

> The whole area of distorted perceptions and expectations, of being unable to commit oneself to the present relationship because of obsolete injuries, provides the context for me to bring up the relationship of these problems to the family of origin. . . . Most often there is an

expressed fear that parents might either die of a heart attack or go crazy
if they were to be brought in. (p. 177)

The best-researched and explicated technique for family-of-origin
visits is found in the natural systems model pioneered by Bowen; it is
based on the concept of "detriangulation," or removing an individual
from a highly charged emotional triangle (see Chapter 1). The therapist
prescribes a series of solo visits for the symptomatic adult to the family of
origin. The visits are prepared in advance with the use of adjunct telephone calls and letters, in which the identified client makes known the
family issues that are causing him/her distress. Any information that has
been covertly passed along between two members of the triangle is
tactfully divulged to the third party.

The symptom bearer leaves the distressing issue open-ended after
broaching it, by avoiding any ultimata or unilateral decisions. Frequently,
he/she is coached to express confusion over the exact nature of the family
tension, while overtly commenting on his/her position in the triangle.
For example, an older daughter who has always been neglected by her
father, in preference to her passive younger sister, may write to her father
encouraging him to continue their enviable closeness. At the same time,
she may state that she has never expressed her feelings openly because of
her "strong and silent" role in the family. She may plan a visit to her
father, suggesting that perhaps if he has any thoughts about the matter he
might share them at that time.

During initial visits to the family of origin, the client in therapy is
instructed to maintain, as much as possible, an "observer" stance in which
the distressing emotional and behavioral patterns are monitored. There is
no attempt to address or change these patterns at first. The object is for
the client to retain a sense of his/her separateness from the family, despite
tension and anxiety. That is, the earliest goal of the family-of-origin visit
is to increase emotional proximity without escalating symptomatic patterns or attempting to change them. In this way, the therapist is pushing
against the rigid intergenerational boundary and making it potentially
more permeable.

Later family-of-origin visits involve gathering personal histories of
intimates and more data about significant events in the family's past.
These data are used in the symptom bearer's therapy to increase understanding of familial rules and mandates supporting chronic triangles. Still
later, as he/she gains in self-confidence and self-direction, the adult
offspring can begin to decline participation in family-wide symptom
patterns and to negotiate quite openly for more functional and supportive
relationships. This degree of interaction will require the parent-offspring
boundary to have relaxed a great deal, allowing for expression of intimate
desires and needs.

Creating Hierarchies: Reviewing the Genogram

In some families, the absence of appropriate hierarchies for decision making and guidance reflects intergenerational enmeshment. In these cases, the therapist needs to begin by creating a boundary between generations so that a hierarchy can be established. In other families, there is evidence of boundaries between grandparents, parents, and offspring, but there are no operating hierarchies. In some families, there is a parent who does not confide extensively in the children, but for other reasons cannot "lead"—for example, the parent is highly anxious, has a poor self-image, is addicted, or is narcissistic. In such situations, the therapist is called on to create a working relationship between an elder and offspring without addressing fusion problems.

One method for inducing a sense of hierarchy where none has existed is to utilize genogramming as an extended intervention. Although most authors have discussed the genogram as a primary assessment tool, several writers have pointed out the therapeutic uses of genogram research. McGoldrick and Gerson (1985) discuss the use of genograms in family sessions to identify family structural patterns and relational pressures more clearly. Wachtel (1982) describes how showing family members their genogram in a session can help to elicit normally suppressed affect regarding chronic or unresolved problems for discussion. A third use for in-session genogram research is creation of a sense of hierarchy for family members. When there has been little guidance, decision making, or problem solving in a stressed family, it can be a very powerful experience to view and discuss the map that details who the family's elders are, facts regarding their life events, and continuities in the family's structure over the decades. The process of viewing and elaborating the family genogram makes it explicit that older members are in a different life stage, are more experienced, and have lived longer; it also emphasizes that they bear the family's values and mandates from previous generations.

Terminating Hierarchies: Personal Authority

There is little recognition in the marital and family therapy literature, or in the literature on life cycle psychology, of the fact that in middle adulthood (the fourth decade) grown sons and daughters are faced with a unique set of personal tasks. Because they are usually parents themselves during this life stage, middle adults must address the long-standing hierarchical boundary that exists with their own parents, now grandparents. If this hierarchy is not terminated, it becomes difficult or even impossible for adults in their 30s and 40s to take on personal authority within their own families. It also becomes difficult to deliver aid to aging parents who may require grown sons and daughters to make decisions with them—or even for them, if they become infirm.

Williamson (1978, 1981) has commented that, as therapists, we are vulnerable to a kind of "intergenerational intimidation" that prevents us from recognizing the importance of terminating hierarchies as well as creating them. By "intimidation" he refers to the child's fear of parental rejection or loss if he/she were to challenge the parent's special prerogatives. It is difficult, and even revolutionary, to take on oneself the task of meeting a lifelong power on a one-to-one basis and requesting parity.

Williamson's thesis—that in middle adulthood the generational hierarchy needs to become more egalitarian—does not mean reversing generations. However, the power and control that elders exercised when offspring were inexperienced and dependent must be renegotiated in order for adult offspring to acquire what he terms "personal authority." Otherwise, relations with elderly parents remain active out of a sense of indebtedness and obligation, rather than one of spontaneous respect and choice. As we have seen in the cases of invisible loyalty and split loyalty, the emotional "pull" of the obligatory relationship contributes to chronic emotional triangles, marital distancing, and familial pressures on children.

It has been suggested that by obtaining feedback regarding his/her adult status, and letting go of powerful childhood parental introjects, the grown offspring becomes the author of or expert on himself/herself—an authority (Paul, 1980, cited in Williamson, 1981). The necessary step in building personal authority thus becomes giving up the desire to be parented. This involves coming to terms with the aging father and mother as individuals, and giving them up as the responsible nurturers of childhood. At this point, the middle adult can now take on emotional responsibility for her own future without looking to the first generation for a sense of self-definition. As Williamson states so beautifully:

> "Leaving home" means no longer being programmed by the transgenerational script. . . . The adult is no longer compelled to work upon the unresolved problems of the previous generations . . . the unachieved goals of ancestors. He is not obligated to carry ritualized in his personal code the highest family values and ideals. It implies that he no longer needs to carry in emotional vaults the rich affective family heritages, whether soaked up through experience or absorbed unconscious to unconscious, through the uncanny conduits of transgenerational communication on human hurt and rage and grief. . . . "Leaving home" means that the adult generation no longer yearns for validation from the older generation, as far as appearance, job, marriage, children, values, and life style are concerned. (1981, p. 445)

In order to make the enormous shift recommended by Williamson, it is not necessary to stage a confrontation with or make demands of the aging elders, nor, indeed, even to require them to change. Rather, the task requires the middle adult offspring to begin to inquire about and to know the parents as individuals. This process entails moving back from the ongoing emotional pressures within the extended family, by becoming an observer and a researcher of the parents. Bowen (1974/1988), without addressing the hierarchy issue directly, discusses in detail how adults increase their sense of separateness and "self" in this process. Working toward peerhood with one's parents as a goal gives this research an important positive focus that goes beyond renegotiating family roles.

The process of becoming a peer to one's aging parents cannot be encouraged by the therapist until the distressed adult has completed certain other life tasks first (hence the staging of this intervention in the fourth decade). They include possessing a social support network (most frequently, a committed relationship) outside the family of origin; a functional vocation; the ability to direct personal time; financial self-sufficiency; consideration of or entry into parenthood; and the awareness of death (Williamson, 1981).

The technique of terminating the parental hierarchy is related to the process technique of mourning, an intervention used with problems of relational fusion. The reason for this connection is that in order to be motivated to renegotiate power and authority with one's parents, one must face the fact that they are close to death and that the self will die too. It is easy to understand most adults' avoidance of the authority issue in the context of our cultural fear of death. Paul (1980, cited in Williamson, 1981) has commented that, since World War II, inhabitants of Western countries have shown phobic death-avoiding behavior and extreme denial of death. Parents, as well as offspring, fear to think of death. Relinquishing the parental roles of control, advising, and validation leaves an elderly individual without a formerly all-absorbing source of self-identity, and thus vulnerable to anxiety. Therefore, the process of moving from "child" to "adult" with one's parents does involve the beginnings of mourning.

On Roles and Stereotypes: Uses of Metaphor

The use of metaphor in family sessions is not unique to transgenerational models; in fact, a significant part of the literature has been produced by certain strategic (Ericksonian) authors. However, one transgenerational model—the symbolic-experiential model—possesses a rich set of ideas for including metaphorical language in family therapy.

Symbolic-experiential interventions were originally formulated for use with clients who expressed themselves in highly symbolic ways, chiefly those with psychotic symptoms. Later, Whitaker proposed that symbolic forms of communication were also especially suited for work with children, who express themselves through play; very intellectualized persons, such as professionals; and individuals in rigid relationships, in which behavior is highly role-dependent and ritualized (see Whitaker & Keith, 1981).

Although systemic family therapists have experimented with use of ritual and metaphor as ways of making new patterns of behavior more meaningful and "palatable" to families, the use of metaphor in transgenerational work is aimed at changing the level of communication in the therapy session. Metaphorical language is more emotionally evocative than analytical reasoning, and elicits more self-observation and reflection during discussion. Therefore, it is especially useful for addressing couples and families whose behavior is stereotyped, gender-stereotyped, or heavily rule-bound. For example, a military wife who is excluded from her husband's work decisions, is made responsible for all aspects of family life, and is financially dependent can be labeled "the good soldier." Calling her by this metaphorical kind of title comments on the duty-bound role in which she is cast, challenges her position by suggesting that she is not dependent but strong, and can evoke spontaneous affect about her position in her marriage.

Diffusing Triangles: Coaching

As Bowen has commented, one way in which to intervene when a family possesses chronically rigid triangles is to "coach" one of the members to begin to observe and later to "detriangle" himself/herself (see Chapter 1). This method of intervention is especially useful when only one member of such a triangle is motivated to make change (Friedman, 1985). Since continuation of a pathological familial "triad" partially reflects the mutual transfer of anxiety among members, allowing one member to achieve distance and a sense of mastery will diffuse a rigid triangle.

The coaching method involves meeting with the most motivated member of the triangular relationship, and tracking the behaviors of the two other participants that increase emotional pressure. As the two other members move to involve the coached one further, the therapist encourages observation, reflection, and strong individual positions to counteract the pressure.

For example, a husband who is pressured to function as a caretaker to a demanding mother-in-law by an insecure wife might begin by relinquishing some of his services. As the wife notes his decreased availability to her mother, she may move to "pull" him back into his caretaker role with criticism and protests. The therapist will point out to the husband these anxiety-laden behaviors, and encourage him to reflect on them so that he can come to recognize them without aid. Other activities that do not include caretaking will be encouraged, so that the husband is maintaining familial contact outside his problematic role. Ongoing pressures and attempts to dislodge him from his separated stance are predicted and discussed. The coaching is continued until the symptomatic triangle is emotionally "diffused"—that is, until the husband is comfortable in his new family position, the wife begins to address her own insecurities about her mother, and the mother assumes more self-sufficiency.

Diffusing Triangles: Self-Delineation

In contrast to the method of coaching, the method of "self-delineation" is a more indirect way of addressing an intense family triangle. Coaching focuses on one individual, and utilizes behavioral prescriptions and self-monitoring to move that member away from the accumulated expectations and emotional reactions that continue the triangle. Self-delineation, a method derived from the contextual model, teaches members of a triangle how to construct individual positions and express them constructively (i.e., without exerting pressures on the other members). As discussed in Chapter 3, it is always an artificial distinction to separate "individualness" from "togetherness." These two experiences of ourselves in intimate relationships reflect a dynamic flux between the need for intimacy and the need for personal competence and autonomy. Self-delineation refers to the "half" of this dynamic continuum that focuses on expressing individuality. Like Bowen's differentiating, or "I" position, self-delineation increases awareness and tolerance in fused relationship systems of individual differences.

Increasing self-delineation involves helping each family member in a triangle to form boundaries between himself/herself and others. However, in contrast to coaching, this process takes place in couple or family meetings. It is in the in-session *experience* of separating oneself from emotionally distressed intimates that self-delineation results. Rather than formulating a plan for achieving greater interpersonal distance in dyadic meetings with the therapist, clients working on self-delineation practice distinguishing their own opinions and reactions from those of others, and exploring the implications with other family members.

Techniques for Process Dysfunctions

Creating Hope: Exoneration

Most therapists have encountered spouses and family members for whom the distressing symptoms appear to be workable, but who experience their problem as hopeless. These individuals struggle with a great deal of shame, anger, and/or grief when they recall painful events and failed relationships. Although they seem willing to explore the possibility of change in therapy, the pervasive sense of deprivation and hopelessness prevents members from focusing clearly on therapeutic alternatives. They may also have difficulty extending comfort and reassurance to one another, including the children, and may overlook areas of strength and small successes. When this process dysfunction interferes with constructive problem solving, the therapist must intervene to restore hope and a sense of familial resources. The method of "exoneration," developed in the contextual model, is a powerful tool for this purpose.

The essential task of exoneration is to "reopen the book" on parents, grandparents, and other significant parenting figures—to re-examine information about their lives in light of what they were trying to accomplish and how they experienced critical family events (Boszormenyi-Nagy & Ulrich, 1981). The goal is to put their behavior in a more human context, rather than focusing on the later consequences of their dysfunctional behavior and decisions. This procedure is often difficult and painful, particularly in families in which abuse, neglect, or abandonment (e.g., suicide) has occurred. However, it is actually the most therapeutic intervention possible, in that it is the only route to preserving damaged trust and emotional attachments.

For example, in a family where the teenage daughter is chronically runaway and promiscuous, and has been managed poorly through the use of physical punishment, there may be little parental trust left and little willingness in the daughter to accept parenting. Such parents may blame their daughter for her behavior, often only to be met with defensiveness. In order to counteract the virulent sense of blame on the part of the parents, and shame in both parties regarding the violence and promiscuity, the focus in therapy will have to be moved from their mutual judgments. They will need to consider what each member was trying to achieve, however disastrous the outcomes might have been. If they can begin to discuss the real intentions that accompanied the hurtful behavior, there will be room to rebuild some trust.

Addressing Cutoff: Rejunction

"Rejunction" is the term contributed by the contextual model for the process of establishing relational consistency. In a couple or family in which one or more individuals avoid or refuse contact with relatives, there is no longer consistent and reliable connectedness between them. During times of familial stress or change, these cut-off relationships cannot serve as a resource for problem solving or inspiration. As noted in

Chapter 3, the therapeutic method of rejunction addresses cutoff by teaching family members how to reapproach each other. In contrast to Bowenian coaching, rejunction is a process that is facilitated with the family of origin participating, rather than alone with the most distressed party. However, rejunction achieves some of the same goals as coaching, by facilitating differentiation and building intimacy so that distressed family members do not need to terminate contact in an attempt to build self-confidence.

Rejunctive work focuses on teaching participants how to talk to each other in such a way as to increase emotional commitment and mutuality (*quid pro quo* and fairness). It begins with the generic family systems intervention of expanding the family's definition of the problem to include multiple perspectives, which is in itself a shift toward mutuality and commitment. Rejunction then comes to involve beginning selective contact, as in visits, letters, or phone calls, in which a distressed member explores potential remaining avenues for cooperation and concern. In rejunctive work, there are often periods of inaction, in which a cut-off family member withholds contact out of confusion, anxiety, or resentment. For example, in families where there has been repeated violence or sex abuse, offspring often feel hopeless about recontacting the abusive parent out of fear that there may be renewed abuse or denial. The therapist does not attempt to short-cut or criticize inaction, but rather to keep the therapeutic focus on what steps can still be tried. If attempts to reconnect with the family of origin are met with negative responses, the therapy continues to explore possibilities for further action now and in the future, and the importance of acting on one's wishes and goals rather than passive resignation.

Addressing Cutoff: Extended Family Reunions

A technique developed by symbolic-experiential therapists, extended family reunions allow families to gather together for a prolonged period (2 to 3 days), expressly to develop a group sense of their own unique organization and issues. The reunion can be seen as the initial stage in rejunction, in which a family is helped to construct a view of its problem, including multiple perspectives. However, the perspective that emerges has the benefit of including many extended family members who have played an important role in the family: siblings, parents' siblings, and grandparents. Clearly, reunions require a great deal of advanced planning, and are held once only or several times at the most.

Whitaker, who has experimented extensively in the past decade with extended family reunions, has stated (Whitaker, personal communication, 1989) that it is crucial to include all the key members of the symptom bearer's family of origin in order to achieve effectiveness. It is not surprising to find that when one member is excluded, important family tensions are obscured. For example, the family may spend a great deal of time discussing the missing member's participation in a family problem, thus finding a focus that cannot become too conflictual in his/her absence. Or absence of one member can contribute to further cut off after the reunion takes place, since all the others will have shared an important problem-solving experience without obtaining his/her perspective.

Extended family reunions differ from family-of-origin consultations in several ways. First, they are intended as a one-time or limited-time intervention. Therefore, exploration and resolution of family tensions must be confined to the 2- to 3-day reunion period, and the family members must be empowered to remain active and accountable with one another afterward. The therapist works with the symptom bearer (and spouse, if he/she is married) to plan a time and place where the reunion can be scheduled. Whitaker (1989) has explored the use of a retreat environment, in contrast to the office, to help create an atmosphere of reflection and self-focus. Often, the person calling to request the reunion is not a client in ongoing therapy, but wishes brief consultation to aid in reconnecting with the family. This method of intervention places the responsibility for change, as well as for the direction of the change, maximally upon the family and its referring member.

Addressing Fusion: The Role of Mourning

Norman Paul's use of therapeutic mourning to correct a number of marital and family problems has been extensively documented (Paul, 1967; 1980, cited in Williamson, 1981). As noted earlier, Paul's view is that since the calamities and war atrocities of World War II, families in Western cultures have had especial difficulty acknowledging death and loss. Loss and death have become alien, ritualized experiences that are avoided through frank denial, retreat into fantasy, and drives for gratification and success to cover over feelings of grief. Many of Paul's pioneering papers in the area of complicated mourning and unresolved grief describe how loss and natural disaster in the life history of distressed families are buried and converted into a range of difficulties, including anxiety, depression, intimacy, and sexual problems.

Fusion in marital and family relationships is one dysfunction that arises in response to loss or perceived loss. Natural systems theorists discuss how fusion operates between poorly differentiated individuals, and how it is transmitted in families through emotional triangles. However, Paul's theory suggests that nodal loss events, especially the death of key family figures, also trigger fusion as a coping mechanism to avoid grief and mourning.

If we view extreme dependency, intense focusing on a partner, and other fusion behaviors as a response to internal feelings of emptiness, anxiety, and loss, then it should be a powerful intervention to induce therapeutic mourning. Object relations theory holds that depression, for example, involves defensive anger turned against the self as a way of holding onto the memories of a loved figure who is gone rather than acknowledging her loss. It follows that acknowledging loss in therapy, and learning to utilize the accompanying sadness constructively, will render fusion unnecessary.

Paul recommends that when unresolved grief underlies dysfunctional behavior, the individual in therapy should be directed to discuss a highly charged loss or death at considerable length. The therapist elicits information about the loss, including specific details about the circumstances at the time; the actual cause of loss or death; the client's whereabouts and how he/she was informed; immediate family reactions to the loss; the funeral and burial itself; and other specifics. The purpose of this detailed review is to reawaken emotional responses to the loss that have been buried by denial or distraction. When this kind of direct questioning is not effective, visual stimulation such as having families view videotape is added. When feelings of sadness, emptiness, loss, or grief are mobilized, the therapist can then help the family members in therapy to use them to productively affirm their own values and needs with one another. The increased self-focus and self-expression will alleviate the chronic externalization and projection that is typical of fusion relationships.

Correcting Distance and the "Revolving Slate"

Overly distant marital or parent–child relationships are characterized by lack of attentiveness, emotional suppression, lack of availability when one member is in distress, an emphasis on "rational" communication and thought, and avoidance of situations in which partners or family members might be thrown together in a highly personal way. As discussed earlier, Boszormenyi-Nagy has pointed out that one common dynamic underlying relational distance is the "revolving slate" phenomenon. In such marriages and families, the distant or disengaged partner often shows coldness, indifference, contempt, or even cruelty and anger toward the vulnerabilities of the spouse or children (Boszormenyi-Nagy & Ulrich, 1981).

From a contextual viewpoint, these symptoms mean that the disengaged member is preoccupied or emotionally bound by prior family legacies, which pressure him/her to preserve a personal commitment to the family of origin rather than to newer relationships. It is as if the distant partner is "distracted" by the "pull" of prior commitments and cannot free himself/herself to attend to the requests of intimates now. This preoccupation is the "revolving slate" in contextual theory: Out of unintended loyalty to old, unsatisfactory relationships, the symptom bearer foists upon his/her marriage and children the very same legacy of unmet needs that he/she has experienced.

It will be recalled that "invisible loyalties" stem from the wishes of growing children to trust and care for their elders and families; it follows that when these efforts to show concern and obtain consideration and approval are rejected, the rejected child or children try harder. The more dysfunctional the family of origin, the more deeply anxious grown sons and daughters can become. Efforts to somehow overcome their sense of indebtedness and inadequacy are expressed by rejecting the very aspects of themselves that were rejected by the family of origin. For example, in a family where a young son was ridiculed by his father for showing insecurity or worry, the now-adult man often seems compelled to keep up a businesslike front at all costs, shaming his children when they show hurt or vulnerability.

In a marriage or family where disengagement and distance are central problems, the most powerful tool for intervention is to uncover the "revolving slate" that exists between one family of origin and the distant partner or parent. The sooner that this individual can acknowlege that he/she felt inadequate and unaccepted in the growing-up family, the sooner that he/she can give up the distancing mechanisms that protect him/her from further demands. For the spouse or children, watching the distant member examine deep feelings of inadequacy, shame, or resentment elicits the personal, intimate quality that has been lacking in their relationships in the past. Discussing the invisible "revolving slate" is a dramatic departure from structural and strategic methods, which seek to correct distance temporarily through the use of assignments to involve the distant member. Of course, the expectation is that when distance is treated via prescription, the increased involvement will prove so satisfying and effective that the family will continue this new pattern in the future. However, when relational distance is a symptom of a demanding and unfair extended family structure, the disengaged member will continue to protect himself/herself through disengagement.

Controlling Projections in Marriage

Projections in marriage, which have been discussed most thoroughly in the object relations literature, are byproducts of fused relationships. When one or both partners in a marriage have not been encouraged to differentiate from intimates sufficiently, there is a tendency for them to avoid taking open positions and expressing themselves directly. As a result, sensitive opinions and reactions are avoided, and one or both partners focus on each other's opinions and behavior instead (natural systems theory discusses how these projections can be diverted onto a child instead of a spouse; see Chapter 1).

Controlling severe marital projections is essentially a case of addressing relational fusion. The therapist can create a therapeutic framework emphasizing review of the past, particularly personal losses that fostered differentiation failure. For example, a dependent wife can be encouraged to examine how she "came to believe" a familial myth that she was incompetent sufficiently enough to remain close to home and support her father after her mother died. A compulsive, workaholic husband who repeatedly pressures his more spontaneous wife about her spending may be directed to consider how his compulsive working was encouraged by his mother and grandparents, who lost all of their family security during the Depression. The loss and grief in many families is carried by a second- or third-generation family member because it has never been contructively faced by previous generations. Eliciting unresolved losses within the here and now forces the buried and denied anxieties that are foisted upon the spouse to become explicit. This explicitness interferes with continued projection and projective identification—the locating of unacceptable feelings and impulses in one's spouse, which are then identified with (e.g., assuming that one's spouse is angry and vindictive, and then focusing upon one's feelings of anger and victimization in return).

Controlling Delegation of Children

Delegation of children is an example of dysfunctional emotional triangling. As the natural systems model has suggested, when there is chronic tension in a family between spouses or between a parent and an extended family member, a common symptom is inclusion of a child to diffuse tension when it becomes intolerable. In many cases, this intergenerational triangling saves the marriage from open dissenion and potential marital crisis.

In order to challenge a family in which one or more children have been pulled into a pathological triangle, and delegated to perform certain roles for the family, the triangle involving each child must be diffused. Less extensive, more problem-focused interventions, such as the strategic method of reframing the problem as "too much love" or "too much parenting," leave such families open to continue expecting their children to deflect adult conflicts. When such expectations continue, future delegations of the symptomatic child or other children are sure to occur.

Methods for diffusing parent–child triangles have been discussed earlier. Using coaching and self-delineation strategies, the therapist can aid one or both parents in such families to achieve greater personal effectiveness within the marriage and families of origin. As personal effectiveness and self-awareness increase, the use of covert triangles to siphon off tension becomes unnecessary. Then, the parents are less dependent on the behavior of their children for a sense of security and confidence.

Sibling Deidentification: The Sibling Session

Although therapists still tend to overlook sibling relationships as a significant source of emotional development, and of dysfunction, there is growing awareness that treating siblings can strengthen individuals and families (Kahn & Lewis, 1988; Schachter, 1982). Methods for intervening in distressed sibling systems are still highly experimental and not well documented. However, several writers have recently attempted systematic descriptions of the use of sibling sessions to address a severely distressed sibling group, or to strengthen sibling alliances.

"Sibling deidentification" is a dysfunction in which one sibling distances himself/herself from another, in order to protect the self from perceived ill-treatment in the family generally or by the sibling in particular. The distancing is achieved, in a child or young adult, not through any rational, thought-out process, but rather by identifying in the self traits that appear to be the opposite of the sibling (Schachter, 1982). The deidentification may be demonstrated also in explicit, behavioral ways: If one sister is uncooperative with the mother, another sister may seek to be the mother's aide and companion. The problems inherent in deidentification are that both siblings lose a sense of shared perspective, common interest, mutuality, and connection.

In families where the children have been divided by this process, sibling sessions can be a singularly powerful arena for enhancing mutuality and alliance. Symbolic-experiential therapists, have for many years separated generations in late-stage family therapy by holding sibling sessions separately from parental marital sessions (Roberto et al., 1987). Lewis (1988) describes how sibling sessions allow siblings to explore mutual perceptions of their parents and family, and thus to construct a sense of solidarity (Kahn & Lewis, 1988).

Sibling sessions should include the entire sibling group regardless of age spread. Issues that promote an intragenerational alliance should be central at first; introducing relational problems should come later, when mutual trust is higher. Concerns that bring siblings closer include scholastic and social achievement; areas in which siblings are insecure but would not go to a parent (e.g., sexuality); managing conflict with peers and each other; parental pressures and symptoms; and family relationships with grandparents and extended relatives. When one sibling is the symptom bearer, contributing to ostracism and distancing by the brothers and sisters, it is especially important to "diffuse the scapegoat" in sibling sessions and to concentrate on child/adolescent issues that they have in common. A second avenue of exploration, in addition to mutual concerns, involves identifying ways the siblings can aid each other in completing developmental tasks. For example, an older sister can improve her connection with a younger brother by coaching him on his spelling drills. A brother can help his sister achieve more autonomy within the family by planning mutual outings in which the parents must adjust to allowing both children to leave home.

·12·

The Gammon Family: A Transgenerational Case History

This chapter provides a case example of an entire course of therapy held with one extended family, and in particular a distressed wife and her husband. The case is provided to illustrate many of the principles of transgenerational family therapy discussed in this book, as well as the kinds of impasses that arise in attempting to treat a larger dysfunctional family system. As Framo (1980) has pointed out, if creating individual change is difficult, then marital change is even more difficult—and, I might add, it follows that creating extended family change is an intricate and multifaceted problem.

The reader will see that change was attempted in stages, as the therapist used a wider "therapeutic lens" to include the distressed wife, her marriage, their children, and her family of origin. The role of the therapist changed over time, moving from quite proximal to more "consultative," as family members became more confident of their goals and direction with one another. As is true of all models of transgenerational family therapy, the course of therapy was longer than we find in ahistorical models: The case presented here spanned a period just short of 1 year. As different relational tensions arose in this case and are here described, commentary is offered describing the theoretical perspective and plan of intervention.

In the Beginning: A Psychosomatic Marriage

Dick Gammon, a 39-year-old accountant, called the therapist's office to request consultation on behalf of his wife, Belinda. A musician the same age as Dick, Belinda had been having a number of health problems over the past 5 years, according to her husband. Although the couple had been married 20 years, Dick stated that he had never seen his wife as uncomfortable and anxious as she had become in the years immediately following the birth of their last (third) child. He made an appointment for both of them, and warned the therapist that he might have to be out of town from time to time on corporate business. Calm and soft-spoken on the phone, he focused completely on his wife's behavior and said nothing about his desire to accompany her or his own feelings about the situation.

On their arrival several days later, the Gammons presented themselves as a conservative, country couple who seemed ill at ease in a clinician's office. Dick wore a suit, loosened his tie frequently, and was largely silent. Belinda was dressed for homemaking activity, and her muted attire completely hid evidence of the artistic streak that made her career. They chatted about the logistical problems of arranging after-school care, which they had put in the hands of their highly responsible oldest child, a daughter who was a high school junior. Both spouses were emotionally quite self-controlled and showed little reaction to any of the issues raised, except for Belinda's occasional delightful humor and laughter.

With little aid from her husband, Belinda gave a history of multiple psychophysiological problems that were plaguing her with discomfort. She had been a migraine sufferer, not for the 5 years that Dick had claimed, but throughout her adulthood. She also stated that she had severe allergies, exacerbated by their decision to reside in the country (Dick's wish). Her thinness and significantly swollen cheeks prompted questions about vomiting. Belinda asserted that she had been having a problem with vomiting whenever she "ate too much"; however, since she did not binge-eat, her pattern was more like that of an anorexic purger. Lastly, she complained of constant nervousness, making her "jittery" and interfering with her sexual capacity in the marriage. In discussion, they clarified that they had had sex only quite rarely throughout the marriage, and that Belinda was panicked by intercourse.

Throughout the hour, Dick appeared interested yet silent, speaking only when spoken to, and then only briefly. He looked more anxious than his articulate wife, as if he were exerting great energy to express himself and disliked the experience. Given the potential danger of Belinda's self-induced vomiting, they agreed to schedule a physical for her, and planned weekly marital sessions with the therapist to explore the nature of her anxiety and stress-related symptoms.

In the first 2 months of marital sessions, this pattern of Belinda's speaking about herself and the marriage while Dick watched anxiously repeated itself continually. When questioned about his opinion of this pattern, Dick stated firmly that he felt if he were not careful, he might add to his wife's distress by "saying things that would upset her." He maintained that he could not predict what these upsetting comments might be, and that he also did not feel he had much to say. When he was directed to respond to his wife's remarks, or to provide any personal reaction to the problems discussed, he shrugged and stated that he agreed with her and was concerned that she found life so stressful. Nor would he venture any statements or recommendations concerning therapeutic goals or plans, beyond "Help give my wife more confidence and freedom from her symptoms." It was clear that Dick experienced only a narrow range of emotionality, and regarded personal dialogue as something dangerous and distasteful.

Belinda responded avidly to the opportunity for marital discussion, and was particularly interested in discussing ongoing tensions with both her family of origin and Dick's. Dick gave a bare minimum of information about his family and upbringing (essentially that he was raised in a farming family, was an only child, had never interacted with his father personally, and had cared for his sickly mother ever since she was widowed). In contrast, Belinda spoke in great detail about her stormy relationship with her family, a small-town business family in which there was constant conflict, verbal and physical abuse, and parent–child tension with herself and her two (also married) sisters.

During this period of 2 months, Belinda experienced rapid relief from her impulses to vomit and her anxiety about food and weight. The vomiting virtually vanished, but a host of discomforts remained—chiefly migraine headaches, sexual aversion, and feelings of depression. Dick spoke little to Belinda in marital sessions or at home, even when asked to do so in front of the therapist. The spouses tended to focus their emotional needs on caring for their children, especially their 13-year-old middle child, a boy who was sullen and withdrawn. Dick also spoke little to the children at home, but stated that he was concerned about how poorly his son handled social and academic stresses.

As the spouses continued with their "battle for initiative" concerning whether they would address the obvious marital and family tensions further, Belinda increasingly asked for help in setting limits with her demanding family of origin. During the third and fourth months of sessions, it emerged that the couple spent all of their scarce vacation time and holidays traveling to Belinda's family and then into the next state to see Dick's mother. These visits (which took place at least quarterly) were interspersed with numerous telephone calls, which troubled Belinda greatly. In contrast, Dick saw these obligatory contacts as beneficial, part of maintaining their filial responsibilities. The difficulty for Belinda was that she harbored intense feelings of anger toward her father and mother; anxiety about her mother; and fear for the youngest sister, who had severe anxiety problems. Discussions about the father's chronic deteriorative kidney disease dominated most family visits, complete with samples of the father's urinary output, which Belinda was asked to view. Her deep negative feelings made pleasant conversation almost impossible, despite the fact that the family clearly preferred cheerful interchange. In fact, Belinda noted that she was frequently told by her parents, "Don't complain—look what happened to the X family" (the specific family in question would change from time to time), whenever she attempted to bring up a personal problem. The more that Belinda voiced these objections in marital therapy, the fewer her medical symptoms became. The migraines became a monthly rather than weekly affair. And, strikingly, Dick seemed to capitalize on his wife's risk-taking behavior by admitting that he felt frustrated that the pair had no private time together. At this point, 5 months into marital therapy, Belinda announced that she was having some "bad memories" that interfered with sexual pleasure and stirred up anger toward her parents. From an object relations viewpoint, Belinda had made the transition from suppressing and somatizing forbidden thoughts and attitudes to experiencing them freely. Dick, who had been projecting many of his own feelings of apprehension onto his wife and labeling her as ill, was beginning to acknowledge that he was vulnerable himself.

It appeared to the therapist that this wife (if not both spouses) felt emotionally quite caught up in a long-term unresolved triangle with her parents. Emotionally drained by a continual, deeply ingrained sense of obligation to them, she expended a great deal of daily thought on their welfare. In the marriage, Dick supported and agreed with this overweening obligation. Unable to choose between time for her family and time for her marriage and herself, Belinda was "bankrupting" what little marital intimacy there was and neglecting personal needs. At this time, Belinda literally seemed without any self-focus. The sole remnant of self-reflection was channeled into her instrumental practice, and this occurred in such a routinized way that she did not seem to feel connected even to her work.

Dick occupied a different position in their marriage. Instead of feeling drained, and feeling torn between the needs of their families and of their marriage, Dick woodenly fulfilled a set of tried-and-true services to his wife and his mother. He provided, showed concern, and listened to their feelings of stress. He did not attempt to connect emotionally with his mother, his wife, or his children, and seemed to believe that he was accruing the love he desired simply by being "true blue." Whereas Belinda was maintaining a dutiful posture with their families out of fear, Dick had long ago buried any parts of himself that went beyond posturing. He felt vaguely cheated and burdened by his loved ones, but he largely attributed these feelings to "work stress," "fatigue," and "infrequent sex."

Structurally, the marriage of Belinda and Dick had little emotional boundary to keep other generations "out" and the couple "in." It reminded one of Whitaker's statement that "grandparents and grandchildren have a common enemy: parents" (personal communication, 1978). Because of the unarticulated pressures present between Belinda's parents, and in the widowhood of Dick's mother, each spouse was essentially more connected to his/her parent(s) than to the partner. In addition, Belinda was closely tied to her high-school-age daughter and 13-year-old son (the 5-year-old child remained somewhat isolated). Again, Dick agreed and actively supported Belinda's focus on the children, which in turn protected his focus upon his mother (Dick's brother, living in the hometown, was largely uninvolved). The lack of marital boundary had existed from the time of courtship, and underlay a host of marital deficiencies such as absence of dating, absence of private intimate conversation, and rigidly divided parental roles in the home.

With these factors in mind, the first goal of intervention was to expand this couple's frame of reference to highlight the interactional components of the stress the spouses experienced. Since many of their stresses occurred in relation to their families of origin, the interactional frame had to include at least three generations: their children, themselves, and their parents and siblings. Since Dick had little family himself, and his mother was not ambulatory, making a transgenerational frame had to occur through observation of his wife's family work and carefully planned contacts between him and his mother.

Creating a Transgenerational Frame

As noted above, at the end of the fourth month of marital sessions Belinda still suffered from multiple somatic problems, but their frequency was episodic. The decrease in active medical problems presented an opening to widen the frame of reference regarding the problems of "stress," "worry," and Belinda's sexual aversions. Ordinarily, this opening is most easily exploited by referring to the family genogram constructed at the outset of therapy. However, Belinda presented an alternate, more metaphorical route into exploration of her familial dysfunction: her "bad memories." Belinda had a few clear and disturbing recollections: an adolescent problem of ritualistic, compulsive behaviors; fear of sleeping unless her door was locked; and fear at age 15 of being pregnant. There was also a memory of her father, incensed by a minor argument, beating her younger sister or yelling at the family. Then there was a vague idea that "maybe" she had been abused—but, despite several weeks of soul-searching, no evidence.

Discussion of these memories vividly brought to light scenes from

Belinda's earlier life, in which her home was a burdensome place occupied by a demanding father, sullen and discouraged siblings, and a tired, depressed mother who confided too much in Belinda. As before, Dick listened to these clarifications with sympathy, but avoided becoming involved or taking a position. He showed absolute respect for his wife's parents, and expressed no negativity himself. Belinda responded to this implacable spousal neutrality with increased depression and marital anger. As she withdrew, she became fixed on her vague concern that she might have been abused. After a month of concern over this, the couple requested to have Belinda undergo hypnotic induction to see whether a specific memory would emerge. As a stipulation, to prevent Dick from maintaining his anxious but self-protective distance, Dick was to sit in on the inductions. In the first induction (there were to be no others, as it turned out), Belinda "remembered" that from early childhood, she and her sisters were administered painful soap-and-water enemas whenever they were upset or ill by their maternal aunt, who lived with them.

Because the relational problems and memories of parental pressure were focused in the past, the therapist moved in the fifth month of marital psychotherapy to bring them into the present. The couple was advised to consider a consultation with Belinda' s family of origin, to clarify further the sources of her sense of obligation and anxiety, and to begin marking a boundary between the family of origin and Belinda's adult married life. To this end, Dick was to participate in the consultation—both to combat his desire to withdraw, and to examine his accommodating position in this enmeshed family.

Two 2-hour back-to-back consultations were scheduled, with parents and siblings (minus their partners and children) to stay in town overnight. Belinda and Dick quickly arranged the meeting with what appeared to be relief.

When Belinda's family of origin arrived, the relief seemed well founded in that, as in other psychosomatic families, members maintained a delightful "chatty" demeanor that discouraged deep discussion. Mother, Aunt Peg, and Belinda maintained eye contact and mutually intervened to speak for one another when stressful topics arose. And the stress arose quickly, because Belinda responded to encouragement by the therapist to tell her family what was going on in therapy by telling all. The remainder of the first consultation yielded much data on how this family reacted to stress. The father immediately agreed with all Belinda said, in a manner remarkably like Dick's. This immediate agreement put a quick end to Belinda's comments about paternal abusiveness, but appeared awkward and strained. The siblings spoke about the family situation in much the same way that Belinda did—emphasizing their individual problems, and looking on the aged parents with intimidation and protectiveness. The middle sister stated that she was a workaholic and had little time to enjoy life. The youngest sister reported that she took multiple medications for anxiety, and felt she needed therapy herself. Neither Belinda nor Dick moved to bring up the problem of the enemas and Belinda's uneasy sense of "abuse." However, her parents, aunt, and sisters did hear her out, and offered their perspectives on the stressful nature of the family's child-rearing history. Belinda did not credit anyone spontaneously for this participation, but did so when asked by the therapist whether she found the discussion helpful. As in most psychosomatic families, the taboo against saying anything negative also seemed to bar positive, affiliative statements as well.

In the second consultation, the atmosphere grew tense again quickly. Belinda's parents wished to know more about her vomiting problem and her marital difficulties. The mother stated that Belinda was quite secretive and rarely informed them of any personal opinions or concerns. This time, it was a parent who identified a problem, only to receive quick agreement (and thereby dismissal). Belinda asserted that she was "shy" about personal matters, and made jokes. The sisters allied with her, echoing Dick's belief that "bringing up personal opinions could just upset Mom and Dad, who have enough problems as it is." The therapist focused on supporting family members' inquiries and initiatives, while voicing respect for their deep mutual concern.

The consultations with Belinda's family of origin revealed that one source of the emotional triangle between parents and daughter lay in her father's deep frustration with his earlier life and her mother's accommodation by doctoring the children, along with her unmarried older sister. Being the eldest, Belinda received the lion's share of this doctoring, and also absorbed what must have appeared as a loving but sad mother's desire for intimacy. The father "gave" Belinda to her mother, channeling his frequent rages onto the youngest daughter. The siblings in this family had attempted to ally with one another by monitoring one another's welfare and showing sympathy, at the same time encouraging one another to keep secrets as a way of gaining privacy and liberty before launching from the family home.

Structurally, this family of origin was enmeshed, with the parents having few friends and almost no extended family contact (the father had cut off his own parents and siblings entirely), save for their active church attendance. They resembled other psychosomatic families in their rigid external boundaries and too-mutable internal boundaries (Minuchin, Rosman, & Baker, 1978; Roberto, 1986). The parents had long before developed a rule not to "air their dirty laundry," and to maintain a positive outlook when upset by comparing themselves to more distressed households. Belinda had chosen a mate who was raised in an isolated family himself and disliked emotional expressivity generally. She had then replicated in her family of procreation a similar pattern of maintaining marital distance, turning to the eldest child, and focusing on the problems of her children.

In these family-of-origin consultations, the therapist sought to expose and highlight these transgenerational patterns as they existed between Belinda and her parents and siblings in the here and now. Because these were consultations and not ongoing family treatment, the therapist avoided prescriptions for change with other family members, and focused on building familial trust for future discussions. The parents were encouraged to ask their questions, and air their concerns for their daughter. Belinda was supported in her self-disclosures; it was pointed out that she ordinarily shut her family out of her problems. The goal of intervention included demarcating a marital boundary around Belinda's marriage, by emphasizing that there was a great deal of information about herself, her marriage, and her children of which the others were unaware. Finally, Belinda and Dick could derive a sense of mastery and success from their efforts to improve relations with her family.

The Midphase: Growing Differences

After Belinda's initial family-of-origin consultation, it was evident that there were several points of disagreement between herself and her sisters, herself and her parents, and herself and her husband. The disagreements centered around Belinda's desire to express her dissatisfactions, past and present, and her family's equally strong desire to avoid unpleasantness and take care of her parents. Similarly, in the marriage, Dick hung back from encouraging Belinda in expressing her needs and wishes, because it violated his own wish to avoid unpleasantness. Although he no longer pathologized his wife, characterizing her as nervous and ill, he was still unwilling to take the next step and personally broach his own desires for the marriage. Belinda's medical problems were now only mildly distressing, but her mood grew more depressed in the face of multiple covert opposition. At the same time, the couple's 13-year-old son, John, became more and more rebellious, refusing to attend school and getting into physical fights there.

The pressures during the sixth, seventh, and eighth months of marital psychotherapy were chiefly transmitted through the triangles in Belinda's family and Dick's family. Her mother called constantly to report on her father's frequent medical emergencies, and his mother called to request aid after injuring her leg in a fall. The spouses responded in their habitual way, by putting their own problems on hold and making more trips to the families' hometowns. In between, Belinda continued to puzzle over her memories of the enemas, as well as the frequent anxiety she experienced when she and Dick attempted to be sexually intimate. Dick slowly began to respond to her anxiety, and to acknowledge that the incidents might have produced a frank phobia in his wife about sexual arousal. The therapist discussed with the couple Belinda's growing self-awareness, as well as the implications for Dick if his wife allowed herself to be more emotionally expressive. Although Dick still seemed to feel extremely vulnerable, the attention to his wife's family of origin con-stituted a "safe" focus for Belinda's sense of frustration and unhappiness. He appeared less defensive, as if he were no longer waiting for some invisible "shoe to drop" on him.

At the end of the eighth month of therapy, the couple was directly identifying individual concerns and goals for change. Dick stated that he wanted more attention from his wife and more involvement with his children. Belinda wanted more information about her sisters' relation-ships with her parents, and about whether either of her sisters were distressed by memories of the enemas. She also wanted acknowledgment from her parents that they would be willing to consider making fewer demands on her and Dick. Since Belinda and her sisters had a history of allying with one another under stress, the therapist suggested that a sibling meeting take place to discuss the problem of the enemas before any further meetings with the burdened, fatigued parents. Again with an appearance of relief, the couple quickly scheduled a third 2-hour con-sultation for the three siblings and Dick.

This time, the atmosphere was not quite so delightful. The foment-ing differences between Belinda and her sisters emerged very clearly when she announced that she had remembered Aunt Peg's enemas under hypnotic induction. Belinda's middle sister, Pam, insisted that Belinda would feel better if she worked more hours to "get her mind off it"; she stated that she herself rarely worried about issues besides her job and her father's precarious health. In fact, Pam and her husband maintained their home 5 minutes away from her parents, partly so that she could "help out with Dad" if her mother appeared tired. She claimed that between job responsibilities and aiding her parents, this left little time to "mope." Belinda took all this in with an appearance of a chastised child, instead of the eldest daughter she was. Dick nodded approvingly at Pam's work orientation and self-discipline.

The youngest sister, Jane, expressed great concern for Belinda's mood and wondered whether she shouldn't simply focus on using medica-tion for relief. She took a very different stance from Pam's regarding the traumatic memories; she felt deeply about the episodes of painful soap-and-water enemas, as well as their father's physical and verbal abuse. She felt so sensitive about these topics that she ruminated about them constantly, feared physical harm often (she had a phobia of flying), and used tranquilizers. Jane agreed with Pam, however, that there was no point to discussing these incidents, because in her case it just agitated her further. Both Jane and Pam vehemently denied any awareness that anything could have happened in their childhoods to injure Belinda or make her think she was pregnant. The meeting ended with repeated statements by Pam and Jane that they could not imagine any incidents upsetting enough to account for Belinda's sexual aversion and feelings of intimidation toward their parents.

The aftermath of this third extended family consultation revealed a great deal of change. Belinda was very disappointed in her two sisters for their persistent confusion about whether "anything really bad had happened" when she herself felt a growing conviction that her memories *were* "really bad." She became increasingly frustrated with Dick as well, who seemed to share Pam's distraction strategies. She began to exclaim that she was actually angry with Dick, with Pam and with her mother, who all took the position that there was no reason to be upset. Her psychosomatic symptoms disappeared, leaving only her aversion to intercourse and a great deal of anger. Dick began to show irritation with her and scheduled a number of business trips out of town. He ceased his recent attempts to intervene with young John, became silent and distant, and stated that he "needed some affection too."

The Late Phase: A Death and a Renewal

In the ninth month after entering marital therapy, Belinda and Dick did not interact much regarding their growing marital differences. While Dick traveled intermittently on business, Belinda agreed to several appearances in regional musical performances on her own. She consistently deferred difficult child-rearing problems to Dick, even though she was tempted to deal with the children herself as she had before. Her psychosomatic problems did not recur, and she seemed to have advanced in the process of "related individuation"—increased autonomy within her intimate relationship network (Stierlin & Weber, 1989). Her energies became chiefly directed toward renegotiating her relationship with her father, who was dying from his chronic illness.

Belinda stated that she felt the need to tell her father a great deal about her positions and feelings regarding many family matters before he died. Although her mother tried to keep her from spending much time alone with him at the hospital, saying that he was too tired, the two of them managed well and discussed further his violent temper during

Belinda's youth. Her father confided in her that he had felt very much alone and overburdened, having cut off his entire family as a young man and raised his own family without support. Although he did not give many details regarding his own disappointing relationship with his family of origin, it appeared that paternal rages and maternal favoritism had created great dissention and envy between him and his siblings (one of whom had become a chronic sex offender).

Shortly after this series of dyadic, father–daughter talks, Belinda confronted her mother with the fact that she had been quite distressed by Aunt Peg's abusive enemas, and that they had caused her physical pain and fear of physical intimacy. Although her mother did not provide much response, and implied that Aunt Peg was just "trying to do what was best," Belinda was relieved at no longer keeping secret her "bad memories." Her father died several weeks later. Instead of being consumed by worry and depression, Belinda stated that she felt she had already mourned for her father, and now wished to concentrate her attention on her marital and family needs. As an example of this, she declared herself interested in undertaking a series of exercises for her sexual dysfunction, with the help of her husband. With this long-delayed attention now finally on him, Dick began to express himself once more, both in and out of therapy.

What of Dick? Persistently, both in his marriage and with his mother and brother, he had been all too willing to give up his own wishes in order to attend to the problems and demands of others. Although he was distant and somewhat resentful, he had never taken the initiative to rework this stalemated situation by asking for more consideration. This passivity seemed related to the advice and teachings of his father, who had spoken to Dick only when necessary, expecting him to become self-sufficient at an early age. Too, the father's emphasis on hard work and on earning one's way in the world conveyed a strong sense that one did not ask for things for oneself—certainly not emotional gratification and affection.

It was during the 10th month of marital sessions that Dick began to present himself more assertively and forcefully with his wife. Using the sensate focus exercises (and eventually nondemand coitus) as an opportunity to be more intimate with her, he began giving her feedback concerning the importance of marital time and affection. His progress was halting, and initially required much encouragement and supportive questioning from the therapist. During that time, a serious illness of his brother's child also presented an opportunity for Dick to express his deep desire for family closeness to his brother. Belinda's willingness to discuss his views was very satisfying to him. Although Dick was not interested in abandoning his family work ethic and self-control, he spoke several times about his realization that men do not allow themselves enough emotion-ality. He and his wife, for the first time in their marriage, arranged to go out together on Saturday nights, leaving the younger children with a babysitter. At this time, the marital therapy terminated.

Case Commentary

The case of the Gammons illustrates well the tremendous power of family legacies over generations to shape and restrict the options that individuals allow themselves in their own lives. Belinda Gammon did not request therapy for unresolved problems with her family of origin, or her parents' families of origin. Rather, she sought therapy for chronic psychophysio-logical illnesses and anxiety. Neither did the therapist attempt to "re-frame" the problem as a dysfunction including her family of origin. Yet the presence of certain transgenerational patterns, such as relational loyalty, avoiding negativity, and obligation to one's parents, emerged quickly within Belinda's schema of what changes she could and could not allow herself to make. Only in the context of renegotiating her position with her parents and siblings—being direct, asking for aid for herself, expressing negative feelings—was she able to begin doing these things in her marriage and in her own self-estimation. In Dick's case, although he did not literally meet with his family of origin, he did not allow himself to make requests of his wife until he had reexamined lessons learned at his father's knee.

It can also be seen from this case description that if the therapist possesses a transgenerational "lens" himself/herself, clinical families do not need to be instructed or pressured to consider the familial components of their symptoms. Rather, the memories, images, self-images, and les-sons learned within the extended family lie very close to the surface, are easily accessible to investigation, and already carry meaning and value to the clients in the office. From such a viewpoint, one hardly needs to conceptualize the case "in transgenerational terms," any more than one needs to consider a day in chronological terms. The elements of past relational systems are always present in present relational systems.

·13·

Cotherapy: A Consultation Team

History of Cotherapy

Use of cotherapy has been reported in the psychiatry, psychology, and social work literatures since the 1920s. Within the field of family therapy, cotherapy has been practiced since the 1940s (Hoffman & Hoffman, 1981). In the present extremely restrictive health care environment, the economic realities of a psychotherapy practice often create pressure for therapists to practice and bill for services individually. Prior to the 1980s, it was possible for therapists to collaborate in family sessions and to receive fair payment from private insurers.

In that less pressured atmosphere, practitioners and theorists experimented extensively with therapeutic collaboration, and found many advantages personally and therapeutically. For example, Whitaker recently commented that David Keith and he began much of their experimenting with cotherapy as a training device, under the umbrella of a medical school department of psychiatry in the early 1970s (Whitaker & Keith, 1986). During this period, they were able to observe and articulate many of the classic principles of developing the two-person consultation team. Unfortunately, the growing demand upon psychotherapists (and upon health professionals in general) not to consult reflects the powerful lobbying of for-profit risk management corporations, including private insurance carriers and health maintenance organizations. These demands currently jeopardize the development of consultation teams, including but not restricted to practicing cotherapy teams. Systemic consultation teams with numbers as large as four participants are less and less feasible outside of grant-funded research and training institutes. In order to protect this form of intervention, our field must undertake sound empirical studies of therapeutic consultation teams to demonstrate their unique capacities for treatment of severe dysfunction, resolution of chronic resistance, and training purposes.

Among the advantages of multiple therapists that have been cited are the following:

1. Facility in training (Cornwall & Pearson, 1981; Latham, 1982).
2. Mutual complementarity and support for participating therapists (McMahon & Links, 1984; Russell & Russell, 1979–1980).
3. Continuity of care in cases requiring intervention in different systems, such as behavioral intervention and medical care (Silber & Bogado, 1983).
4. Modeling for couples and families intimacy, autonomy, and healthy conflict (Epstein, Jayne-Lazarus, & DeGiovanni, 1979; Hannum, 1980).
5. Division of roles within a therapy session (Hannum, 1980; Mueller & Orfanidis, 1976).
6. Construction of a "binocular," multiversal systemic view of relational problems (Ferrier, 1984).
7. Increased creativity on the parts of participating therapists (Whitaker & Keith, 1986).
8. The ability to use a number of therapeutic interventions within the session that require more than one individual therapist (Hannum, 1980).
9. Preventing, or breaking, a therapeutic impasse (Whitaker, 1989).

Cotherapy, or inclusion of a second psychotherapist into a treatment session, was first used in the same way that primary care physicians might invite a colleague to give a second opinion on a difficult medical case. From an interactional viewpoint, we might say that the second physician was invited in to break a treatment impasse stemming from the first professional's incomplete understanding of the problem. For example, a resident surgeon examining a postoperative client might feel puzzled about why a wound was not healing rapidly enough. He/she might then invite in a colleague to view the wound and offer observations. The colleague might discover on reviewing the case that the client's diabetes and overweight were interfering with proper healing, and might recommend modification of diet and insulin.

Consequently, cotherapy practiced in the 1950s and 1960s followed the medical model of "two physicians, two opinions." However, in the 1960s, as the viewpoints of psychotherapists became increasingly less individualistic and more systemic, the use of cotherapy began to include exploration of other functions. An early conceptualization was that the inclusion of another observer *set a boundary* between the therapist and the couple or family, preventing the therapist from becoming confused or inducted into complex familial interaction cycles. Whitaker (1989) has described this realization as it took place in his practice at the Oak Ridge Plutonium Facility:

> It led me to structure therapy sessions so we worked with patients together and at least could discuss the psychotherapy from the vantage point of a shared experience. It was only later that I discovered the other assets of co-therapy, which are probably more important: assets such as the freedom to back away and look at what is happening, and the freedom to plunge in and not be afraid of what is happening—to you *and* the patient. A third asset that went unrecognized was that co-therapy also served as a secret system for learning how to talk about emotional experiences, since you could objectify a subjective experience shared with someone else. (p. 18)

Early experimenters found that this boundary was quite effective in helping to preserve the freedom to observe without becoming too quickly entrenched in one specific role desired by the family. As Whitaker stated, "Freud's concept was of an equilateral triangle of mother–father–child. Cotherapist, or parents, should relate *to each other*, and then the child [or clients] can relate to *their relationship*" (Whitaker & Keith, 1986; italics added). In other words, family therapists began to discover that a cotherapist team was a powerful source of support in creating a therapeutic suprasystem with families.

Later, in the 1970s and 1980s, earlier conceptualizations of the role of the therapist (and collaborators) were increasingly reworked to include the idea of "the therapist within his/her context," rather than the therapist and colleagues as separate entities observing the family from a neutral diagnostic position. This "contextualization" of the therapist's role reflected mounting awareness in the social sciences that, just as there is no objectivity in physical sciences and experimental method, so there is no objectivity in the construction of social science principles and their application to psychotherapy (Dell, 1986; Maturana & Varela, 1980).

Accordingly, the writing of family systems theorists also began to reflect awareness that the presence of a therapist creates a "therapeutic suprasystem" of therapist plus family, whose dynamics are unique to that configuration of persons. Adding a cotherapist, therefore, magnifies the complexity of interactions, creating further unique dynamics that can only occur with *that* configuration of persons. As one example of this new awareness, systemic theorists in the late 1970s began to discuss the idea that the presence of multiple therapists creates a "binocular" (two-sighted) view of family process—a view that is unique to consultation teams of two or more therapists.

The Therapeutic Suprasystem

Although systemic writers posit that therapeutic consultation teams began at Milan's Centro per il Studio della Famiglia (Boscolo, Cecchin, Hoffman, & Penn, 1987), they are speaking only of the four-person team rather than the cotherapy team of therapist plus colleague (which, as I have pointed out, is considerably older). This point must be emphasized even further, as many systemic teams now utilize only two therapists for efficiency. However, the systemic writers are the ones who have most extensively described the internal workings of the "suprasystem" that is created when consultation team meets family.

The suprasystem provides a multiplicity of views not only from the family's end, but from that of the therapists as well. As one metaphorical description states, "As long as there was one person who could be immersed in the family and one person who could watch—one who leaned out the window and one who sat on that person's feet—a depth dimension could be achieved" (Boscolo et al., 1987, p. 25). The aim is to create a "binocular," or two-sighted, view (or larger) of any event in a session. This aim reflects findings in first- and second-order cybernetics about the importance of new information in the creation of social meaning (and therefore social change). According to Gregory Bateson, philosopher and student of first-order cybernetics, a dysfunctional social system perpetuates its own symptomatic interactions because it is "closed" to new information by the fact that its members can only feed in a certain number of familiar views and positions. These views have achieved, in a dysfunctional system, a "fit" that causes confusion, distress, and rapidly escalating cycling of behavior. In order to decrease the "fit" of a social system's component views, and thus its capacity to escalate behavior cycling, new information must be introduced from outside the closed loop of interactions so that new behavioral options become apparent.

For example, in a family in which the mother feels she must monitor and care for an adult son who does not show responsibility, the son's passive and dependent behavior confirms the view of the mother that she must monitor him. However, if new information were to be inserted by the divorced father that on visits to his home, the son acts quite withdrawn, a channel of information is opened for the mother to reconceptualize the problem in a new way that contains alternatives. For example, she may decide that his behavior is not "dependent" but "spoiled," and may determine that instead of monitoring him herself, she will insist that the father give him more time and attention.

Another aspect of therapeutic consultation teams is that they are able to engage in collaborative analysis and planning. For example, a research case study identified that in observing one consultation team operating in a university setting, "emphasis was on . . . *hypothesizing* about the family organization and the role of the symptom(s) within it; *analyzing* the family reaction to various interventions . . . and *planning* an outline of what to do in the upcoming session . . ." (Roberts, 1981, p. 74; italics added).

The function called "hypothesizing" has also been discussed extensively in the systemic literature (Selvini Palazzoli, Boscolo, Cecchin and Prata, 1980). It is the process of formulating a working map of the positions of each spouse or family member in regard to presenting symptoms, so that antecedents and maintaining factors can be addressed most completely. When more than one therapist participates in hypothesis formation, the multiple views that enter into conversation enhance the completeness of systemic formulation. Likewise, analysis of familial responses to team interventions becomes multilateral, and therefore richer and more complex. Finally, the plan that is constructed for further interventions contains information from several sources and is more complex (increasing the potential for delivering new data, which will stimulate more truly innovative planning strategies).

A key difference between the consultation team and the family in treatment is that the therapy team is more flexible than the family component of the suprasystem. The therapy team joins and separates more easily, maintains a less rigid boundary with others, and shows other characteristics of a healthy family. This live demonstration of flexibility creates experiential alternatives for family members, while the therapists actively intervene in the more rigid and closed cycles of behavior that the family has developed (Roberto, 1991).

All of these characteristics of consultation teams, described in the systemic family therapy literature, pertain as well to cotherapy teams of two. Since it is the two-person cotherapy team that is central to the practice of transgenerational marital and family therapy, the next section examines the implications of these findings for the functioning of cotherapy dyads.

The Two-Person Consultation Team

When there are two therapist observers present in a room rather than one, there are two sources of information available from outside the "closed loop" of family interaction rather than one. As time passes during the course of therapy, the views of a solo therapist tend to begin to "fit" with pressures and forces from within the family to maintain the family's own organization and belief system. The presence of another therapist counteracts these pressures, and tends to slow or prevent this particular "fit" from occurring and therefore neutralizing the novelty of the therapists' views.

For example, it is common that when a solo therapist enjoys a family and finds the members' beliefs compatible with his/her own, the therapist may become reluctant to challenge their positions and ideas as the relationship with them grows more familiar. Instead, he/she may feel understanding of each member's motives and desires. The therapist is being "inducted" into the family's dominant belief system because of confluences between the members' experiences and his/her own. Concurrently, the therapist may discover that he/she no longer possesses novel ideas regarding the nature of their problem, or ideas for experimenting with or solving the problem. If a cotherapist is present, his/her views are likely to be discordant with the first therapist's. The second therapist will then observe the first one's increasing comfort level with the family's problem, and will be able to comment on his/her observations. This commentary punctuates or highlights the first therapist's "otherness" from the family, and allows him/her renewed distance to assess the changes that will need to be made.

In sum, in the interchange that takes place between two therapists and a couple or family, it is more difficult for either therapist to assume a vacant role posed by the family and thus to be "inducted." When one therapist begins to accommodate to family rules and to assume a conforming role, the other therapist can block this process by interacting with the first therapist, commenting on the process, or interrupting with his/her own observations. The "binocular view" established by the pairing of therapist plus colleague is much like the process of human vision, which involves the interaction of two separate but connected eyes that each focus on the environment and relay information from a slightly different vantage point. Extending the biological metaphor, we can say that this process creates depth of observation, just as two eyes establish depth perception.

The Tetrad versus the Triad

It was Murray Bowen who speculated that the most enduring configuration of human relationships is not the dyad, but the triangle. As evidence, he described how distressed dyads tend to expand to include a third party, which appears to decrease their subjective sense of tension (see Chapter 1). However, I believe that it is also common for each individual in a distressed dyad to seek out a personal ally, as in the case when married partners each consult an individual therapist, or when dissatisfied parents each cultivate special closeness with one child. This arrangement, a foursome, may be called a "tetrad."

In a therapeutic tetrad, interaction is actually more stable than in a triangle, in that *at no time is any individual excluded from an alliance* (Roberto, 1988). If two or more individuals in a family are in conflict, each cotherapist can encourage and support the point of view of a different party. Or one cotherapist can highlight a particular position in the family, while the other cotherapist listens along with the rest of the family. In couples therapy, each cotherapist can at times side with one spouse or represent the viewpoint of one spouse (the cotherapists will, however, need to shift these alliances frequently).

A tetrad contains the possibility of four emotional triangles, and any one participant can be included in three triangles. For example, the husband in a couple that is consulting a husband–wife cotherapy team can enter into three triangles: husband–male cotherapist–female cotherapist; husband–wife–male cotherapist; and husband–wife–female cotherapist. Therefore, according to the criteria of natural systems theory, it is possible for a tetrad to develop very stable long-term interactions along the paths of its component triangles. However, a key differencebetween tetrads and triangles lies in the fact that if one individual becomes excluded from a dysfunctional triangle, he/she must expand into another triangle with additional parties in order to contain the tension. In a tetrad, when tensions escalate, the fourth participant can form an alliance with the excluded "third person."

For example, let us consider a marital therapy in which the husband is in a very emotionally intense triangle with a deferential wife and a female cotherapist. Perhaps he has difficulty in considering his wife's opinion when making family decisions, and in showing respect for her contributions to the marriage. The female cotherapist is in a position to challenge his assumptions about his wife and the conditions of their marriage. At times her challenges may heighten emotional tensions, especially if the wife feels compelled to support her husband's authoritarian stance when she is uncertain or stressed. At these times, the spouses can move closer in their positions with each other, and can attempt to extrude the third party—in this case, the female cotherapist. In the tetradic arrangement of cotherapy, the male cotherapist can ally with the female cotherapist and support or augment her position while the spouses are in their alliance, or at times when a client spouse feels put off by a therapist.

John and Maria sought marital therapy because Maria had had a brief extramarital affair, and John had recently discovered its existence when he found a diaphragm in her purse. Although the marriage had been extremely distant for almost its entirety (5 years), John was angry and felt that Maria had no cause for her infidelity. Maria, on the other hand, tended to withdraw when John became angry, and did not explain or discuss her perceptions or wishes for the marriage. Her passivity enraged John, who interpreted it as rejection and indifference.

When the male cotherapist began to encourage Maria to make known her intentions and wishes at this point in the marriage, John's anger increased. He saw the therapist's efforts as implicit agreement with what he perceived as Maria's "devil-may-care" attitude, and tried to express his dismay by shouting down his wife whenever she attempted to speak. The female cotherapist undertook to address John, assuring him that "silence does not always mean consent," and that his wife's presence in the marital therapy bespoke a real attachment. This alliance allowed John to contain his hurt and anger somewhat, and to commit himself to the painful work of marital discussion without having to extrude either the male cotherapist or his wife.

I believe that it is because of the multiple triangles contained within a tetrad that each cotherapist is able to shift positions (and therefore alliances) within a therapy session without causing negative reactions in the family. If a solo therapist attempts to make the same shift of position within a session, the person with whom he/she has been aligning experiences the shift as an exclusion. The discomfort of feeling "excluded" can increase tension between participants, and may even cause the "excluded" member to seek out another ally outside the therapy. This new ally expands the number of problem triangles in the distressed family, and interferes with control of the treatment process.

Sophia, Tony, and their 17-year-old daughter, Rochelle, were in family therapy in order to get help for Rochelle, who was severely depressed 6 months after getting an abortion in secret. In fact, she did not feel able to inform her parents or the solo therapist about the abortion itself until the third session. When she did inform them, the parents (who also had a secret) stated that they already knew, having examined her room carefully and found medications after the surgery.

While Tony moved quickly to support his daughter, telling her that his main concerns were her withdrawal and depression, Sophia burst forth with considerable disapproval and disappointment. She stated that her religious faith made such a decision abhorrent, that she felt Rochelle was less than the daughter she had hoped, and that her grandchild had been taken away from her. She wept in deep pain. Of course, Rochelle was greatly shocked, seeing that the outcome of her risky disclosure was as bad as she had feared. The therapist, recalling that Rochelle's father appeared available to support her, moved to acknowledge the mother's disappointment and to try to reframe it in such a way that Sophia did not have to reject her daughter.

After the family therapy session, nonetheless, Rochelle became inconsolable and extremely anxious. She called her boyfriend (who lived in another state), arranged to stay with his family for the remainder of the summer, and bought her airline tickets before the family returned to the next session.

It takes a very highly trained and seasoned solo therapist to predict such incidents, and to plan therapeutic shifts carefully so that feelings of exclusion are kept to a minimum. Often such reactions occur anyway, despite careful planning, and the solo therapist must attempt to utilize a fourth person to stabilize the situation. In clinical commentaries, the fourth person may be one of the following: a consultant brought in for one to several sessions; a supervisor or peer supervisor; an extended family member; an observer behind a mirror; or a fictitious observing team. The real presence of a cotherapist, however, precludes the problem of the "excluded" member's reaction entirely. In the case just described, while one cotherapist acknowledged the concern and distress of Sophia, the other cotherapist could either have taken Rochelle's position or further explored the possibility of Tony's mediating between mother and daughter.

Interventions with a Cotherapy Team

Up to this point, the chapter has described many therapeutic functions that are made possible by a cotherapy team. This section leaves training functions aside and focuses on therapeutic functions. There are a number of therapy interventions that are possible only in a therapeutic dyad or team.

Shifting the Focus of a Session

During the course of therapeutic conversation, there are times when a specific issue does not produce useful ideas or alternatives. This can reflect a timing obstacle, as when a couple or family is not ready to discuss a problem; a situational obstacle, such as missing members; or other transitory factors. At times when one cotherapist pursues an avenue that is not proving fruitful, the second cotherapist can actively change the focus of discussion. Alternatively, the second one can make a process comment to the first, remarking that the avenue does not seem fruitful, and perhaps speculating as to the reasons.

Mirroring Familial Patterns

When there is an unresolved conflict within a couple or family, two cotherapists can mirror the conflict by taking the roles of participants. In the process, they are able to model a different way of interacting in regard to the disagreement—one that involves productive negotiation and better-differentiated views. There is a systemic version of this technique called the "reflecting team," which involves constructing a "Greek chorus" of voices that mirrors the current conflict until the family itself chooses a resolution (Papp, 1980).

Each cotherapist chooses a different position to reflect. The cotherapists then proceed to have the disagreement, with the couple or family watching. In the process, each cotherapist can demonstrate more effective ways to represent his/her position, or comment to a family member on his/her thoughts about the position. Together, the two cotherapists then attempt to reach a resolution, or "agree to disagree" if immediate closure is undesirable.

Role Switching

In an attempt to clarify the way in which a family member experiences his/her role in the family, the presence of a cotherapist allows one to "take the place" of the member in question for a brief period. This "role switching" is not so much a strategic ploy as a deliberate emotional shift from the neutrality and distance of the observer to the involved, subjective experience of that member.

For example, in a family with an alienated teenager, one therapist can allow himself/herself to imagine what it is like to be the teenager in that home. At the same time, the other cotherapist keeps the controlling functions of directing the conversation in the room, tracking familial interactions, and performing other "gate-keeping" activities. This technique allows a therapist access to experiential information about family roles, which will help clarify why a particular role is difficult to address or change.

Supporting and Confronting

When one or several family members are especially rigid and resistant to change, one cotherapist can take on the task of challenging any such members. At the same time, the other cotherapist can split off into a supportive stance, to "cushion" the stress of challenge. This division of labor in a therapy session is particularly useful for rigid individuals, who may tend to escalate a position under stress if challenged too directly. Here, the presence of two therapists means that challenges can be given directly, since the second cotherapist offers an alliance to mitigate any escalation.

Setting Boundaries and Protecting Boundaries

In families where there are poorly defined boundaries around internal relationships, or intrusion between individuals, it is often difficult to focus needed attention on those relationships or individuals. For example, in an enmeshed family, one therapist often tries to address one member, only to have another member "answer for" him/her.

In such instances, one cotherapist can focus on eliciting information from an individual or key dyad, while the other cotherapist observes with one or more other members. In one variation of this intervention, the other members are asked not to respond until the first one has shared perceptions with the observing cotherapist (Hannum, 1980). This technique is a splitting off of two therapeutic functions: setting boundaries and eliciting multiple viewpoints. Its advantage lies in the freeing up of the first cotherapist to proceed with eliciting information at crucial moments.

Creating Gender Balance

Dual-sex cotherapy teams have the capacity to respond to couples' gender problems in many more ways than a solo therapist can. Of course, this is dependent on the understanding that each cotherapist possesses of gender issues within marriage, the family's culture, the cotherapists' culture, and the current practice of family therapy. If the cotherapists are knowledgeable, they have the ability to replay, examine, renegotiate, and create alternatives to gender imbalances in the marriage or family being treated. Ideally, tensions in the family centering around severe imbalances are "taken on" by the cotherapy team in a mirroring fashion, and each cotherapist can take a definite position on the options for male and female members of that family.

For example, in a marriage where the husband has considerable economic power over an educated wife, who has given up her earning power to support his career and the home, a male and female cotherapy team is able to experience their power imbalance from a vantage point that is somewhat "more equal." The female cotherapist, who has chosen to pursue a "more equal" status by maintaining a professional identity, will be able to challenge and question the wife on the consequences of her voluntary dependency on the husband. She will be able to interact with the husband on a "more equal" footing, and test his willingness to negotiate in a truly egalitarian relationship.

The male cotherapist, if he is able to maintain an egalitarian relationship with his partner, shows the husband new options for mutually respectful problem solving. If he is sufficiently open to his own concerns about and difficulties in sharing power with women, he can also comment on the confusion and lack of guidelines for men who are trying to make this shift. Moreover, the wife can interact with a man who is openly examining these problems and acknowledging their validity.

In the process of establishing these connections, it is probable that each cotherapist will experience gender tension with the other, since these dilemmas are also present in the cotherapists' own families and families of origin. The cotherapists, if they are aware of their own problems in negotiating power, intimacy, and autonomy with the opposite sex, can comment on tensions that arise and can even weave them into the evolving discussions with husband and wife. The couple or family in therapy is given the opportunity to observe another dual-sex pair struggling with the same gender tensions and creating alternatives together.

Complex Prescriptions

Cotherapy teams, like larger consultation teams, are able to deliver complex therapeutic messages to families by splitting up the components of such messages. In the case where a family shows disagreement over the proper course of action concerning a problem, messages or prescriptions must be complex in order to address the concerns of each spouse or family member. For example, in a family where a son is depressed, the father may believe that he requires more constructive activity, while the mother may believe that he requires more attention and nurturance. Any message to the family regarding solutions must take both sets of beliefs into account in order to be truly systemic. A solo therapist attempts to reflect all of these beliefs at different times within a session, or all together in one summarization of possible solutions. The partners in a cotherapy team are able to represent different beliefs for a specified period of time.

Complex messages from a cotherapy team can take several forms. One form is the "disagreement," in which one cotherapist represents one dominant point of view while the second cotherapist reflects another. The cotherapists go on to disagree and negotiate for their respective goals while the family observes. A second form is the "expansion," in which one cotherapist takes a side, the other protests that both sides are correct, and the first cotherapist then agrees with the second. The message to the family is that no one view is more valid than the other in the eyes of the cotherapy team. A third form is "parallel positioning," in which one cotherapist offers suggestions that encourage the view of one member, while the second cotherapist offers different suggestions that encourage the view of another member. "Parallel positioning" supports differentiation of family members without entering into disagreement. It also allows for directives and assignments when family members do not agree on the definition of a problem.

Developmental Stages of a Cotherapy Team

A cotherapy team can be likened to a marriage. Like a marriage, the team proceeds through stages of relationship—from the initial decision to make acquaintance, into a more long-term cooperative venture in which each partner expects to contribute personal direction and to gain support and personal growth. At each developmental stage, there are predictable issues that arise and need to be addressed in order for the cotherapy team to remain vital, creative, and cohesive. In this section, I discuss some of the major stages of cotherapy development as I have experienced them in my training and practice experiences. The stages outlined here do not pertain to cotherapy teams comprised of a supervisor and a trainee, as these teams are not really peerships, but rather are hierarchical training relationships. A supervisor–trainee team operates more like a supervisory relationship or like a training consulting team, in which issues of hierarchy, control, authority, responsibility, and intimacy reflect the unequal status of the participants. (See "Cotherapy as a Training Procedure," below.)

Initial, Task-Oriented Phase

A cotherapy team initially emerges from each therapist's need for consultation and stimulation. The situation may reflect an external demand, such as a cotherapy-oriented training program typical in symbolic-experiential schools, or a perceived need by the therapists. The desire for consultation is tied to the performance of psychotherapy interventions, so that the pair begins on a task-oriented basis. We feel that this is not true of husband–wife cotherapy teams, which often begin not as a means of consultation, but out of the spouses' desire to share their work with each other (a relational decision).

In its initial phases, a cotherapy relationship focuses on the problem of inclusion, or forming connectedness or belonging. Each partner tends to focus on the exchange of information regarding his/her past history, personal preferences, and philosophy of therapy. There may be intellectual debate about theoretical differences. However, the exchange of information takes place, as it does for any new couple, within a context of creating inclusion.

Similarities and areas of agreement are emphasized, as are mutual goals for the cotherapy experience and goals for the couples or families being treated. There are few intensely emotional interactions. Both parties control the information, so as to create a favorable impression regarding the future of the relationship and to maximize cohesion. Where there is tension or difference, it is often attributed to the difficulty of the case being treated, or to behavior by family members in treatment. An appearance of alliance is maintained. In this respect, the a cotherapy team at this phase resembles a dating pair that is not motivated or ready to explore areas of disagreement.

Early-Phase Role Negotiation

Once the partners in a cotherapy team have elected to work together on a continuing basis, they are no longer simply providing consultation to each other. Rather, by virtue of committing themselves to one or more ongoing cases, they have formed a commitment to each other as well. The issue of inclusion is no longer pertinent, and instead the partners begin in an implicit way to negotiate their individual roles in the team. Much as in a marital dyad, tasks are allocated for conduction of the therapy, or (often) divided between the two cotherapists.

In an early-phase cotherapy team, important roles are typically divided in a relatively rigid and unchanging fashion. For example, one cotherapist will be more instrumental and directive, with the other tracking the family members' affect and commenting on emotional dynamics. Or one cotherapist will form an alliance with a particular member, while the other consistently supports a different member or different generation in the family. Attempts by one cotherapist to go beyond "his"/"her" role produce tension and conflict between the partners, as in an early marriage. The cotherapists have not yet examined their personal contract with each other, or negotiated it. The cotherapists also begin to struggle with differences in desired level of intimacy, both with each other and with the treatment couple or family.

Interdependency

As a cotherapy team continues to work together, it is inevitable that the heretofore rigid individual roles must be addressed, so that the partners can take on each other's tasks, positions, and plans when necessary. A treatment team is more effective if each partner has access to many different methods of intervening, so that each can "spell" the other. In order to do so, the partners must each be willing to share roles that were previously divided. If the cotherapists are able to make their positions on the team more flexible, they will achieve greater interdependency, or mutuality. Interdependency is experienced as a comfortable level of intimacy, as a sense of cooperation, and as give and take.

The shift toward greater interdependency is often conflictual, since each cotherapist is challenged to abandon preferred modes of thinking and behaving and to learn new and unfamiliar skills. For example, a cotherapist who has been more active and interrogative in the past may be asked by the partner to assume a more reflective posture while he/she pursues a therapeutic issue that he/she feels is important. A cotherapist who has operated autonomously in each session, formulating his/her own plans and ideas, may be asked to become more affiliative and to plan further interventions cooperatively.

A number of cotherapists split up and cease working together at this stage in their professional relationship. We believe that this is a stressful period that some clinicians do not wish to navigate with every professional partner, just as some marriages do not survive major modification. However, cotherapy teams that have passed through the stage of greater interdependency show tremendous creativity and effectiveness. Each partner has a range of behaviors available to him/her when therapeutic impasses occur, or when one cotherapist is "stuck." Such teams may stay together for the span of a long professional career—witness the cotherapy teams of Carl Whitaker and David Keith, Luigi Boscolo and Gianfranco Cecchin, Salvador Minuchin and Braulio Montalvo, Peggy Papp and Olga Silverstein, and Norman and Betty Paul.

Cotherapy as a Training Procedure

Not all transgenerational training programs use cotherapy in their curricula. Cotherapy training teams are particularly common in programs that teach the symbolic-experiential training model; other models tend to utilize the supervisory relationship as the main source of clinical learning and feedback. For example, the natural systems model utilizes coaching of the solo therapist, in order to teach him/her to observe personal relational limitations and to expand and correct them with his/her own family of origin (Carter & Orfanidis, 1976; Kerr, 1981). The object relations model also depends on the use of the supervisor–supervisee relationship in order to encourage the growth of the individual therapist. In addition, this model utilizes training analysis for the purpose of identifying and resolving stagnant familial problems that affect the trainee's relationships and professional identity.

In training institutes that do utilize cotherapy as a primary educational tool, there are two forms of cotherapy teams. One is the assigned team, in which two trainees are paired (or pair themselves) and treat a family together for the duration of the case or for the training year. The second form is the supervisor–trainee cotherapy team, in which a trainee is paired with an experienced senior clinician. In the latter case, the trainee is in a position to actively observe and model the senior clinician in the process of the team's development.

Trainee cotherapists have the advantage of sharing the training experience, and the stress of supervision, with a partner. There is a sense of learning together, and of creating new and exciting interventions and strategies as a team. Like members of the systemic consultation team, trainee cotherapists form a group identity and a feeling of cohesion. There is less anxiety in treatment of early cases because responsibility is shared. Trainee cotherapists also gain experience at conflicting and negotiating preferred roles and operating parameters for the team, which will be invaluable experience at the worksite with future colleagues.

Compared with training where all work is done on a solo basis, cotherapy offers much more information for the developing professional. From the first, trainees are not seeing the majority of their couples and families alone. Individuals are therefore less secretive and defensive about their work, since each trainee's attempts are more visible to his/her peers. Likewise, each trainee is able to discuss and learn from the mistakes that peers make; this allows observational learning to occur. Sharing the anxiety and self-consciousness of peers who are unsure of a treatment plan helps to prevent each trainee from forming rigid and premature convictions about his/her own work. Finally, experiencing the emotional give and take of the cotherapy team teaches trainees respect for the enormous pressures in distressed couples and families, where members are also unsure of their place in the group.

The supervisor–supervisee cotherapy team does not possess the degree of openness and flexibility of the trainee team, because the senior clinician already possesses an orientation and well-formed beliefs regarding the therapy process. To the degree that the senior is confident in these beliefs, he/she is less oriented toward experimentation. There is more implicit guidance within the cotherapy session, and the trainee cotherapist accommodates to the supervisor's preferences because of the experienced difference in their statuses. Over the course of the training year, this status difference should ideally lessen so that the trainee, formerly less proactive, becomes equally active. As Whitaker has noted of his own experience as supervisor:

> There comes a point in the co-therapy relationship where the trainee co-therapist stops feeling insecure and starts feeling like a teammate.

> . . . The family sees it too, and responds to the therapists as a team. This is my dream . . . of how children ought to see the parents. (Whitaker & Keith, 1986)

Whereas the trainee cotherapy team is more likely to experience conflicts centering around competition and the division of roles, which tend to be symmetrical escalations (like marital fights), the supervisor–trainee cotherapy team experiences conflict in regard to authority and problems of initiative. This type of conflict is complementary and is often more implicit and less openly visible. For example, two trainees may find themselves arguing over the definition of a problem in a clinical family. One may argue that a child's symptoms, for instance, reflect lack of parental cooperation in his/her rearing, while the other feels that one parent is more involved and responsible than the other. The cotherapists in such a situation are vying for control of the conceptualization and planning of the therapy, and for delineation of who will intervene at what times.

In a supervisor–trainee team, such arguments are unlikely to occur until much later, when the trainee feels like more of an equal. Initially, the trainee is apt to be awed by the experience and self-confidence of the senior cotherapist, and thus may not be inclined to compete. Rather, in this type of team a core difficulty is the trainee's fear of taking initiative with the senior cotherapist present. The trainee may hang back, offer fewer observations, and try to support and back up the senior cotherapist instead. Tensions surround the supervisor's encouragement of active participation when the trainee is self-conscious.

Training programs that utilize cotherapy as a training tool often arrange both trainee and supervisor–trainee teams. Each provides instruction in a unique fashion, and allows the trainee to experience and manage different types of team conflict for future use. I believe that as cotherapy in private practice becomes more difficult in the face of capitated mental health care programs, training institutes will consider de-emphasizing cotherapy as a training tool. I further believe that this would be a grave error, however awkward it becomes to bill for cotherapy in the current marketplace. Cotherapy, a quite personal and emotionally rewarding form of consultation team, is also an invaluable learning tool that can never be replaced in the supervisory session or classroom.

·III·

TRAINING THE TRANSGENERATIONAL FAMILY THERAPIST

·14·

Transgenerational Family Therapy for the Trainee

The use of a therapy experience during the training years is a time-honored procedure. It has been recommended both for increasing the trainee's self-knowledge and social effectiveness before licensure, and also for deepening and personalizing the training experience. In Freud's time it was considered essential for a training analysis to be performed, so that the trainee would be free from personal wish–defense complexes and neurotic anxieties before entering into transference relationships with analytic clients. Freud felt so strongly about this requirement that he attempted a self-analysis, in the absence of a senior analyst to analyze him.

Currently, psychotherapy during the training years in marital and family therapy programs is often recommended, although not required. Recent guidelines from the American Association for Marriage and Family Therapy's Commission on Accreditation's site visitors' procedures have further recommended that boundaries between faculty–student relationships and therapist–client relationships be preserved, so that faculty members do not see their own trainees in therapy. This guideline is also a departure from the practice of earlier analytic institutes, where faculty members frequently saw their own students for a training analysis. In this chapter I discuss the forms of therapeutic experience currently available to trainees in marital and family therapy programs; the effects of obtaining therapy during the training years; and the potential advantages for professional development and effective practice.

Within the transgenerational training institutes, there are two major forms of marital and family therapy available to the trainee: (1) Bowenian coaching techniques; and (2) marital or family therapy with one's own spouse, family, and family of origin participating. There is no formal research to date comparing these two forms of trainee psychotherapy in terms of their relative effectiveness or other characteristics, such as ap-

195

plicability to specific trainee problems. Since coaching interventions are endemic to institutes teaching natural systems theory, it is probable that the same factors that influence a trainee's choice of institute (theoretical orientation; identification with a specific faculty member; personal therapeutic style) also influence his/her choice of personal therapy experience.

Coaching Marital and Family Therapy Trainees

Murray Bowen initiated the use of "coaching," or aiding an individual in efforts to change himself/herself in the context of the nuclear and extended family, at Georgetown University in the late 1960s. Coaching was a natural outgrowth of natural systems theory, which stipulates that when only one member of a family is motivated, intervening to educate that member about family dynamics can produce system-wide change. Bowen informally observed that in his own training program, trainees who opted to receive coaching for personal concerns tended to progress faster not only personally, but also professionally in their clinical effectiveness (Bowen, 1974/1988).

A number of institutes have introduced variations in methods for coaching trainees. For example, Carter and Orfanidis (1976) reported inclusion of formal family-of-origin work into the didactic and supervisory portions of their postgraduate curriculum. Whitaker, at the University of Wisconsin School of Medicine from 1964 to 1984, utilized formal family-of-origin presentations for each residency group, followed by experiential discussion. Marital and family trainees at the Menninger Clinic program are coached individually upon request, as a therapeutic experience.

Coaching as a training intervention aims to aid the individual student *in work to be performed with his/her nuclear and extended families* (Carter & Orfanidis, 1976). The emphasis of psychotherapy is not on the interaction between trainee and coach, as it would be in marital or family therapy. Rather, the significance of the trainee–coach relationship is made secondary to the importance of the trainee's ongoing, long-term bond with his/her family of origin. The very term "coach" denotes a person outside one's "team" who observes and teaches, but does not play. Strong emotionality (such as irritation or anxiety) and urges to express one's view of important relationships are guided toward the relationship producing the emotionality, not toward the coach. Coaching is also action-oriented, so that increasing understanding of the tensions within one's multigenerational relationships is accompanied by home visits, letters, and other direct communications and acts.

The goal of coaching for the family therapy trainee is to facilitate an adult–adult, dyadic, person-to-person relationship with each available member of the extended family. This work includes one's family of procreation (the spouse and children); in fact, it usually begins there, because most married trainees are highly motivated to preserve their marriages. The second field of inquiry is the nuclear family of parents and siblings. Many postgraduate trainees, in their 20s and 30s, have not yet renegotiated personally effective relationships with parents in their adult lives (Williamson, 1981). In addition, sibling relationships are so de-emphasized in our culture that early, "frozen" childhood perceptions often dictate the interactions among otherwise adult siblings. These neglected areas are fruitfully researched in the process of coaching. Trainees are aided in re-evaluating their views of sibling position in the family, forming alliances with siblings who were previously cut off or battled, and showing a positive stance toward other siblings' coping strategies within the family.

Still later in the coaching process, although much relevant information arises from the very first construction of the family genogram, the trainee begins to inquire into the lives and experiences of the maternal and paternal grandparents and greatgrandparents. I believe that this tertiary level of inquiry often produces the most lasting effects, because it is out of this information that acculturated, third-generation American therapists obtain their first glimpse into the worldwide historical, cultural, and economic forces that molded and shaped the family of origin and its traditions until the present day. Family patterns and rules that have been incomprehensible until this point in coaching may become clarified and contextualized for the first time in the trainee's life experience. At times, these patterns are equally incomprehensible to the trainee's parents, so that initial nuclear family discussions shed little light in themselves. Research into the grandparental and great-grandparental generations involves more long-term and indirect procedures, such as finding gravesites; tracing family members through organizations; contacting elderly cousins or great-uncles; tracking written materials, such as diaries or family Bibles; and visiting regions or countries where previous generations resided.

This chapter does not attempt to describe the specific strategies for coaching, which have been elaborated in the extensive natural systems literature. However, it may be edifying to follow Carter and McGoldrick's (1980) earlier description of coaching as a five-stage process: forming the coaching alliance; a psychoeducational stage; re-entering the family of origin; reworking family relationships; and a following-through stage.

In order to form a coaching alliance, the training coach must take a position that the trainee is not "outside" his/her family system, but rather, is an integral part of it. Because family therapy trainees do not yet have an understanding of systemic theory, they also do not experience themselves as "part of" rule-bound family systems. Most trainees cultivate an analytical stance toward their own families, and make judgments or diagnoses of important family members rather than observational descriptions. The coach initially allies with the trainee by constructing the family genogram (see Chapter 8); taking a lengthy family history; tracing conflictual family patterns over several generations; and eliciting guesses about how other members might view specific family problems. The tone of this first stage is informational and reflective, as it is in early-stage Bowenian family therapy.

The psychoeducational stage is a stage often administered by itself in didactic training groups. For example, at the Eastern Virginia Family Therapy Institute, the first 2 months of the advanced externship training year focus on readings from natural systems theory and papers describing family-of-origin work by professional colleagues (e.g., Bowen, 1972/ 1988), followed by presentation of one's own family genogram. In the psychoeducational phase, the trainee elaborates information in the original genogram by adding important nodal events in the life history of the family of origin. Conflictual patterns are examined to identify key triangles that have formed around them, and the functioning of these key triangles is discussed.

For example, a hard-working male trainee whose father is a physician may discover that his father's younger brother died at a young age from a serious illness and that his father felt responsible for taking care of the family. He may find, upon examining his father's relationship with his grandparents, that his father gained authority with the grandparents by becoming a successful physician. The trainee may have gained similar acceptance with his parents and grandparents by becoming a physician. After identifying these triangles of father–uncle–grandparent and father–uncle–self, the trainee may gain a further sense that tensions between himself and his own father reflect unresolved grief problems.

During the psychoeducational stage, few tasks or actions are prescribed. In fact, the early inquiries during genogram construction and this second stage of coaching usually elicit familial responses in themselves. One of my trainees found that requests for her parents' date of marriage yielded several months of embarrassed evasions, after which her mother acknowledged for the first time that the parents had married when pregnant with the trainee. One powerful and evocative method for receiving information is sending audiotapes to each parent with a request that each "describe what s/he remembers of his/her life up until the birth" of the trainee (Whitaker, personal communication, 1978).

It is considered unwise to attempt to modify ongoing relationships during the psychoeducational stage, because the trainee does not yet have a well-formulated idea of the origins and functions of long-term family triangles. Therefore, any efforts to make dramatic statements or changes may intensify chronic conflicts and solidify problem triangles, instead of defusing them. Furthermore, it is necessary for the trainee to learn skills for containing intense emotion and combating stress before venturing to shift tense familial triangles. Otherwise, it is possible that the trainee will evoke family pressures, succumb to personal anxiety, and repeat already dysfunctional ways of countering the anxiety (e.g., by cutting off emotionally from the family of origin).

The third stage of coaching involves re-entering the family of origin from a different, more self-aware stance. In this more self-aware or differentiated stance, the trainee is encouraged to begin approaching individual family members with whom there is conflict, distance, or severe tension. The goal of differentiation, as it is in all natural systems therapies, is to form a personal dyadic, adult-to-adult relationship with each member. The form of this re-entry is dosed and timed, depending upon the severity of the tension between trainee and family member.

The re-entry work is usually begun with the trainee's parents, whether the trainee is still living at home or not. If a parent is deceased, the re-entry work is accomplished by approaching the deceased parent via letter or graveside visit (Williamson, 1978). A parental relationship, or one with a "psychological parent" (e.g., a close aunt), that is highly emotional requires timed interventions. Many trainees have the impulse to stage a dramatic confrontation of some kind, either to defend their decisions, to force immediate understanding, or to challenge someone to change. Such confrontations are, in fact, further expressions of anxiety and have no place in re-entry assignments. The task of re-entry requires affirmation of already existing bonds; positive connotation of family attempts to give support; and demonstration of one's interest in becoming more personally involved.

The trainee must cultivate an attitude of curiosity and observation of the parents' ways of connecting, rather than one of judgment, and an attitude of self-assertion rather than defensiveness. Specific assignments during this stage often include letter writing to renew communication with a disengaged parent; searching for a divorced biological parent whose whereabouts are uncertain; and exchanging information about one's current life with parents or siblings. If a trainee has typically maintained only secondhand contacts with someone—for example, if he/she has received news of a sister only by talking to their mother—the trainee is guided to contact that person directly and to eliminate the third member from the emerging dialogues.

The fourth stage of coaching involves the trainee's doing the work of resolving recurring dysfunctional interactions, by focusing on his/her own behavior. Rather than focusing on the contribution of significant others to ongoing tensions, the trainee refocuses after each contact on his/her hidden expectations of each family member and efforts to change them rather than changing himself/herself. For example, a young man may follow each telephone contact to his mother by expecting his mother to take more initiative in confiding her concerns and her past. He may repeatedly show interest in her, only to place her in the position of lowering her guard while he waits to receive her disclosures. If she is reluctant to divulge unpleasant family issues, she will in all likelihood feel pressured to take a step that is intolerably anxiety-provoking. In this case, the trainee would be advised to cease pressuring his mother for self-disclosure, and to begin opening up his own concerns and problems during conversations with her. For this trainee, the process of sharing his own problems would be a different and more differentiated way of achieving his goal of closeness with his mother, and would produce a different context in which for her to take the first step toward openness.

The key to working on differentiation is, as Bowen has noted, to be able to maintain an individual stance *while staying connected emotionally to one's family of origin.* As Fogarty (1972) has pointed out, in relationships where there is a moderate level of anxiety or "emptiness," people tend to want relief from the accompanying negative affects of anger, hurt, and dissatisfaction. When feelings of helplessness and dissatisfaction are high,

> The desire to change some other person consumes one and fills his head. This is disguised emptiness—an attempt to run away from personal emptiness by focusing on others. . . . One must also deal with the over-responsible person who runs from his own emptiness by his efforts to help the other person. (Fogarty, 1972, pp. 80–81)

I feel that the overresponsible position is one common to marital and family therapy trainees, who often base their choice of career on their having previously filled a caretaker role in their own families of origin.

The final stage of coaching involves following through on planned changes that have begun. The orientation of transgenerational therapies is that adult and family development is a lifelong cycle, with the challenge and potential for continuous self-discovery and relational deepening. From this vantage point, in coaching my colleagues and I encourage trainees to value small, incremental changes over time. Initially, family systems concepts are tremendously exciting for trainees, and they may have considerable motivation to "work on" their families. Yet the investment in taking risks with intimates waxes and wanes, in coaching as well as in therapy. There are times in the coaching process when trainees believe that no more can be accomplished in terms of relational change, or when they are discouraged by chronic family impasses. Many trainees have difficulty recognizing the potential gains offered by extended family work, and shy away from it. Others are enthusiastic about multigenerational researches, but avoid discussing the implications of their family roles for their marriages and children.

The key to fruitful following through in coaching is to allow a long-term view of relational change, and to pace the coaching sessions further apart over time. At the beginning of a training year, coaching sessions are often held on a biweekly basis. At the end of the year, these sessions may take place only once every 2 months, or after long hiatuses in which the trainee attempts new positions with the family of origin. Transgenerational therapists see the process of differentiation as a lifelong task, and have been known to report on their progress at professional meetings (Dammann, 1990).

Marital and Family Therapy with Trainees

Much less has been systematically published in the marital and family therapy literatures on the use of family therapy for trainees. I believe that the therapists associated with each training institute utilize the techniques familiar to them, whether with trainees or with clinical families. The varieties of transgenerational therapies available to trainees include object relations family therapy; contextual family therapy; symbolic-experiential family therapy; and the variants applied by Norman Paul, James Framo, and Donald Williamson. Since the techniques involved do not explicitly vary from those used for clinical practice, I do not reiterate them here. The central questions relevant to therapy with trainees are these: Does it promote self-knowledge and maturation? Is this maturation necessary for, or pertinent to, the effectiveness of trainees in practice? Does the experience of family therapy affect a trainee's view of the therapy process with clinical families? I believe that the answer to all these questions is a definite affirmative.

Training Therapy and Self-Knowledge

It has been said that "a client can only become as differentiated as his/her therapist." Contrary to the medical orientation that one need not suffer a disease process to treat it, from a family systems viewpoint a therapist cannot teach what he/she does not know. If therapist(s) and the client family form a working metasystem in the process of therapy, then the beliefs and constructions of one subsystem affect the other. To the extent that a therapist is unaware of emotional dynamics within himself/herself, such as relational cutoff, distancing, fusion behaviors, or projection, he/she is less able to identify them and intervene when they occur in a clinical family.

As in the technique of coaching, one function of marital and family therapy during the training years is to make the trainee aware of unresolved issues with the family of origin, as well as of predominant roles he/she plays within the nuclear and extended families. If these roles are being replicated in the trainee's marriage, or compensated for via a "revolving slate" in the marriage (Boszormenyi-Nagy & Krasner, 1986), such patterns are also examined in marital/family therapy. The goal of such examination is to prevent the trainee from blindly repeating such roles and tensions, via countertransference, in therapy with clinical families.

This is not to say that countertransference reactions can be eliminated or prevented in the practice of family therapy. For example, a trainee who has come from a physically abusive family of origin will have a specific set of responses to an abusing parent within a clinical family, which exceed in emotional intensity the responses of a trainee who has not experienced abuse. According to object relations theory, our own internalized images of important others, formed quite early in family interaction with parents and siblings, carry emotional loadings which are activated whenever real relational events resemble the images we have formed (see Chapter 4). A training experience in marital and family therapy brings these images and their accompanying affect to the fore, so that the trainee is highly aware of their existence. Although these images can be changed during the process of therapy by modifying one's family-of-origin relationships in the here and now, the process of identifying such images also makes the trainee less susceptible to uncontrolled countertransference reactions.

> Sylvia, a 50-year-old professional counselor, enrolled in a 2-year postgraduate training program for further specialization in marital and family therapy. During the second year of training, which had a heavy practice and supervision component, she found herself treating many more couples and families than she had in the past. The didactic component of the first training year led her to make a systemic shift in her thinking. Instead of interviewing the occasional parenting pair, or couple, as she had previously, she was now choosing to treat her clients in marital and family sessions whenever possible, and scheduled up to 10 such sessions per week in her part-time practice. In individual and group supervision of her cases, she began to notice that she did not encourage fathers to attend family sessions, and experienced considerable anxiety when she spoke to a husband or father about scheduling sessions. She decided to seek personal psychotherapy in order to understand her anxiety problem.

Sylvia was in her third marriage, to a successful business executive who travelled extensively. Despite his frequent departures, Sylvia's therapy was a marital psychotherapy with a number of midphase family-of-origin consultations. The consultations included her widowed mother, her two sisters, and her mother's sister, who resided in a different state. Quite early in her marital sessions, Sylvia declared that she saw her marriage as a distant, institutional relationship that had been entered into by both partners for purposes of convenience—companionship and economic security. Her husband agreed. It emerged that Sylvia had never known her own father, who was excluded and excluded himself from family activities, and that she had no brothers or uncles. She was, quite literally, unsure what sort of attachment was possible with adult males. She commented on the then-popular joke, "A woman without a man is like a fish without a bicycle." Her husband, who had married late in life and had a heavily conflicted relationship with his own mother, viewed Sylvia as an ornamental but irritating business requisite for travel and entertaining.

The consultations with Sylvia's mother, younger sisters, and maternal aunt (who lived with the mother) disclosed that the mother had valued her marriage highly, but had not demonstrated her attachment in front of the children because of long-term depression during her childbearing years. The aunt felt that this depression was strongly related to the fact that both had been orphaned young, when their parents were killed in an auto crash. Afraid to become too happy, Sylvia's mother had kept to herself until her own husband's death from heart disease, and the aunt had never married. Sylvia became aware that behind her alienation from men and confusion regarding the value of intimacy, there was a multigenerational legacy of loss, fear of loss, and fear of happiness. As she articulated for herself the "loner" stance that she had cultivated to cope with these confusions, she began to challenge her husband to commit himself more to her. She also found herself more comfortable with—even eager to include—husbands and fathers in family therapy, and to ally with them.

Training Therapy and the Therapist's Role

Gus Napier (1983) commented that one vital component of a successful and effective marital or family therapy is the empathy that exists between therapist and client family. He remarked that although the field has developed a strong regard for the use of positive reframing and positive connotation in empowering families and building competencies, there has been an accompanying distance between therapist and family. To some extent, this distance is a product of early strategic and systemic theories, which called for a boundary of privacy and mystery surrounding the therapy team in order to protect systemic planning and interventions.

In addition, the marked professional distance advocated by many strategic and systemic practitioners reflected early formulations of the concept of "neutrality," which discouraged individual alliances between therapist and family member. As recently as 1989, Stierlin remarked that well-maintained therapeutic neutrality should leave family members unsure whom the therapist is allied with (Stierlin & Weber, 1989). From a transgenerational view, the optimal role of the therapist resembles more Boszormenyi-Nagy's concept of "multidirectional partiality"—an ability to ally with and include the viewpoint of *each* family member.

Napier's point was that in the pursuit of more systemic formulation and protection of the consulting team, family therapists also prevent themselves from working "up close" in an emotional field with those who seek their aid. At times, it is the empathic connection that chiefly allows the client family to maintain the trust and courage needed to confront serious family dysfunctions (such as violence or sex abuse) and cataclysmic events (such as divorce, loss, and death). The ability to work "up close" in an emotional field with client families is, to some extent, learned. I do not believe that even the process of coaching teaches this ability, which is closely linked to the concept of "use of self." Use of self, the ability to insert one's own personal responses and focus into ongoing emotional interactions, is one skill best developed in a training family therapy experience.

When a trainee enters personal marital or family psychotherapy in order to clarify relational tensions or individual distress, he/she is also typically at a point in training where therapy skills are rudimentary and technique-oriented. The process of training seeks to advance systemic skills, but also to advance the trainee's ability to access important nonspecific skills, such as the capacity for humor, self-observation, receptivity to supervision, cognitive "openness" (ability to shift a hypothesis), timing, and spontaneity. These nonspecific skills constitute aspects of the self that are important coping mechanisms in the face of stress, sudden change, and confusion. In fact, they are aspects of the self that are often underdeveloped in members of distressed families seeking treatment. These aspects of self are specifically those that can best be encouraged, modeled, nurtured, and strengthened *within the context of a personal therapy relationship with one's own family therapist*. To a large extent, these skills are very difficult to teach in a didactic setting, or even in a group supervisory setting that is essentially task-oriented. I believe that family therapy for the family therapy trainee is an underutilized resource—one that possesses considerable power to produce the self-knowledge and strong personal identity necessary to aid families in distress.

References

Anderson, C. M. (1986). The all-too-short trip from positive to negative connotation. *Journal of Marital and Family Therapy, 12,* 351–355.

Balint, M. (1968). *The basic fault: Therapeutic aspects of regression.* London: Tavistock.

Bateson, G. (1972). *Steps to an ecology of mind: Collected essays in anthropology, psychiatry, revolution, and epistemology.* San Francisco: Chandler.

Benedek, T. (1959). Parenthood as a developmental phase: A contribution to libido theory. *Journal of the American Psychoanalytic Association, 7,* 389–417.

Benjamin, L. S. (1974). Structural Analysis of Social Behavior. *Psychological Review, 81,* 392–425.

Bion, W. R. (1961). *Experiences in groups and other papers.* London: Tavistock.

Boscolo, L., Cecchin, G., Hoffman, L., & Penn, P. (1987). *Milan systemic family therapy: Conversations in theory and practice.* New York: Basic Books.

Boszormenyi-Nagy, I. (1962). The concept of schizophrenia from the point of view of family treatment. *Family Process, 1,* 103–113.

Boszormenyi-Nagy, I. (1965). A theory of relationships: Experience and transaction. In I. Boszormenyi-Nagy & J. L. Framo (Eds.), *Intensive family therapy: Theoretical and practical aspects* (pp. 33–86). New York: Hoeber.

Boszormenyi-Nagy, I. (1966). From family therapy to a psychology of relationships: Functions of the individual and fictions of the family. *Comprehensive Psychiatry, 7,* 408–423.

Boszormenyi-Nagy, I. (1972). Loyalty implications of the transference model in psychotherapy. *AMA Archives of General Psychiatry, 27,* 374–380.

Boszormenyi-Nagy, I. (1976). Behavior change through family change. In A. Burton (Ed.), *What makes behavior change possible?* (pp. 227–258). New York: Brunner/Mazel.

Boszormenyi-Nagy, I. (1989, March–April). In focus [Interview with D. S. Williamson]. *Family Therapy News,* pp. 8–9.

Boszormenyi-Nagy, I., & Framo, J. L. (Eds.). (1965). *Intensive family therapy: Theoretical and practical aspects.* New York: Hoeber.

Boszormenyi-Nagy, I., & Krasner, B. R. (1986). *Between give and take: A critical guide to contextual therapy.* New York: Brunner/Mazel.

Boszormenyi-Nagy, I., & Spark, G. M. (1973). *Invisible loyalties: Reciprocity in intergenerational family therapy.* New York: Harper & Row.

Boszormenyi-Nagy, I., & Ulrich, D. N. (1981). Contextual family therapy. In A. S. Gurman & D. P. Kniskern (Eds.), *Handbook of family therapy* (pp. 159–186). New York: Brunner/Mazel.

Bowen, M. (1980). Key to the use of the genogram. In E. A. Carter & M. McGoldrick (Eds.), *The family life cycle: A framework for family therapy* (p. xxiii). New York: Gardner Press.

Bowen, M. (1988). The use of family theory in clinical practice. In M. Bowen, *Family therapy in clinical practice* (2nd ed., pp. 147–181). Northvale, NJ: Jason Aronson. (Original work published 1966)

Bowen, M. (1988). On the differentiation of self. In M. Bowen, *Family therapy in clinical practice* (2nd ed., pp. 467–528). Northvale, NJ: Jason Aronson. (Original work published anonymously, 1972)

Bowen, M. (1988). Toward the differentiation of self in one's own family of origin. In M. Bowen, *Family therapy in clinical practice* (2nd ed., pp. 529–547). Northvale, NJ: Jason Aronson. (Original work published 1974)

Bowen, M. (1988). *Family therapy in clinical practice* (2nd ed.). Northvale, NJ: Jason Aronson.

Bowlby, J. (1969). *Attachment and loss: Vol. 1. Attachment.* New York: Basic Books.

Bowlby, J. (1973). *Attachment and loss: Vol. 2. Separation: Anxiety and anger.* New York: Basic Books.

Brazelton, T. B., Koslowski, B., & Main, M. (1974). The origins of reciprocity: The early mother–infant interaction. In M. Lewis & L. A. Rosenblum (Eds.), *The effect of the infant on its caregiver.* New York: Wiley–Interscience.

Carter, E. A., & McGoldrick, M. M. (Eds.). (1980). *The family life cycle: A framework for family therapy.* New York: Gardner Press.

Carter, E. A., & Orfanidis, M. M. (1976). Family therapy with one person and the family therapist's own family. In P. J. Guerin, Jr. (Ed.), *Family therapy: Theory and practice* (pp. 193–218). New York: Gardner Press.

Cornwall, M., & Pearson, R. (1981). Cotherapy teams and one-way screen in family therapy practice and training. *Family Process, 20,* 199–209.

Dammann, C. (1990). *Discussion of "The whole story: The healing dimension of social history."* Distinguished Lecture presented at the 12th Annual Meeting of the American Family Therapy Association, Philadelphia.

Dell, P. F. (1986). In defense of "lineal causality." *Family Process, 25,* 513–521.

Dicks, H. V. (1963). Object relations theory and marital status. *British Journal of Medical Psychology, 36,* 125–129.

Duhl, F. J. (1981). The use of the chronological chart in general systems therapy. *Journal of Marital and Family Therapy, 7,* 361–373.

Epstein, N., Jayne-Lazarus, C., & DeGiovanni, I. S. (1979). Cotrainers as models of relationships: Effects on the outcome of couples therapy. *Journal of Marital and Family Therapy, 5,* 53–59.

Fairbairn, W. R. D. (1952). *An object-relations theory of the personality.* New York: Basic Books.

Fairbairn, W. R. D. (1954). Observations on the nature of hysterical states. *British Journal of Medical Psychology, 27,* 105–125.

Ferrier, M. (1984). Teamwork: Process, problems and perspectives. *Journal of Strategic and Systemic Therapies, 3,* 17–23.

Fogarty, T. (1972). Fusion in the family system. In F. Andres & J. Lorio (Eds.), *Georgetown Family Symposium* (pp. 45–52). Washington, DC: Georgetown University Press.

Fraiberg, S. (Ed.), & Fraiberg, L. (Collaborator). (1980). *Clinical studies in infant mental health.* New York: Basic Books.

Framo, J. L. (1965). Rationale and techniques of intensive family therapy. In I. Boszormenyi-Nagy & J. L. Framo (Eds.), *Intensive family therapy: Theoretical and practical aspects* (pp. 143–212). New York: Hoeber.

Framo, J. L. (1972). Symptoms from a family transactional viewpoint. In C. Sager & H. Kaplan (Eds.), *Progress in group and family therapy* (pp. 271–308). New York: Brunner/Mazel. (Original work published 1970)

Framo, J. L. (1980). Marriage and marital therapy: Issues and initial interview techniques. In M. Andolfi & I. Zwerling (Eds.), *Dimensions of family therapy* (pp. 49–71). New York: Guilford Press.

Framo, J. L. (1982). Family of origin as a therapeutic resource for adults in marital and family therapy: You can and should go home again. In J. L. Framo (Ed.), *Explorations in marital and family therapy* (pp. 171–190). New York: Springer.

Framo, J. L. (1982). The integration of marital therapy with sessions with family of origin. In J. L. Framo (Ed.), *Explorations in marital and family therapy* (pp. 191–224). New York: Springer. (Original work published 1981)

Freud, S. (1964). Analysis terminable and interminable. In J. Strachey (Ed.), *The standard edition of the complete psychological works of Sigmund Freud* (Vol. 23, pp. 209–253). London: Hogarth Press.

Friedman, E. H. (1985). *Generation to generation: Family process in church and synagogue.* New York: Guilford Press.

Friedman, H., Rohrbaugh, M., & Krakauer, S. (1988). The time-line genogram: Highlighting temporal aspects of family relationships. *Family Process, 27,* 293–303.

Goodrich, T. J., Rampage, C., Ellman, B., & Halstead, K. (1989). *Feminist family therapy: A casebook.* New York: Norton.

Guerin, P. J., Jr. (1976). Study your own family. In P. J. Guerin, Jr. (Ed.), *Family therapy: Theory and practice.* New York: Gardner Press.

Guerin, P. J., Jr., & Pendagast, E. G. (1976). Evaluation of family system and genogram. In P. J. Guerin, Jr. (Ed.), *Family therapy: Theory and practice* (pp. 450–464). New York: Gardner Press.

Guttman, H. (1989). *Marriage at midlife.* Paper presented at the 11th Annual Meeting of the American Family Therapy Association, Colorado Springs, CO.

Haley, J. (1977). Toward a theory of pathological systems. In J. Haley, *Reflections on therapy and other essays* (pp. 94–112). Washington, DC: Family Therapy Institute.

Haley, J. (1986). The art of being a failure as a therapist. In J. Haley, *The power tactics of Jesus Christ and other essays* (2nd ed., pp. 81–89). Rockville, MD: Triangle.

Hannum, J. W. (1980). Some cotherapy techniques with families. *Family Process*, 19, 161–168.

Hare-Mustin, R. T. (1987). The problem of gender in family therapy theory. *Family Process*, 26, 15–33.

Hoffman, L. W. (1981). *Foundations of family therapy*. New York: Basic Books.

Jackson, D. D., & Weakland, J. H. (1961). Conjoint family therapy. *Psychiatry*, 24(Suppl. 2), 222–248.

Kahn, M. D. (1988). Intensive sibling relationships: A self-psychological view. In M. D. Kahn & K. G. Lewis (Eds.), *Siblings in therapy: Life span and clinical issues* (pp. 3–24). New York: Norton.

Kahn, M. D., & Lewis, K. G. (Eds.). (1988). *Siblings in therapy: Life span and clinical issues*. New York: Norton.

Keith, D. (1987). *The healthy family*. Unpublished manuscript.

Kerr, M. E. (1981). Family systems theory and therapy. In A. S. Gurman & D. P. Kniskern (Eds.), *Handbook of family therapy* (pp. 226–264). New York: Brunner/Mazel.

Kerr, M. E. (1985). Obstacles to differentiation of self. In A. S. Gurman (Ed.), *Casebook of marital therapy* (pp. 111–154). New York: Guilford Press.

Klein, M. (1957). *Envy and gratitude*. New York: Basic Books.

Klein, M. (1975). *Love, guilt and reparation and other works: 1921–1945*. London: Hogarth Press.

Latham, T. (1982). The use of co-working (co-therapy) as a training method. *Journal of Family Therapy. 4*, 257–269.

Lewis, K. G. (1988). Young siblings in brief therapy. In M. Kahn & K. G. Lewis (Eds.), *Siblings in therapy: Life span and clinical issues* (pp. 93–114). New York: Norton.

Luepnitz, D. A. (1988, September–October). Bateson's heritage: Bitter fruit. *Family Therapy Networker*, pp. 48–53, 73.

Mahler, M., Pine, F., & Bergman, A. (1975). *The psychological birth of the human infant: Symbiosis and individuation*. New York: Basic Books.

Maturana, H. R., & Varela, F. J. (1980). Autopoesis: The organization of the living. In H. R. Maturana & F. J. Varela, *Autopoesis and cognition: The realization of the living* (pp. 62–123). Boston: Reidel.

McGoldrick, M. (1982). Ethnicity and family therapy: An overview. In M. McGoldrick, J. K. Pearce, & J. Giordano (Eds.), *Ethnicity and family therapy* (pp. 3–30). New York: Guilford Press.

McGoldrick, M., & Gerson, R. (1985). *Genograms in family assessment*. New York: Norton.

McMahon, N., & Links, P. S. (1984). Cotherapy: The need for positive pairing. *Canadian Journal of Psychiatry, 29*, 385–389.

Minuchin, S., Rosman, B., & Baker, L. (1978). *Psychosomatic families: Anorexia nervosa in context*. Cambridge, MA: Harvard University Press.

Mueller, P., & Orfanidis, M. M. (1976). A method of co-therapy for schizophrenic families. *Family Process, 15*, 179–191.

Napier, A. Y. (Chair). (1983). *Coming of age: Reflections on the journey*. General session presented at the 41st Annual Meeting of the American Association for Marriage and Family Therapy, Washington, DC.

Neill, J. R., & Kniskern, D. P. (Eds.). (1982). *From psyche to system: The evolving therapy of Carl Whitaker.* New York: Guilford Press.

Olson, D., Portner, J., & Lavee, Y. (1985). *Family Adaptability and Cohesion Evaluation Scales—III (FACES-III).* St. Paul: Department of Family Social Science, University of Minnesota.

Papp, P. (1980). The Greek chorus and other techniques of paradoxical therapy. *Family Process, 19,* 45–57.

Paul, N. L. (1967). The role of mourning and empathy in conjoint marital therapy. In G. H. Zuk & I. Boszormenyi-Nagy (Eds.), *Family therapy and disturbed families.* Palo Alto, CA: Science & Behavior Books.

Perlmutter, M. S. (1988). Enchantment of siblings: Effects of birth order and trance on family myth. In M. D. Kahn & K. G. Lewis (Eds.), *Siblings in therapy: Life span and clinical issues* (pp. 25–45). New York: Norton.

Piercy, F. P., Sprenkle, D. H., & Associates. (1986). *Family therapy sourcebook.* New York: Guilford Press.

Roberto, L. G. (1986). Bulimia: The transgenerational view. *Journal of Marital and Family Therapy, 12,* 231–240.

Roberto, L. G. (1987). Bulimia: Transgenerational family therapy. In J. A. Harkaway (Ed.), *Family therapy of eating disorders* (pp. 1–11). Rockville, MD: Aspen.

Roberto, L. G. (1988). The vortex: Sibling relationships in eating disordered families. In M. Kahn & K. G. Lewis (Eds.), *Siblings in therapy: Life span and clinical issues* (pp. 297–313). New York: Norton.

Roberto, L. G., Keith, D. V., & Kramer, D. (1987). *Breaking the family crucible: Symbolic-experiential family therapy.* Workshop presented at the 45th Annual Meeting of the American Association for Marital and Family Therapy, Orlando, FL.

Roberto, L. G. (1991). Symbolic-experiential family therapy. In A. S. Gurman & D. P. Kniskern (Eds.), *Handbook of family therapy* (2nd ed., pp. 444–476). New York: Brunner/Mazel.

Roberto, L. G., & Mintle, L. M. (1989). *Treating military families.* Workshop presented at the 47th Annual Meeting of the American Association for Marriage and Family Therapy, San Francisco.

Roberts, J. (1981). Two models of live supervision: Collaborative team and supervisor guided. *Journal of Strategic and Systemic Therapy, 1,* 68–84.

Russell, A., Russell, L. (1979–1980). The uses and abuses of co-therapy. In J. G. Howells (Ed.), *Advances in family psychiatry* (Vol. II). New York: International Universities Press.

Sager, C. J. (1976). *Marriage contracts and couple therapy.* New York: Brunner/Mazel.

Schachter, F. F. (1982). Sibling deidentification and split-parent identification: A family tetrad. In M. E. Lamb & B. Sutton-Smith (Eds.), *Sibling relationships: Their nature and significance across the life span* (pp. 123–151). Hillsdale, NJ: Erlbaum.

Scharff, D. E., & Scharff, J. S. (1987). *Object relations family therapy.* Northvale, NJ: Jason Aronson.

Selvini Palazzoli, M. (1974). *Self-starvation: From the intrapsychic to the transpersonal approach to anorexia nervosa.* London: Human Context Books.

Selvini Palazzoli, M., Boscolo, L., Cecchin, G., & Prata, G. (1980). Hypothesizing–circularity–neutrality: Three guides for the conductor of the session. *Family Process, 19,* 3–12.

Silber, T. J., & Bogado, P. (1983). Pediatrician and psychiatrist as co-therapists. *Adolescence, 18,* 331–337.

Slipp, S. (1984). *Object relations: A dynamic bridge between individual and family treatment.* New York: Jason Aronson.

Slipp, S. (1989). A differing viewpoint for integrating psychodynamic and systems approaches. *Journal of Marital and Family Therapy, 15,* 13–16.

Sonne, J. C., Speck, R., & Jungreis, J. (1962). The absent-member maneuver as a resistance in family therapy of schizophrenia. *Family Process, 1,* 44–62.

Stierlin, H. (1974). *Separating parents and adolescents.* New York: Quadrangle.

Stierlin, H. (1977). *Psychoanalysis and family therapy.* New York: Jason Aronson.

Stierlin, H., & Ravenscroft, K. (1972). Varieties of adolescent separation conflicts. *British Journal of Medical Psychology, 45,* 299–313.

Stierlin, H., & Weber, G. (1989). *Unlocking the family door: A systemic approach to the understanding and treatment of anorexia nervosa.* New York: Brunner/Mazel.

Sullivan, H. S. (1953). *The collected works of Harry Stack Sullivan.* New York: Norton.

Sutherland, J. (1985). *The object relations approach.* Paper presented at the Sixth Annual Symposium on Psychoanalytic Family Therapy, Washington School of Psychiatry, Bethesda, MD.

Toman, W. (1961). *Family constellation.* New York: Springer.

Toman, W. (1988). Basics of family structure and sibling position. In M. D. Kahn & K. G. Lewis (Eds.), *Siblings in therapy: Life span and clinical issues* (pp. 46–65). New York: Norton.

Wachtel, E. F. (1982). The family psyche over three generations: The genogram revisited. *Journal of Marital and Family Therapy, 8,* 335–343.

Walters, M., Carter, B., Papp, P., & Silverstein, O. (1988). *The invisible web: Gender patterns in family relationships.* New York: Guilford Press.

Whitaker, C. A. (Ed.). (1958). *Psychotherapy of chronic schizophrenia.* Boston: Little, Brown.

Whitaker, C. A. (1975). Psychotherapy of the absurd: With a special emphasis on the psychotherapy of aggression. *Family Process, 14,* 1–15.

Whitaker, C. A. (1976a). The hindrance of theory in clinical work. In P. J. Guerin, Jr. (Ed.), *Family therapy: Theory and practice* (pp. 154–164). New York: Gardner Press.

Whitaker, C. A. (1976b). The family is a four-dimensional relationship. In P. J. Guerin, Jr. (Ed.), *Family therapy: Theory and practice* (pp. 182–192). New York: Gardner Press.

Whitaker, C. A. (1982a). Functions of marriage. In J. R. Neill & D. P. Kniskern (Eds.), *From psyche to system: The evolving therapy of Carl Whitaker* (pp. 166–175). New York: Guilford Press.

Whitaker, C. A. (1982b). Psychotherapy of marital conflict. In J. R. Neill & D.

P. Kniskern (Eds.), *From psyche to system: The evolving therapy of Carl Whitaker* (pp. 189–195). New York: Guilford Press.

Whitaker, C. A. (1982c). Gatherings. In J. R. Neill & D. P. Kniskern (Eds.), *From psyche to system: The evolving therapy of Carl Whitaker* (pp. 365–375). New York: Guilford Press

Whitaker, C. A. (1982d). Three types of craziness. In J. R. Neill & D. P. Kniskern (Eds.), *From psyche to system: The evolving therapy of Carl Whitaker* (pp. 36–37). New York: Guilford Press.

Whitaker, C. A. (1985). *The normal family.* Unpublished manuscript.

Whitaker, C. A. (1989). *Midnight musings of a family therapist.* New York: Norton.

Whitaker, C. A., Felder, R. E., & Warkentin, J. (1965). Countertransference in the family treatment of schizophrenia. In I. Boszormenyi-Nagy & J. Framo (Eds.), *Intensive family therapy: Theoretical and practical aspects.* New York: Hoeber.

Whitaker, C. A., & Keith, D. V. (1981). Symbolic-experiential family therapy. In A. S. Gurman & D. P. Kniskern (Eds.), *Handbook of family therapy* (pp. 187–224). New York: Brunner/Mazel.

Whitaker, C. A., & Keith, D. V. (1986). *Conversation hour: Cotherapy.* Workshop presented at the 44th Annual Meeting of the American Association for Marriage and Family Therapy, Orlando, FL.

Whitaker, C. A., & Napier, A. Y. (1977). Process techniques of family therapy. *Interaction, 1,* 4–19.

White, M. (1983). Anorexia nervosa: A transgenerational system perspective. *Family Process, 22,* 255–273.

Williamson, D. S. (1978). New life at the graveyard: A method of therapy for individuation from a dead former parent. *Journal of Marriage and Family Counseling, 4,* 93–101.

Williamson, D. S. (1981). Personal authority via termination of the intergenerational hierarchical boundary: A "new" stage in the family life cycle. *Journal of Marital and Family Therapy, 7,* 441–452.

Winnicott, D. W. (1965). *The maturational process and the facilitating environment.* London: Hogarth Press.

Winnicott, D. W. (1971). *Playing and reality.* London: Tavistock.

Winnicott, D. W. (1975). Transitional objects and transitional phenomena. In D. W. Winnicott, *Collected papers: Through paediatrics to psycho-analysis.* London: Hogarth Press. (Original work published 1951)

Wynne, L. C., McDaniel, S. H., & Weber, T. T. (Eds.). (1986). *Systems consultation: A new perspective for family therapy.* New York: Guilford Press.

Zimmerman, N., Collins, L. E., & Bach, J. M. (1986). Ordinal position, cognitive style and competence: A systemic approach to supervision. *The Clinical Supervisor, 4,* 7–23.

Zuk, G. H., & Boszormenyi-Nagy, I. (1967). *Family therapy and disturbed families.* Palo Alto, CA: Science & Behavior Books.

Index

Absent-member maneuver, 128
Abusive behavior, 64, 140, 157
Acculturation, 30
Addiction, as psychological absence,
    104
Adolescence
    and return of the repressed, 63–64
    sexuality in, 105
    turmoil in, 18
Aggressive behavior; see Siblings, vio-
    lence in
Alliances
    in cotherapy, 189
    in tetrads, 182–183
    therapeutic, 203–204
    in trainee coaching, 197–198
    in triangles, 11, 71, 73
"Alpha" bias, 27
Ambivalence, 147
American Family Therapy Association,
    1, 41
Anderson, Carol M., 135
Anger, 43, 63, 88
    and depression, 159
Anniversary reaction, 116
Anorexia, 94, 165
Anticipatory mourning, 40
Anxiety
    and change, 35
    in emotional triangles, 11, 17, 84–
        85
    in marital conflict, 101
Assessment, of extended family, 121–
    134; see also Interview

case examples of, 123–125, 128
    early-stage, 127–128, 144, 146
    later-stage, 132–134
    reasons for, 123
Attachment problems; see Bonding,
    affective
Autonomy, 29
    and accountability, 46
    in marriage, 101

B

Basic fault, 60–61, 64
Basic self, 12–13, 15–16
Bateson, Gregory, 2, 179
Belief systems, 23, 28, 34, 75, 105
    loyalty to, 30–31
"Beta" bias, 27, 30
Binocular view, 178–179, 181
Birth order, 14, 77–78
Bonding, affective, 26, 29, 31, 75
    between parent and child, 103
    between siblings, 76–78, 88
Boszormenyi-Nagy, Ivan, 24, 41–42,
    45–48, 59, 136
    and "feedforward," 109
    and "revolving slate," 149, 159
Boundaries
    and cotherapy, 186
    family, 27–28, 32–33, 74
    generational, 27, 32, 86, 89, 151
    lack of, 104, 168
    and self-delineation, 50

213